╫ 119 √

Contemporary theoretical debates reveal contradictory views on the foundations of knowledge: hermeneutics challenges epistemology, politics challenges science, identity theory challenges critical theory, pragmatism challenges formalism, and so on. Horace Fairlamb contends that philosophy's foundationalist quest has usually been misconceived as a choice between a "super-science" and anarchy. Through an examination of the history of foundationism and detailed analyses of the work of such leading thinkers as Fish, Foucault, Derrida, Gadamer, and Habermas, Dr. Fairlamb argues for a conception of foundations that is neither reductive nor arbitrary. Providing a sophisticated critique of contemporary foundationist debate, this work contributes significantly to the current revaluation of theoretical discourse with implications for philosophers as well as literary theorists.

D0003911

Literature, Culture, Theory 8

❖❖❖❖❖❖❖❖❖❖❖❖❖❖❖❖❖❖❖❖❖❖❖❖❖❖❖❖❖❖❖❖❖❖❖❖❖❖❖

Critical conditions

Literature, Culture, Theory

General editors

RICHARD MACKSEY, *The Johns Hopkins University*

and MICHAEL SPRINKER, *State University of New York at Stony Brook*

The Cambridge *Literature, Culture, Theory* series is dedicated to theoretical studies in the human sciences that have literature and culture as their object of enquiry. Acknowledging the contemporary expansion of cultural studies and the redefinitions of literature that this has entailed, the series includes not only original works of literary theory but also monographs and essay collections on topics and seminal figures from the long history of theoretical speculation on the arts and human communication generally. The concept of theory embraced in the series is broad, including not only the classical disciplines of poetics and rhetoric, but also those of aesthetics, psychoanalysis, semiotics, and other cognate sciences that have inflected the systematic study of literature during the past half century.

Critical conditions

Postmodernity and the question of foundations

HORACE L. FAIRLAMB

University of Houston-Victoria

CAMBRIDGE
UNIVERSITY PRESS

Published by the Press Syndicate of the University of Cambridge
The Pitt Building, Trumpington Street, Cambridge, CB2 1RP
40 West 20th Street, New York, NY 10011-4211, USA
10 Stamford Road, Oakleigh, Melbourne 3166, Australia

© Cambridge University Press 1994

First published 1994

Printed in Great Britain at the University Press, Cambridge

A catalogue record for this book is available from the British Library

Library of Congress cataloguing in publication data
Fairlamb, Horace L.
Critical conditions: postmodernity and the question of foundations / Horace L. Fairlamb.
p. cm.—(Literature, culture, theory)
Includes bibliographical references and index.
ISBN 0 521 45047 0 (hardback) ISBN 0 521 45665 7 (paperback)
1. Postmodernism (Literature) I. Title. II. Series.
PN 98 P67F35   1994
149—dc20   93-25034 CIP

ISBN 0 521 45047 0 hardback
ISBN 0 521 45665 7 paperback

Contents

Preface

This project attempts to address the problem of the foundations of knowledge and meaning, an issue that has recently received much attention. The list of authors discussed in the following chapters shows the interdisciplinary nature of the problem and its relevance for a host of debates being conducted in different disciplinary terms. Yet, while the problem of foundations will be familiar to the veterans of these debates, the strategy of this book is perhaps less obvious than appears on the surface, in which case some prefatory remarks are in order.

This volume is part of a larger project which links epistemology, hermeneutics, and critical social theory. Whereas I hope to provide separate treatments of epistemology and critical theory in subsequent volumes, the current focus stresses the linkage between the most basic assumptions of foundational discourse and the politics of the modern/postmodern debates. Thus this approach runs the risk of being both insufficiently theoretical for the more abstract concerns of epistemology, and insufficiently wide for the complexity of social theory. I believe, however, that my intermediary strategy is justified by my central argument about the issue of foundations. In its simplest form, the argument holds that the much politicized debate between modern and postmodern perspectives rests on a deeper, even more pervasive misunderstanding of the issue of foundations. For diagnostic purposes, however, both the political and foundational aspects of the problem are important: the foundational question because it highlights the starting points for understanding and argument; the political implications because they reveal the problems that follow from misleading assumptions about foundations.

My Introduction summarizes the larger argument on the foundationist debate. (I depart from the more common usage, "foundationalism" and "conventionalism," with "foundationism" and "conventionism.") I argue that this debate has traditionally and currently been misconceived as a false dilemma (the strong foundational antithesis or antinomy) which forces a choice between too narrow and too loose notions of grounds. The too strong version hopes to reduce knowledge and meaning to some epistemic or hermeneutic principle. The too weak version merely repudiates the necessity of any particular constraints on knowledge or meaning. Foundations, in other words, are thought to be a one-or-none proposition. I argue that both of these options are too extreme, and that they represent a false dilemma insofar as the real significance of foundations lies between these alternatives.

In my view, foundationism only errs when it hopes to reduce the conditions of knowledge to *one kind* of foundation instead of explaining the different but equally necessary conditions of knowledge and meaning. Likewise, while the foundational antinomy (the one-or-none dilemma) offers only reduction or anarchy, I suggest that the point of foundationist theory is to account for the necessity and significance of three kinds (the *heterology*) of epistemic conditions: formal, objective, and conventional. If I am correct, then to require that foundations be either reductive or arbitrary systematically misleads, and certain predictable problems should follow. The theme of my eight chapters is that the problems found in many major theorists are in fact consequences of misconceiving the foundationist question along the lines of this false dilemma.

Specifically, the central essays show how – through the strong foundationist antithesis – the emerging postmodern positions continue to be shaped by the foundationist conception they are trying to subvert. My argument examines (a) how both defenders and critics of foundations are still infected with the traditional reductive ideal of epistemology, (b) how anti-foundationists attempt to critique the traditional notion of foundations without having a sufficiently clear notion of their own theoretical presuppositions and constraints, and (c) how a heterological model of critical conditions avoids those problems.

The key to the argument is the introductory thesis about the heterology of critical conditions, without which the purpose of the subsequent chapters is liable to misunderstanding. The risk is that my reader will assume that the individual discussions are supposed to be entirely representative of the various thinkers discussed or be fit substitutes for critiques already available. But the focus of the argument is not on authors per se. Being an argument about the structure of foundational discourse, the specific thinkers discussed are chosen only to exemplify typical discursive strategies, their theoretical constraints, and their practical implications. My point, therefore, is neither representational completeness regarding individuals nor comprehensiveness of overview regarding the critical literature about them. While my discussions attempt to provide enough of their work to represent the thrust of the discursive strategies in question, I do not claim to represent the entire range of these authors' works and thought, nor all their subsequent revisions and recantations. In short, this is not a survey of postmodern thinkers but an analysis of how certain strategies fail to address foundational problems.

An equally important limitation of this project is its relation to the material reserved for other works, including one more exclusively focused on the history of epistemology, and another devoted to critical social theory. The theoretical apparatus of my present argument is, by necessity, largely compressed into the introduction and conclusion. And while my critiques dialectically exemplify my defense of heterological foundations, like all dialectical arguments mine is often more symptomatic and negative than systematic. That is, my analyses often show what happens when one does *not* share the assumptions and theoretical commitments I have summarized in the introduction. I hope, however, that the heterological pattern of foundational discourse is powerful enough to be visible through the different critiques.

Still, some may consider the lack of a full blown epistemological presentation of my commitments to be a more than negligible void. Strategically, however, I believe that the dialectical presentation of this argument is justified for reasons of reception as well as for reasons of space. A purely theoretical approach to foundations at this point in time is likely to be welcomed by only half of the parties involved in the foundationist debates, a suspicion to which the currency of anti-theory, anti-epistemology, and anti-system all give credence. If the underlying thesis must finally be made in stages, I believe that it makes sense to begin by discovering in the context of contemporary debates the widespread need for a more fully theoretical understanding of critical conditions.

Acknowledgements

The many versions of these chapters have profited from the intelligence and consideration of Ed Freedman, Dan Jaeckle, Richard Macksey, Michael Sprinker, Jeffrey Geller, Dolora Ann Wojciehowski, Angelika Rausch, Paisley Livingston, Virgil Lokke, John McNamara, and others. From the Cambridge staff and series editors, the encouragement and patience of Kevin Taylor, Richard Macksey and Michael Sprinker were more than generous. An early version of the project owes much to Ernst Behler's National Endowment for the Humanities summer seminar of 1987 on the Romantic origins of literary theory. The University of Houston-Victoria lent consistent support over the years. Mark Poster graciously made available the resources of the University of California at Irvine's Institute for Critical Theory in the summer of 1991. The hospitality and support of the University of Oregon Humanities Center was much appreciated during the final stages of the project. Susan Tesar's thoughtful editing helped improve the manuscript substantially. And from the earliest stages of the project, Richard Macksey's interest and advice have been an indispensable support.

As a final note, even with the satisfactions of a dialogue as stimulating as today's, one cannot help regretting that the negativity of one's role so often neglects the debts that remain invisible. Thus my attention to limitations overlooks the extraordinary virtue of Rorty's reawakening of metaphilosophy and the exemplary professionalism of Fish's classes.

❖❖❖

Abbreviations

❖❖❖

AP   Stanley Fish, "Anti-professionalism," *New Literary History*, vol. XVII (1985).

AT   Stanley Fish, "Consequences" in *Against theory: literary studies and the new pragmatism*, ed. W. J. T. Mitchell, Chicago, 1985; pp. 106–131.

BI   Stanley Fish, "Being interdisciplinary is so very hard to do," *Profession 89*, New York: Modern Language Association, 1989.

CP   Richard Rorty, *Consequences of pragmatism*, Minneapolis: University of Minnesota, 1982.

FR   Michel Foucault, *The Foucault reader*, ed. Paul Rabinow, New York: Random House, 1984.

ITC   Stanley Fish, *Is there a text in this class?: the authority of interpretive communities*, Cambridge, MA: Harvard University Press, 1980.

OG   Jacques Derrida, *Of grammatology*, Baltimore: Johns Hopkins University Press, 1974.

PC   Jean-François Lyotard, *The postmodern condition: a report on knowledge*, Minneapolis: University of Minnesota Press, 1984.

PH   Hans-Georg Gadamer, *Philosophical hermeneutics*, ed. David E. Linge, Berkeley: University of California Press, 1976.

PK   Michel Foucault, *Power/knowledge: selected interviews and other writings 1972–1977*, ed. Colin Gordon, New York: Random House, 1980.

PM   Richard Rorty, *Philosophy and the mirror of nature*, Princeton University Press, 1979.

TM   Hans-Georg Gadamer, *Truth and method*, New York: Crossroad, 1988.

Introduction

Throughout a remarkable number of contemporary disciplines there is a vigorous interest in the questions of foundations, an interest that is by turns nervous, skeptical, and controversial. This interest is a product of numerous intellectual cycles of various wave-lengths, but certainly it represents the coincidence of both the post-structuralist skepticism of recent decades as well as a postmodern crescendo of skepticism that began with Nietzsche, if not with Romantic challenges to the Enlightenment. Thus we find today not only a postmodern culture, but also a postmodern philosophical skepticism, a hermeneutics of suspicion, which has challenged the Enlightenment legacy's progressivism, universalism, and rationalism.

Postmodern skepticism appears as a crisis, a break, and one whose reach lays claim not only to modernism, but to Western philosophy as a whole. It is a crisis, moreover, because while its roots are not new, serious challenges to the rationalist-scientific tradition of the West have remained, for much of this century, safely marginalized as the exorbitances of the poets, fideists, and nihilists. But that has changed: the anti-rationalist impetus no longer emerges solely from the academic and cultural margins, but through the very legacy of analytic philosophy itself.

The linguistic turn: philosophy discovers language

How is it that analytic philosophy came to put so much stock in the linguistic approach to philosophical problems? In philosophy's search for the foundations of knowledge, language has traditionally been thought an obstacle to something more reliable. As epistemology and science idealized the authority of logic and facts, they spurned the ambiguity and colloquialism of natural language. Just as Plato looked beyond the linguistic perplexities of his *Cratylus* toward certain intellectual grounds, Descartes and Bacon looked beyond the idols of

1

language to the quantified verifications of science, while Kant simply ignored linguistic perplexities for the pure reason of concepts. What could have so altered this legacy of rigor? The roots of the linguistic turn lie in the history of modern foundationist thought.

After the breakup of scholasticism's Aristotelian synthesis of concepts and senses, modern epistemology dispersed its search for ultimate foundations between the mind (rationalism), the senses (empiricism), and the representations of thoughts (nominalism). Of these three, nominalism is inherently anti-foundationist insofar as it tends to collapse representational authority into the very process of representation, in which case transcendent foundations are suspected if not denied. Against this more skeptical line, modern strong foundationists turned to the subject and object for the most promising philosophical grounds. The rationalist line culminated in Kant's Transcendental Subject and Pure Reason, the universal categories by which the mind ordered the world, while empiricism placed its faith in the integrity of its verificationist methodology, culminating in the confidence of positivism. But finally, as Kant's categories began to appear less immediate and necessary under the scrutiny of his critics, and as science's pronouncements began to seem more theory-laden and discursive, language seemed less the dispensable and transparent medium of philosophy's insights than the very locus of philosophical perplexity.

Against the background of this foundationist legacy, the linguistic turn appeared to promise (to ideal language philosophers at least) an old style epistemology of privileged grounds, even as it circumvented or explained away metaphysics. Here lies the linguistic resurgence of strong foundationist theory. Just as modern philosophy was born in dissatisfaction with classical metaphysical approaches to philosophical foundations, so philosophy in the twentieth century came to believe that rationalist epistemologies were too abstract, and scientific practice too concrete to expose the roots of philosophical issues. According to Richard Rorty, the linguistic turn grew out of the belief "that philosophical problems are problems which may be solved (or dissolved) either by reforming language, or by understanding more about the language we presently use."[1] Language and linguistic analysis became of central philosophical importance. The linguistic

---

1. *The linguistic turn: recent essays in philosophical method*, University of Chicago Press, 1967, p. 3.

turn became, Rorty notes, the last major revolution in philosophical paradigms, the last hope for finding the proper philosophical grounds that would either answer or dissolve the big questions.

The revolution, however, did not go as planned. Despite its popularity, the linguistic turn failed to specify the larger significance of language for the question of philosophical foundations. Philosophical problems either did not reduce to linguistic solution, or reduced to a proliferation of linguistic explanations – from the formal to the ordinary – challenging the coherence of linguistic philosophy's methodological integrity. Linguistic theory and analysis not only did not solve most philosophical problems, but raised new questions no less fundamental, and therefore no less troubling for the question of foundations, such as "the more difficult topic of how changes in the vocabulary used in formulating substantive theses produce changes in the vocabulary of metaphilosophy."[2]

Yet, the origins and failure of the linguistic turn may signal something deeper, an insight into the question of foundationism itself. Indeed, the linguistic turn appears almost fated by a genetic logic. Modern epistemology began with a bifurcation into rationalist appeals to subjective certainty (Descartes to Kant) and objectivist appeals to objective givenness (Bacon to Popper). Given the failure to get formality out of objectivity or objectivity out of formality, the translation of Kant's conceptual determination of experience into a *linguistic mediation* of knowledge seems to follow naturally enough. As Rorty put it: "The point about the so-called 'linguistic turn' in recent philosophy is supposed to be that whereas once we thought, with Aristotle, that necessity came from things, and later thought with Kant that it came from the structure of our minds, we now know that it comes from language" (*CP*, 26). This origin of linguistic philosophy is significant both historically – in the genealogical struggle of ideas – and semiologically – in defining the formal conditions of philosophical authority and postmodern explanation.

In fact, as if to demonstrate the formal or semiotic conditions of thought, the dispersion of linguistic philosophy constitutes a micro-cosm of foundationism itself: rather than converging on a privileged ground or method, linguistic philosophy recapitulates the heterology of foundationist elements in a variety of linguistic guises. Between Russell's logical atomism and contemporary speech-act theory, for

2. *The linguistic turn*, 39.

instance, one finds grounds ranging from the phenomenal atoms given by experience, to formality of syntax, and the pragmatically and culturally relative practices of language games. Linguistic foundationism has generated its own heterology of objective, formal, *and* conventional constraints on knowledge. The diaspora of linguistic foundations into syntactic formulae, referential theories, pragmatic conditions, language games, speech acts, interpretive communities and such indicates the historical approximation of linguistic philosophy to the heterological conditions of thought, the semiotic elements of objectivity, formality, and historical contingency.

For many, the inconclusiveness of linguistic philosophy implies the truth of postmodern conventionism, of hermeneutic relativism, of the belief that language is an unreliable index of a deeper reality. For postmodernists, the linguistic turn has become the ubiquitous occasion for anti-foundationist deconstructions of meaning.

The hermeneutic turn: hermeneutics dis-covers philosophy

For traditional philosophy, the structure of epistemic authority descended from the privileged elements at the peak of the hierarchy of principles (e.g. in defending his logical atomism, Russell declares that "Descartes' method [of analyzing into privileged elements] is on the whole a sound one"[3]). To violate one's hierarchy of explanatory priorities threatens a viciously circular argument, the only solution to which is a final appeal to immediate foundations. In Rorty's view, the most persuasive analyses of the nature of philosophical authority suggest that this hierarchical view is fundamentally mistaken. In his influential *Philosophy and the mirror of nature*, Rorty extends his view of linguistic philosophy (i.e. as the last strong foundationist revolution) into a sweeping repudiation of epistemology as foundationist theory, declaring the foundationist project defunct.

Contrary to tradition, the work of Quine, Sellars, and Kuhn shows that epistemic authority is holistically and historically dependent upon pragmatically and culturally relative contexts, in which case no privileged principle can account for what is taken as knowledge or

3. From the "Facts and propositions" section of "The philosophy of logical atomism." *The Monist*, 1918; reprinted in *Contemporary analytic and linguistic philosophies*, E. D. Klemke (ed.), Buffalo, New York: Prometheus, 1983; p. 208.

meaning. Where traditional epistemology sought such privileged grounds, the holistic critique of strong foundationism suggests that

we will not be able to isolate basic elements except on the basis of a prior knowledge of the whole fabric within which these elements occur ... Our choice of elements will be dictated by our understanding of the practice, rather than the practice's being "legitimated" by a "rational reconstruction" out of elements. This holistic line of argument says that we shall never be able to avoid the "hermeneutic circle." (PM, 319)

The hermeneutic circularity of epistemic holism negates the hierarchical model of privileged elements, and suggests instead an expanding horizon of mutually coherent and interdependent elements that can only be explored dialectically, never finally reducing to certain conditions or transcendental criteria. This is the hermeneutic turn from epistemology, the breach of modernist foundations with a postmodern *heterology* of elements.

Instead of trying to replace the failed epistemological theories of old, Rorty urges philosophy to do hermeneutics instead.

In the interpretation I shall be offering, "hermeneutics" is not the name for a discipline, nor for a method of achieving the sort of results which epistemology failed to achieve, nor for a program of research. On the contrary, hermeneutics is an expression of hope that the cultural space left by the demise of epistemology will not be filled – that our culture should become one in which the demand for constraint and confrontation is no longer felt. (PM, 315)

Philosophically considered, postmodernism embodies the fall from absolute frameworks, after which language – as the medium of foundationist contingency – is taken to be a chronic opportunity for repeated lapses. In Derrida's words:

However the topic is considered, the *problem of language* has never been simply one problem among others. But never as much as at present has it invaded, *as such*, the global horizon of the most diverse researches and the most heterogeneous discourses, diverse and heterogeneous in their intention, method, and ideology ... a historico-metaphysical epoch *must* finally determine as language the totality of its problematic horizon. (OG, 6)

Postmodernism is the time for which language is the game. The heralds of the postmodern condition have turned the traditional vices of mediate truth and conflicting perspectives into the virtues of liberal understanding of significant flux, and of openness to the questionability of past knowledge and to the creativity of future truths. In its post-strong-foundationist spirit, contemporary hermeneutics embraces the instability of signs, the relativity of premises and contexts. In response to this skeptical tendency, hermeneutics itself has shifted its center of gravity from the positive to the negative, from confidence to suspicion, from its original interest in correct interpretations to self-reflection on its own contingencies, from the sure elimination of error to the *questionability* of the grounds of understanding.

Nor is this skeptical and opening movement without force. There is, to begin with, its effect upon strong foundationist thought. Targeting the structures of philosophical order, Derrida remarks that "in a classical philosophical opposition we are not dealing with the peaceful coexistence of a *vis-à-vis*, but rather with a violent hierarchy ... To deconstruct the opposition ... is to overturn the hierarchy at a given moment."[4] It is for this power of displacement that Rorty has cast hermeneutics as the nemesis for strong foundationist philosophy, as the subverter of epistemology rather than its fulfilment.

Yet as postmodern thought has emerged, it appears that hermeneutics faces its own problems regarding the status of its global claims. Saying how and why hermeneutics can confront traditional foundationist theory without using the older terms is not as easy as some would-be innovators have suggested.[5] Once one has characterized the philosophical canon as foundationist, one wonders what could successfully deconstruct that tradition *in principle* (rather than just in isolated cases) if not another foundationist theory of equivalent universality. The standard explanation is to say that postmodernism substitutes practice for theory (as do the literary anti-theorists,[6]) but that suggestion faces the problem of either (a) being local and leaving the *principle* of strong foundationism untouched by ad hoc textual analyses, or (b) being universal and accounting for its own universal implications while denying universalism. In this regard, the postmodern condition is less the transcendence of universalisms than a

---

4. *Positions*, University of Chicago, 1981, p. 41.
5. On this point, Derrida has been exceptionally acute in recognizing the continuity between traditional foundationism and the postmodern discourse, especially: "Structure, sign, and play" reprinted in *The structuralist controversy: the languages of criticism and the sciences of man*, eds. Eugenio Donato and Richard Macksey, Baltimore: Johns Hopkins Press, 1970; *Of grammatology*. Baltimore: Johns Hopkins Press, 1976; pp. 85–6.
6. "Against theory"; "A reply to our critics"; "Consequences"; all in W. J. T. Mitchell's *Against theory: literary studies and the New Pragmatism*. Chicago, 1985.

contest of universalisms, a contest that reveals a profound crisis of foundationist theory, and the need to revise the notion of how philosophical foundations operate.

A contest of universalisms

On the one hand, science and epistemology have traditionally sought to transcend the relativity of context to achieve foundational universality. Thus Popper defends the privilege of an empirical foundationism by arguing that "the growth of scientific knowledge may be said to be the growth of ordinary knowledge *writ large* ... [for] science is one of the very few human activities – perhaps the only one – in which errors are systematically criticized and fairly often, in time, corrected ... in other fields there is change but rarely progress."[7] In the name of a linguistic formalism, Michael Dummett awards to Frege's innovations the canonical mantle of "first philosophy":

philosophy has only very recently struggled out of its early stage into maturity: the turning point was the work of Frege ... What has given philosophy its historical unity, what has characterized it over all the centuries as a single subject, is the range of questions which philosophers have attempted to answer ... Only with Frege was the proper object of philosophy finally established: namely, first, that the goal of philosophy is the analysis of the structure of *thought*; secondly, that the study of *thought* is to be sharply distinguished from the study of the psychological process of *thinking* and, finally, that the only proper method for analyzing thought consists in the analysis of *language*.[8]

Husserl, Lévi-Strauss and others could be cited in the same vein, i.e. as pretenders to the discovery of the ultimate grounds of knowledge-truth-meaning. It is the very foundationist ideal of closing off philosophical and hermeneutic questionability – either with some theoretical structure or some methodological security – that the hermeneutic revolution seeks to challenge.

On the other hand, hermeneutics has responded to traditional claims for transcendence – largely through the influence of Heidegger, Gadamer, and Derrida – with a claim to its own universality: that of contextual and historical contingency, the universal questionability of philosophical grounds. For it is precisely at the foundational moment, the moment when empirical and formal theories lay claim to the heart

---

7. *Conjectures and refutations: The growth of scientific knowledge*, New York: Harper & Row, 1963, p. 216.
8. *Truth and other enigmas*, Cambridge: Harvard, 1978, p. 457.

of truth, that hermeneutics steps in and discovers the questionability of *all* epistemic assumptions.

Against the ideals of scientific and epistemological closure Gadamer claims that "philosophical hermeneutics takes as its task the opening up of the hermeneutical dimension in its full scope, showing its fundamental significance for our entire understanding of the world and thus for all the various forms in which this understanding manifests itself" (*PH*, 18). Hermeneutic universality does not appeal to privileged grounds, but to the instability of all grounds: "The real power of hermeneutical consciousness is our ability to see what is questionable" (*PH*, 13). This ability is no mere cleverness; its reality derives from the openness of human experience, for it "is clear that the structure of the question is implicit in all experience" (*TM*, 325). On the one hand, it appears that hermeneutics displaces the universalism of science and philosophy; on the other hand, hermeneutics claims a universalism for its own ontological originality. With a touch of foundationist ambiguity, Gadamer dubs his project "philosophical hermeneutics."

Thus postmodern skepticism walks through the door of linguistic philosophy armed with a negative, critical universalism. For hermeneutic questionability, ideas that are supposed to be "indubitable" for traditional epistemology or "objective" for science only appear so when their assumptions are not under scrutiny, either through forgetfulness, habit, or convenience. By showing that "the given" is contingent upon the particular historical question which it answers, philosophical hermeneutics posits an infinite regress of foundational questionability. Hermeneutic universality implies the *historicity* of all argument, i.e. philosophy's dependence upon a context of questions which – through the assumptions that underlie doubt and belief – structure the authority of the given with precritical prejudices.

Moreover, it is no small irony that the most significant site of hermeneutic questionability lies in the philosophical closure attributed to the *foundational moment itself*. For insofar as hermeneutics successfully questions the ultimate closure of philosophical authority, so the historical residues of language – the residues that bear the traces of the original questionability from which philosophy springs – will remain for hermeneutics an open book, i.e. open to debate in a somewhat untraditionally genealogical, contextual, and irreducible sense of openness.

Hermeneutics' challenge to traditional foundationist philosophy is disturbing, therefore, to the degree that philosophy must take the problem of language seriously, for it is language that is supposed by hermeneutics to keep the origins of philosophical authority open. And for Gadamer as for Derrida, that degree is total: "interpretive language and concepts are … an inner structural element of under-standing. This moves the whole problem of language from its peripheral and incidental position into the center of philosophy" (*TM*, 274). Not surprisingly, then, the hermeneutic challenge has thrown the issue of critical conditions into notable disarray. If critical authority cannot turn to metaphysical permanence, transcendental subjectivity, scientific objectivity, formal systematicity, methodological closure, or any other transcending constraints for its authority, are we not left with nothing firmer than Nietzschean perspectivism and an anarchy of wills to power? Might not the respectable looking Trojan Horse of philosophical hermeneutics be filled with sophists, gamesters, and fascists?

These doubts cannot be dismissed lightly. As the career of post-structuralist theory shows in abundance, the hermeneutic turn brings with it a surfeit of troubling questions about hermeneutic question-ability and critical conditions, of which there may be some ir-responsible versions, but which include rigorous versions as well.[9] But if one takes hermeneutic questionability seriously, one question is of particular philosophical interest, the question implied by the contest of universalisms. When conceived philosophically, as Gadamer poses it, hermeneutics raises the problem of *its own* foundationist question-ability, an issue certain postmodern skeptics have overlooked: how is it that hermeneutics can warrant both its own universality (of questionability) and postmodern anti-universalism at the same time? Is not the historical-conventional subversion of foundationism, if it claims to be universal, itself a global theorization of the necessary nature of language, if not of reality? What, finally, is the authority and scope of the postmodern critique of philosophical foundations?

9. E.g. Is there really nothing outside language? Is *Hamlet* really Norman Holland's greatest creation as a reader-response? Does that mean that literary criticism is, as the rank and file version of hermeneutics, (a) the science of rules that has no rules as Hayden White suggests, and (b) incapable of extraprofessional critique as Fish suggests? Can the pragmatic conditions of communication yield tran-scendental moral constraints upon social-critical discourse as Apel and Habermas have argued? Does the universality of questionability only subvert all *other* universalities, such as the formal conditions of language and the objectivity of science, or does the universality of questionability imply that maybe *some* things may not actually be questionable, though we cannot know what they are?

The paradox of hermeneutic universalism

Gadamer's elevation of language to the center of philosophical authority constitutes the paradox of *centralizing the decentering of foundations*, a paradox which lies at the heart of the postmodern crisis of criticism. On the one hand, hermeneutic universality threatens the traditional notions of critical foundations with the universality of questionability; on the other, this universality of questionability (presupposed by postmodern anti-foundationism, localism, pragmatism, etc.) cannot be accounted for in anti-theoretical, local, and conventional terms. For if hermeneutic questionability is local, how could it be universal? If it is not theoretical, how could its necessity anticipate future practices? If it is merely conventional, why could it not simply be refused? Hermeneutics cannot escape its own foundational questionability.

This problem determines what conclusions we can draw from the critique of foundationism. Does the claim of hermeneutics to universality (a) *transcend* the errors of traditional foundationism, (b) *revise* the notion of foundations, or (c) merely *repress* its own totalization into a new and unaccountable form of theory? Can one have a universalism of openness without some sort of universalism of closure? These problems pervade Derrida's notion of the General System, Fish's "no consequences" thesis, Gadamer's notion of the perfect interiority of language, Habermas' notion of quasi-transcendental grounds for critique, Lyotard's goal of scientific dissent, and Foucault's anarchic injunctions to "substantial resistance." Indeed, the universality of hermeneutic questionability is the philosophical crux of postmodern critique.

In their satisfaction with deconstructive practices, postmodern innovators have not taken the issue of foundations seriously enough, but have too readily adopted an anti-foundationist stance. This precipitousness is twofold.

First, anti-foundationism too often suggests that strong foundationism achieved its hegemony over philosophy through some sleight of hand rather than through appeal to actual discoveries about the conditions of thought. Notwithstanding some more restrained moments, the willingness of postmodern skeptics to dismiss essentialism, foundations, theory, logical and necessary conditions, and objectivity at one blow indulges the fantasy that Plato, Aristotle, Descartes, Bacon, Kant and Hegel defended the philosophical canon against radical skepticism and relativism merely by force of false consciousness, a highly unlikely assumption.

Secondly, postmodern critics often assume too quickly that the failure of strong foundationism automatically accrues to the credibility of various forms of radical skepticism, and that the lack of an ultimate standard of rationality leaves nominalism, skepticism, and relativism free to carry the field. But this false dilemma merely hides the theoretical problems of radical skepticism and relativism behind the problems of reductive foundationism. Unexplained are the pragmatic conditions of hermeneutic and deconstructive authority, conditions which allow that postmodern critique is always already a possibility. Even *given* their critique of strong foundationism, most postmodern critics beg the question of the theoretical conditions of hermeneutic universality and the critique of strong foundationism.

But then why should postmodern critics worry about the grounds of their critiques as long as they are safe in the knowledge that such conditions are always already available? The reason has to do with the work of *engaging the tradition* as referred to above by Derrida. Merely to assume that foundationism has not worked and that we need merely to stop doing it only perpetuates the very problem of strong foundationism in a new form: the problem of prematurely ceasing to examine the conditions of one's discourse. Rather than totalizing the failure of foundations, the more productive strategy is to seek the strategic error of past foundationisms. Here is where postmodernism's "no-depth" theory of authority serves no one's long-term interests. In the absence of deep critique, anti-foundationism must assume the demise of key issues which, though out of sight, are far from buried. As a discouragement from depth analysis rather than an incitement to it, the paradox of hermeneutic universality has remained repressed, unaccounted for, and overshadowed by a utopian optimism about the possibilities of post-logocentric understanding.

Naturally, the paradox of hermeneutic universality is most problematic in the arguments of the most extreme anti-foundationists, some of which will be examined in the following chapters. Perhaps most commonly, anti-foundationists suggest that discursive authority can be adequately understood in terms of conventions, even in the cases of philosophical and scientific discourse, for which reason traditional epistemological questions are simply dismissed rather than re-examined. Thus despite considerable differences between their overall views, the arguments of Gadamer, Kuhn, Rorty, and Fish have the effect of privileging the deconstructive authority of historical conventions as much as science privileged verification or as epistemology privileged clear and distinct ideas.[10]

Thus to explain scientific progress, Kuhn argues that "explanation must, in the final analysis, be psychological or sociological. It must, that is, be a description of a value system, an ideology, together with the institutions through which that system is transmitted and enforced."[11] And Rorty maintains that "if anything 'replaces' epistemology it is the history and sociology of science" (*PM*, 226). And Fish claims that "the one thing a historically conditioned consciousness cannot do [is] scrutinize its own beliefs, conduct a rational examination of its own convictions – for in order to begin such a scrutiny, it would first have to escape the grounds of its own possibility" (BI, 107). Or as Gadamer says of the explanatory sufficiency of language: "The phenomenon of understanding ... shows the universality of human linguisticality as a limitless medium that carries *everything* within it – not only the 'culture' that has been handed down to us through language, but absolutely everything – because everything (in the world and out of it) is included in the realm of 'understandings' and understandability in which we move ... " (*PH*, 25); "With [the] area of what lies outside the realm of human understanding and human understandings (our world) hermeneutics is not concerned" (*PH*, 31). Such critical tactics – which are linch-pins for debunking objectivity and foundational invariance – often lead to an anti-foundationist universalism, a sweeping "everything is nothing but," which can be quite oblivious to the self-contradictory totalizations they imply in turn.[12]

The problem with the foundationist debate is that it has been left in

---

10. The point is not to represent all of these thinkers as similar in their conclusions. Rather, the point is to indicate how much credence is given to the linguistic and contextual mediacy of discourse as a tactic for deconstructing traditional and modern notions of foundations. Such tactics may appear in a variety of arguments that are otherwise substantially different.

11. In Imre Lakatos and Alan Musgrave, (eds.), *Criticism and the growth of knowledge*, Cambridge University Press, 1970; p. 21.

12. True, paradoxes may be benign, but this paradox is benign only if postmodern anti-foundational critique does not turn out to rest on what appear to be universalist claims, which it often does. Also, it must be noted that the most contradictory uses of these points are often indulged by epigones rather than by the originators. It is these less rigorous, more reductive versions that need to be critiqued, not that postmodern critique in general needs to be rejected.

the strong foundationist terms of a choice between an ultimate foundation and none at all (the one-or-none thesis), whereas neither of these positions is tenable. As a result, post-strong-foundationists become anti-foundationists. Anti-foundationism, in turn, leads to the postmodern preoccupation with critical practices in a spirit of localism and anti-theory that occults the question of the theoretical conditions presupposed by these practices.

An examination of the arguments of Gadamer, Rorty, Lyotard, Fish, and others, however, reveals their fundamental dependence on universalized claims, and hence the theoretical incoherence of their anti-foundationism as usually stated. But furthermore, their discourse also shows – both in the force of their claims and in the pattern of their contradictions – an unidentified heterological foundationism, an operation of necessary *critical conditions* that subverts *both* the error of strong foundationist closure and the totalization of strong conventionalist relativity. Consider, for example, certain discursive invariances – chosen for their genealogical and formal importance – that show the continuity between Habermas' well-known neo-foundationist project and certain thinkers normally associated with postmodern thought.

In his project to rationally ground social critique, Habermas posits a scheme of discursive modes whose critical authority suggests a neo-Kantian confidence in what he calls "quasi-transcendental" conditions of rationality:

There are three categories of processes of inquiry for which a specific connection between logical-methodological rules and knowledge-constitutive interests can be demonstrated. This demonstration is the task of a critical philosophy of science that escapes the snares of positivism. The approach of the empirical-analytic sciences incorporates a *technical* cognitive interest; that of the historical-hermeneutic sciences incorporates a *practical* one; and the approach of critically oriented sciences incorporates the *emancipatory* cognitive interest that, as we say, was at the root of traditional theories.[13]

In their greater skepticism about transcendental constraints, postmodernists suspect that the invocation of such categories defies the infinite questionability of hermeneutics. Do not transcendental categories imply the transcendence of history? Habermas' qualifying

---

13. *Knowledge and human interests*, Boston: Beacon, 1968, p. 308.

prefix "quasi-" is intended to indicate the empirical character of his categories, though postmodernists do not excuse claims of trans-cendence for being hypothetical, since transcendence violates the historicity of language. And yet, if we look at the way Habermas' categories function in his argument, we might find that deconstructors, strong interpretivists, and hermeneutic theorists have comparably "quasi-transcendental" elements at work in their arguments.

Gadamer, for instance, expects no less from an Aristotelian counterpart to Habermas' list, the three cognitive modes of *technē* (science), *epistēmē* (epistemology), and *phronēsis* (hermeneutics). No mere relic of Greek metaphysics, this set of distinctions allows Gadamer to critique both (1) the methodological abstractions of technology and (2) the self-refuting immediacy of epistemological theories, and do so by way of (3) the universality of questionability and interpretive praxis, i.e. the universality of *phronēsis* (hermeneutic indeterminacy). Nor should we be surprised at Gadamer's appeal to such distinctions, given his own Heideggerean genealogy. Heidegger's explanation of the hermeneutic circle includes the three aspects of the "pre-understanding" on which interpretation is based: *Vorhabe*; *Vorsicht*; and *Vorgriff*. According to Hubert Dreyfus, these terms distinguish the "totality of cultural practices" (conventional grounds), the "vocabulary or conceptual scheme we bring to any problem" (formal coherence), and any "specific hypothesis which ... can be confirmed or disconfirmed by the data" (objective grounds).[14] As aspects of pre-understanding these distinctions, no less fun-damental than Habermas', indicate the need to distinguish similar kinds of epistemic authority.

But perhaps even more surprising to some, one finds in Foucault a comparable willingness to resort to quasi-transcendental discursive distinctions. While commentators such as Dreyfus and Rabinow express a common belief that after "the *Archaeology* [*of knowledge*] he turns sharply away from the attempt to develop a theory of discourse," other commentators such as Deleuze are willing to attribute to Foucault an ongoing – and even neo-Kantian – commitment to epistemic distinctions that function quasi-transcendentally.[15] Thus one

---

14. See Hubert L. Dreyfus' discussion, "Holism and hermeneutics" in Robert Hollinger's anthology, *Hermeneutics and praxis*, Notre Dame, 1985; pp. 233–4.

15. Hubert L. Dreyfus and Paul Rabinow, *Michel Foucault: Beyond structuralism and hermeneutics*, Chicago, 1983; p. xxv. Despite the experimental character of

finds in the late Foucault interviews and in his *History of sexuality* a moral theory structured in three fundamental modes:

> Three domains of genealogy are possible. First, a historical ontology of ourselves in relation to truth, through which we constitute ourselves as subjects of knowledge [epistemology]; second, a historical ontology of ourselves in relation to a field of power through which we constitute ourselves as subjects on others [technology]; third, a historical ontology in relation to ethics through which we constitute ourselves as moral agents [hermeneutics].
>
> (FR, 351)

Though Foucault hails the specific intellectual rather than the general one, these distinctions may have a certain transcendence of their own, the kind of theoretical authority most commentators associate with his earlier, not-quite-structuralist phase. Furthermore, such a possibility may underlie other claims as well: "Truth is a thing of this world: it is produced only by virtue of multiple forms of constraints. And it induces regular effects of power" (FR, 72). How much regularity, finally? How "local" are these possible domains of genealogy? Disclaimers nothwithstanding, it is not clear that the specificity of meaning and power Foucault is known for is utterly incompatible with formal constraints of a foundationist character.

Heidegger, Gadamer, Habermas, and Foucault all acknowledge discursive conditions to hermeneutic understanding and their critical projects. Likewise, the anti-foundationist reading of the hermeneutic turn is too simplistic, even by its own critical commitments. Willingness to abandon one's assumptions is one thing; denying that they are there is another. While it is true that hermeneutics discovers the openness at the horizon of all understandings, it is also true that a philosophical hermeneutics defines that openness between the

---

Foucault's late work, which might suggest that Foucault's relation to theoretical foundations was not a settled question, some of his followers have been content to assume that the theoretical underpinnings for Foucault's histories are not a serious issue, since such underpinnings are the kinds of structures whose ultimacy he calls into question. Yet the assumption that their status is of secondary importance is no safer than any other assumption, and therefore needs to be argued more thoroughly than it has. Much to the contrary, as I argue in Chapter 6, the neo-Nietzschean emancipatory potential of Foucault's work depends on its relation to the theoretical structures which his more anarchist followers believe him to have critiqued. Indeed, Foucault's theoretical ambiguity accounts for why there are attributed to him utterly contradictory political and moral implications. For that issue, and to save him from the nihilism he explicitly eschews, the theoretical status of his discourse is crucial.

formal (*epistēmē*) and objective (*technē*) constraints that language mediates, constraints that are the necessary conditions of hermeneutics itself.

From foundationism to critical conditions

Postmodern anti-foundationism misidentifies the foundationist error, a misunderstanding which takes secondary problems for the essential problem.

Why foundations to begin with? Through philosophy's dialectic of skepticism and belief, the idea of foundations has traditionally implied a privileged principle by which epistemic authority is defined. Most of the candidates for that privilege were sought in the structure of thought (formality), in what is exterior to thought (objectivity), or in what appears self-evident to thought (certainty). Likewise, most epistemologists understood their task to be defending the crucial determinant of knowledge, and thereby *reducing* knowledge to the authority of a single element.

Peirce noted that the history of philosophy and science shows the reductive ideal to be oversimplified. Epistemology should not seek its foundations exclusively in the certainty of pure forms or in an empirical objectivity that transcends thought, but rather in the process (*semiosis*) by which thought unites these formal and objective elements in the historically conditioned mind of the interpreter(s). For Peirce the great lesson of modern epistemology (which Kant and Hegel only imperfectly understood)[16] is that thought can only be explained as a signifying product of three kinds of elements, each of which is a necessary condition. When phenomenology discovers the conditions of experience, including cognition, it always finds formal, objective, and historical elements woven together in semiosis. Kant's insight that thought constitutes itself is thus revised from his *a priori* model to a semiotic-pragmatic model where all knowledge derives from the *intermediacy* of different epistemic elements in experience.

Once the foundations of thought are rendered as a sign process, epistemology must be rethought. Epistemology cannot be reductive because these three different kinds of constraints are equally functional,

---

16. "Kant (whom I *more* than admire) is nothing but a somewhat confused pragmatist" (5.525); "I consider Hegel's three stages as being, roughly speaking, the correct list of Universal Categories" (5.53).

equally fundamental, and equally irreducible. Semiosis is not a hierarchy of dependences: it works by mediating thought between formal, objective, and historically contingent elements. Given that each element is a necessary epistemic condition, the traditional reductive approach was destined to fail in its efforts to make one privileged element the controlling determinant of knowledge. Though epistemology is still foundational, it is no longer reductive.

Nor is epistemology pure reason. Though epistemology discovers what constitutes experience, it does so *through* experience, not prior to it. Moreover, semiosis renders all cognition hypothetical, inter-dependent, intertextual, and hermeneutic. And what is true for the character of thought is true for philosophy itself. Philosophical authority, Peirce concludes, "should not form a chain which is no stronger than its weakest link, but a cable whose fibers may be ever so slender, provided they are sufficiently numerous and intimately connected" (5.265).

Why, then, is this post-traditional view not simply anti-founda-tionism? In Peirce the notion of foundations survives as the idea of necessary conditions, i.e. those elements that resist the reductions of strong foundationism. Likewise, in this view, much postmodern anti-foundationism appears constituted by half-truths. For even if strong foundationism was always in error, the error was not in seeking foundations at all, but in seeking a reductive version of them. The crucial error of traditional foundationism is not certainty, universality, or objectivity. Rather, the key error of foundationism is *explanatory reduction*, the error of thinking that one can explain knowledge monologically or wholly on the basis of formality (rationalism), objectivity (positivism), or historical conventions (hermeneutics).

On this point hangs the success of post-strong-foundationist philosophy. For as long as the issue of foundations is taken to involve either finding the privileged foundation/method or rejecting any necessary constraint on knowledge, philosophy will continue its unhappy contest between explanatory reduction and hermeneutic relativism.

Contrary to the contests of the faculties, however, if the strong foundationist error is explanatory reduction, then hermeneutics and epistemology are not incompatible. Since the universality of epistemic conditions does not refer to an ultimate principle, but rather to necessary conditions of thought, then we can say that thought always needs an accounting of both its formality and its context. In that case, hermeneutic universality means that there must always be a context of interpretation, while formalism means that every practice is defined by the formal conditions that make it possible. What we cannot say is that contextuality rules out necessary conditions (as Gadamer, Rorty, and Fish imply), or that formal conditions of some practices hold for all practices (as Habermas and Apel maintain).

Epistemic formality refers to the fact that all practices have their formal conditions, and the more general the practice, the more general the conditions. For epistemology, the *only* universal practice is thought itself – the medium of analysis – whose only universal conditions are formality, objectivity, and history. These ultimate constraints include formality insofar as thought is representational, objectivity insofar as experience has material constraints, and conventions insofar as analytic thought always has its uniquely historical and social context. (I refer to the historical element as truncated into the hermeneutic *conventions* of social and linguistic understanding.) This multiplicity of critical conditions shows that epistemic authority is always constitutive and open-ended. Against traditional epistemology, this heterological foundationism derives from the universality of its own disclosure, its openness to the various contingencies of practice and indeterminacies of history and context.

This post-reductive epistemology points to several ways in which anti-foundationism continues to distort the issue of knowledge due to strong foundationist habits. Objective conditions are not univocal, though they are not dispensable either. Formal conditions need not "stand outside" practice in order to be presupposed by that practice. Indeed, they are *inside* practice in the same sense that syntax is inside one's speech. Of course, one may choose not to speak; but if one speaks a language one invokes its syntactic logic, whether to be straightforwardly employed or to be ironically transformed. Here formality must be disengaged from its strong foundationist past. Instead of functioning as the anatomy of certainty as Descartes would have it, or as the limit to all experience as Kant proposed, the formal conditions of thought and significance constitute a heterology of logical *possibilities* of signification. By displacing the "exterior boundary" or "universal essence" conceptions of strong foundationism with the heterological conception of formal possibilities, formality appears as epistemically enabling rather than reductive and confining.

The strong foundationist legacy was not in error to seek the logical conditions of knowledge, but only in assuming that philosophical authority converged upon a single principle of explanation, upon systematically closed and uniquely necessary conditions for knowledge, or upon immediate knowledge of such conditions. Freed of this reductive fallacy, logical conditions can assume their proper relation to practice, i.e. as enabling logics whose critical force depends at once on formal possibilities and contextual conditions. As Derrida paraphrases Peirce, such a theorization of formal critical conditions "is a matter of elaborating ... a formal doctrine of conditions which a discourse must satisfy in order to have a sense, in order to mean, even if it is false or contradictory. The general morphology of that meaning (*Bedeutung*, *vouloir-dire*) is independent of all logic of truth" (*OG*, 49). Evaluation, including truth and falsity, is always a function of the whole that is constituted historically by formal conditions.

The heterological epistemology to which semiotics and the history of foundationist philosophy point is revolutionary just because it blocks the traditional *reductive* ideal of an ultimate principle of explanation. Rather than converging on a single ground, knowledge and meaning are projected *between* inner (formal) and outer (objective) constraints.[17] It is this semiotic (in)determination of language between inner and outer elements that underlies the critique of reductive foundationism and the reconstruction of philosophy.

Hermeneutics and heterological epistemology

It is this dynamic balance of critical conditions that postmodern anti-epistemological, anti-theoretical critique tends to miss (and thus obscure) in its haste to bury strong foundationism. Ironically, hermeneutic universalism seduces postmodern thought into the traditional one-or-none notion of epistemic constraints, the false dilemma of strong foundationism or arbitrary conditions for knowledge. Thus in the name of hermeneutic universality Gadamer and Fish struggle to collapse all significance into the historicity of language and convention, while against postmodernism Habermas struggles to find a universal paradigm of rationality by which to demarcate social

---

17. Foucault acknowledges this heterological origin of knowledge in language's occulting of absolute origins: "we have seen how labour, life, and language acquired their own historicity, in which they were embedded ... [a] historicity that, in its very fabric, makes possible the necessity of *an origin which must be both internal and foreign to it.*" *The order of things*, New York: Random House, 1970; p. 329; (my emphasis).

legitimacy. Even thus, the invariance of epistemic grounds competes with the variance of meaning. And so postmodernism obscures the theoretical conditions of its own, and indeed of all, critical authority.

What, then, *are* the limits of hermeneutic universality?

Since all thought is a sign process, all thought is interpreted and inferential; thought is indeed universally questionable, as Gadamer says. This becomes a reflexive feature of hermeneutics: the process of questioning itself has no origin, no end, no essential form. Unlike the more specifically defined sciences, hermeneutics – as Heidegger, Gadamer, and Rorty maintain – has no method. Its historical substance renders it self-consuming, as Gadamer observes: "the task of hermeneutics, seen philosophically, consists in asking what kind of understanding, what kind of science it is, that is itself changed by historical change" (*TM*, 276).

Yet this is a universality that easily misleads. If one were to focus only on the decentering movements of postmodern hermeneutics, it would appear as if all transcendental constraints have been repudiated, as postmodern anti-foundationist rhetoric suggests, especially in its aggressive displacements of science and epistemology. But the "universal scope of the hermeneutic problem" does not finally render science, epistemology, and transcendence obsolete, as the defenders of hermeneutics themselves admit in their most candid moments. Thus Rorty concedes that epistemology and hermeneutics "do not compete, but rather help each other out" (*PM*, 346); and Gadamer admits that science "will continue along its own path with an *inner necessity beyond its control*, and it will produce more and more breathtaking knowledge and controlling power" (*PH*, 10; my emphasis); and Kuhn and Feyerabend will defer to the local technological success of science that somehow, for them, does not add up to truth. For all its deconstructive power, hermeneutic historicity is not adequate even for the critical purposes of the partisans of hermeneutics. There is always a given residue that is not *merely* history, not *merely* what interlocutors happen to agree to, something with an "inner" formality or an "outer" expediency that is not yet hermeneutic, not yet put to use. And this is why anti-foundationism remains incoherent and inadequate to its own critical force.

Here philosophical hermeneutics needs a few more epistemic teeth. Hermeneutics' historicity and its dialectical character, finally, are not *due to* the absence of a proper method; that feature is not the cause but the *effect* of hermeneutics' critical conditions, its inner necessity, which is also its formal openness. That is, hermeneutics is conditioned by the heterology of its own objective and formal constraints – the constraints it mediates historically. Indeed, the infinitude of question-ability is universal just because formal and objective constraints on power, knowledge, and meaning are at once necessary and different, and thus irreducible.

Semiotically viewed, hermeneutics is constituted by formal and objective constraints on our represented world, producing culture, tradition, texts, i.e. the conventional substance of our historical contexts: "To exist historically means that self-knowledge proceeds from what is historically pre-given, what we call, with Hegel, 'substance'" (*TM*, 269). Textuality and meaning do have substance, not because history gives it to them (whatever that might mean), but because the necessities of formal and objective constraints transcend our discretion, however their mediation may evolve with experience. The instability of language occurs *within* the necessary constraints of meaning, reinterpreting but not dispensing with objective exteriority to linguistic form and the formal invariances that, like tomorrow's experiment and everyone's mathematics, remain possible grounds of meaning.

Our organization of experience between formal and objective constraints has a local determinacy that is the work of hermeneutics, history, and sociology to identify. As contextually determined, hermeneutic products are always conventional, practical, and unique: "the text, whether law or gospel, if it is to be understood properly, i.e. according to the claim it makes, must be understood at every moment, in every particular situation, in a new and different way. Under-standing here is always application" (*TM*, 275). Because it is infinite, "The illumination of [the hermeneutic] situation ... can never be entirely completely achieved" (*TM*, 269). When hermeneutic philoso-phers say that such a mediate condition is historical in substance they merely point to what semioticians theorize as the formal process of semiosis, a process "repeated continually throughout our familiar experience" (*PH*, 15). But that infinite disclosure, that hermeneutic universality, is *necessary* just because it is formally structured between pure form and objectivity, the necessary "inner" and "outer" constraints, the critical conditions of all hermeneutic interpretation.

In the reconciliation of epistemology and hermeneutics, then, epistemology shows to hermeneutics the heterological structure of its openness to the world – the necessity of its inner and outer constraints

– while hermeneutics shows the practical or *applied* character of all thought as interpretation. On the one hand, linguistic or hermeneutic conventions of understanding practically mediate the necessary constraints of objectivity and formality. On the other hand, that process is never finished, and therefore perpetually requiring further applications of the self-transforming conventional substance of history. Given its hermeneutically practical character, Kant's philosophical reflection – "reason turned back upon itself" – never completes the final examination.

Much of the current divisiveness of postmodern critical theoretical discussions results from the failure to find in the critique of traditional epistemology a theoretical and critical space between foundationist reductions and hermeneutic relativism. Anti-foundationism, however, only substitutes historicist reductions for strong foundationist ones. If, on the other hand, philosophy's critical conditions are multiple, irreducible, and historically interpreted, then there are necessary conditions for critical practice, the same conditions revealed and presupposed by the critique of strong foundationism.

Fish's strong conventions: the mind's own world

> The mind is its own place, and in itself
> Can make a Heav'n of Hell, a Hell of Heav'n.
>
> (Satan), *Paradise Lost*

A. Conventionism in literary critique

One of the more confusing aspects of the last four decades of critical and philosophical discourse has been the tendency for literary theory to get more epistemological just as philosophers were getting more literary. In the same decades in which Wittgenstein, Quine, Sellars, and Austin were relaxing their notion of philosophy's legitimacy, literary critics were trying to bolster theirs.[1]

With the skepticism of post-structuralist excursions into the interpretive instabilities of the human sciences, however, a number of the more theoretically inclined critics soon suffered the same disillusionment and frustration that postmodern philosophers felt with the bolder claims of positivism, analytic philosophy, and ideal-language philosophy. It is not surprising, therefore, that postmodern

---

1. Early in the fifties, R. S. Crane noted the Chicago School's search for "a more critical approach to criticism itself, in something like the Kantian sense of 'critical': a consideration of criticism, as a mode of inquiry, that would go behind the doctrines of different schools and try to uncover the basic assumptions about literature and literary study on which these are founded" (*Critics and criticism*, Chicago: 1952; p. v). Northrop Frye recalls being surprised when, early in his career, he discovered "how general was the agreement that criticism had no presuppositions of its own, but had to be 'grounded' on some other subject." (*Contexts for criticism*, ed. Donald Keesey, Mountain View, California: Mayfield, 1987; p. 268). His monumental *Anatomy of criticism* attempts to suggest that "there is surely no reason why criticism, as a systematic and organized study, should not be, at least partly, a science" (*Literary theories in praxis*, ed. Shirley Staton, Philadelphia: University of Pennsylvania, 1987; p. 111). Then structuralism arose to promise a transdisciplinary methodology for all the human sciences. For a time it appeared that criticism was not too late for scientific respectability.

philosophers and critics, sharing a skeptical sensibility, turn to similar strategies in their critiques of strong foundationist theories.

In particular, the later work of Stanley Fish illustrates an important and instructive turn from his earlier explorations of a number of current theoretical models (e.g. linguistics, stylistics, speech-act theory, reader-response theory) to a conventionist model of literary criticism. As a strong interpretivist, Fish characterizes his development as anti-foundational:

[Formerly] I wanted to put my accounts of *the* reader's experience on as firm a ground as the ground claimed by the champions of the text by identifying the *real* reading experience in relation to which others were deviations or distortions. What I finally came to see was that the identification of what was real and normative occurred within interpretive communities and what was normative for the members of one community would be seen as strange (if it could be seen at all) by members of another. (*ITC*, 15–16).

Having put behind him his foundationist search for a privileged theoretical model, a paradigmatic origin or ground of meaning, Fish resolved to explore how readers constitute the rules of interpretation by virtue of consensus among "interpretive communities." This change of terms is no mere semantic trick, hiding another privileged formality behind the notion of convention. Being conventional, the structure of consensus is historical, contextual, unformalizable, untotalizable.

For Fish, the conventionism of interpretive communities explains and guarantees the insufficiency of all other theoretical models. In this view, all literary theoretical models – and thus the efforts of all strong foundationist critics – suffer from being but one possible set of conventional constraints, one possible language game, one possible practice. A theorized ideal reader may or may not be the historical reader; a syntactical structure may or may not control the figures of speech in a given text – such issues remain open to interpretation. As opposed to such qualified claims, however, interpretive communities *must* agree on their rules in order for the rules to work. As Wittgenstein suggests, there is no such thing as a private language. As interpretive communities are a condition of meaning, their presence becomes a powerful argument for the conventionality of meaning formation. And so Fish concludes that all rules of reading must be conventional.

The fact that all interpretations are mediated by the local conventions of their practitioners appears to refute a certain kind of totalizing strategy practiced by strong foundationists. Whereas objectivists want to suggest that there is something outside our language that constrains our thinking and the truth of our speech, interpretivists such as Gadamer and Fish claim instead that there is *nothing outside language* to which objectivists can lay claim. In Gadamer's words: "There is always a world already interpreted, already organized in its basic relations, into which our experience steps as something new ... Understanding is language-bound" (*PH*, p. 15). Or as Derrida says, there is nothing outside the text. Or as Fish likes to put it, there is nowhere to stand outside interpretation. In any case, the point is to enclose all understanding within the conventional parameters of the interpreter's horizon of meaning, whatever its inevitable prejudices and historical limits of vision.

By defending the primacy of interpretive communities over hermeneutic theory, Fish repudiates foundationist theory in the name of conventions and history. His attempts to develop this position, however, repeatedly show the inadequacies of conventionism in two ways. First, his arguments fail to account for *all* of the constraints of interpretation (some of which are non-conventional); second, this ignorance of non-conventional constraints leads to a new form of reduction, reduction to conventional authority. Indeed, Fish's intolerance of all non-conventionist explanations of meaning and authority dramatizes a contradiction in strong conventionism, and of anti-foundationism in general: the more narrowly he makes his case for conventional constraints – as opposed to all others – the more universalist he becomes. Like the radical skeptic who wants to believe absolutely in the impossibility of absolute belief, strong conventionism becomes a crypto-totalizing discourse that contradicts in practice what it preaches.

Though Fish's position presumes to be a pragmatic one, its dogmatic adherence to conventionism cripples its critical force through all its transformations. In the following discussion, I examine the flawed first premise of Fish's position – the strong foundationist antinomy of *one-foundation-or-none* – and work toward an understanding of its implications for the practice and institution of criticism.

1. Literary anti-theory

When literary theorists of the seventies began to feel exhausted by the search for the foundations of literary criticism, Stephen Knapp, Walter Benn Michaels, and Stanley Fish turned against the very possibility of literary theory. In their project, these "anti-theorists" identified literary theory as, in Fish's words:

an effort to govern practice in two senses: (1) it is an attempt to *guide* practice from a position above or outside it ... , and (2) it is an attempt to *reform* practice by neutralizing interest, by substituting for the parochial perspective of some local or partisan point of view the perspective of a general rationality to which the individual subordinates his contextually conditioned opinions and beliefs ... Only if this substitution is accomplished will interpretation be principled, that is, impelled by formal and universal rules that apply always and everywhere rather than by rules of thumb that reflect the contingent practices of particular communities. (*AT*, 110)

But Fish's argument against general hermeneutics indulges two totalizations of its own. First, Fish does not intend his attack to be limited to such literary theoretical critics as Northrop Frye, the structuralists, and E. D. Hirsch, Jr. with their projects of literary formalism, general hermeneutics, and "validity in interpretation." Fish considers the pattern to apply in linguistics, social theory, legal theory, or anywhere else where interpretation is the issue. Furthermore, because Fish assumes that theory necessarily conforms to the pattern of strong foundationist reduction, it can be argued against in principle: "The argument *against* theory is simply that this substitution of the general for the local has never been and will never be achieved. Theory is an impossible project which will never succeed" (*AT*, 110).

The issue of foundations and theory, however, is not finally what Fish makes of it. In brief, interpretation is not a question of substituting the general for the local, but of *applying* the general locally or of finding the general *in* the local. The problem is that Fish insists on Platonizing foundations as "above or outside" the text. By polarizing the issue between Plato and Fish, Fish reduces the notion of foundations to a straw man, thereby distracting the issue from a suitable definition of theory, foundations, and hermeneutics.

In the wake of structuralism, Fish's Platonic definition of theory as an interpretive position outside practice is *already* obsolete. Fish's work on interpretive communities parallels work by the literary Marxists, feminists, and semiotic deconstructors for whom theoretical and practical interests are not mutually exclusive, and for whom theory is the more valuable for getting *into* practice rather than for getting outside it.[2] To tilt against Platonic transcendence and practical

---

2. Some Marxist and feminist literary theorists have turned to theory, not to escape practice, but rather to show the practical consequences of foundationist ideas.

neutrality is to tilt against a very unpopular straw man that can hardly claim to represent fully the many current interests of theory.

Faced with the phenomenon of "negative theory" – a theory of vigorously non-reductive intent – Fish admits the equivocal nature of theory, but concludes that the negative theorists do not change the crux of the matter. Why? Because that is not how Fish has defined theory: "The fact that there are two kinds of theory (or, rather, theoretical discourse – *antifoundationism really isn't a theory at all*; it is an argument against the possibility of theory) complicates the question of consequences [of theory], although in the end the relationship of both kinds of theory to the question turns out to be the same" (*AT*, 112; my italics). Even on its face this claim is incoherent, suggesting that negative theory is and is not theory (isn't really theory but has the same implications as theory, which cannot exist). The fact that negative theorists have persuasively critiqued strong foundationist reductions with their own foundationist inquiries into the logical conditions of knowledge and meaning is good reason to reject Fish's Platonic straw man, a definitional point on which his whole argument hangs. It even suggests that negative theory is just what Fish has in mind.

But Fish *wants* the Platonic theory-convention antinomy without which his strong conventionism makes no sense: "So, even though the thesis that theory has no consequences holds only when the consequences are of a certain kind [i.e. transcendental], they are the only consequences that matter, since they are the consequences that would mark theory off as special" (*AT*, 125).[3] Why define theory so

Likewise, for Fish to suggest that Derrida's deconstructions are not theoretical would obscure the source of their greatest power: i.e. that the targets of his deconstructions are so *fundamental*. Or as Foucault deconstructs the theory/practice dichotomy in a generalization of his own: "truth isn't outside power, or lacking in power ... [Truth] is a thing of this world" (*FR*, 73).

3. Must the syllogism stand outside practice to be special? Must physics stand outside the physical world to have a theory? Is Aristotle's theory of logic redundant because the syllogism normally works in a context with particular content? Or isn't it true that Aristotle's theory is special just because it identifies an *inner logic* of thought that enables us to understand better the practical force of thought? As a practice, theory is theory when it identifies in a general way the abstract structures of practices of more specific contexts. Theory abstracts, but it need not force a *choice* between the general and the contextual, or even a priority between them. Transcending practice is neither the ultimate point of theory nor what makes it special, which is the point of the pragmatic challenge to epistemology: to be interesting, a theory need only identify what works in practice – and for epistemology, as generally as possible.

that theory can only be special if it is outside practice, and hence impossible? Why assume that Plato had the only true theory of theory, if his was wrong? Why should we forget about the alternative tradition of theory from Aristotle's critique of transcendentalism to Peirce's critique of Kant, just because such theories of theory are not "special" enough to qualify as straw men? However misguided may be those Platonic literalists who think that theory stands outside practice, the point is not to accept their rhetoric as the essence of theory, but rather to reform the notion of theory as, for example, science has. Here begins a pattern of contradiction that plagues Fish and much of postmodern anti-foundationism: by refusing to allow revisions of theory, Fish essentializes theory in the most transcendental way possible – i.e. as necessarily outside practice – with self-consuming consequences for his unfolding theory of hermeneutic practice.[4]

In particular, two kinds of problems follow from this theoretical error. First, Fish must force everyone less conventionist than himself into the false dilemma of essentialism and conventionism in order to reduce hermeneutics to conventions. Secondly, this strong conventionist reduction constitutes an anti-universalist universalism, totalizing the possibilities of theory and meaning in the name of contextuality.

2. From argument to interpretation

Whereas Fish's anti-theory arguments reveal his theoretical premises, his essay "Demonstration vs. persuasion: two models of critical activity" reveals the central rhetorical strategy of his subsequent

---

4. Indeed, Fish's identification of theory with a position outside practice is even more debilitating than Rorty's identification of epistemology with an ultimate standard of knowledge, for Rorty at least left himself the concept of theory to use in a pragmatic way, and finally concedes a complementary relation between epistemology and hermeneutics. But Fish denies himself that option. Instead, he winds up saying at different turns that anti-foundationism is and isn't theory, and that theory explains foundational history but has no consequences – until finally, like Rorty, he winds up taking back the punch of his thesis and even admits the inevitability of theory's consequences: "But certainly we have gone too far, and it is time to admit what everyone knows: theory has consequences; not, however, because it stands apart from and can guide practice but because it is itself a form of practice and therefore is consequential for practice as a matter of definition" (*AT*, 125).

work. Beginning with the traditional rhetorical distinction between demonstration (rational appeal) and persuasion (irrational appeal), Fish fashions a two-fold model of literary criticism in which the irrational functions turn out to be the more basic. The original rhetorical distinction becomes a critical distinction between arguments *from* assumed grounds and principles of reason, and foundationist arguments *about* grounds. By arguing that literary criticism is ultimately about grounds, Fish's model of literary criticism appears to put all grounds into question at once, as if all constraints on meaning were theoretically contingent, and only arbitrarily determined by the conventions of the interpretive community.[5] Thus Fish appears to reduce discursive authority to the accidents of convention.

This argument claims that literary criticism, when it is most interesting, is not rational but rather *about* rationality: i.e. criticism is finally irrational or persuasive not when it departs from reason, but when it determines reason by the choice of first principles:

we try to persuade others to our beliefs because if they believe what we believe, they will, as a consequence of those beliefs, see what we see; and the facts to which we point in order to support our interpretations will be as obvious to them as they are to us. Indeed, this is the whole of critical activity, an attempt on the part of one party to alter the beliefs of another so that the evidence cited by the first will be seen *as* evidence by the second.

(*ITC*, 365)

In the best literary criticism, one does not *demonstrate* conclusions on the basis of already accepted first principles; rather, one persuades one's interlocutor of the best total framing of the relevant material, including all principles in dispute. Rather than forcing obedience to rules of reason from given premises, Fish argues, criticism decides those first principles, and does so necessarily by persuasion.[6]

5. According to the traditional rhetoric of debate, critical argument is supposed to be a matter of arguing a conclusion from the basis of shared premises and according to shared standards of method. In this view, demonstration argues rigorously according to the rules of reason from whatever is assumed to be true. Persuasion, on the other hand, is traditionally thought to be an irrational appeal to the will, an appeal that is outside the authority of reason, whether directed toward rational conclusions or not. Demonstration depends, therefore, on the authority of the rational rules for getting from premises to conclusion. Persuasion is irrational insofar as it does not reduce to the rule of reason, nor requires it to succeed.

6. Furthermore, this foundational implication raises the stakes of criticism to their highest point: "Obviously, the stakes are much higher in a persuasion than in a

But despite the cogency of Fish's version of what happens in literary critical interpretations – or maybe because Fish's model appears to be as coherent as it does – the foundational theorist might still ask what Fish has shown about the limits of reason. Fish has shown that it is possible to challenge *some* principles of reasoning, and that certain choices of constraints are conventional. But has Fish utterly dispelled the question of non-conventional critical conditions within which such persuasions and meanings must take place? Has Fish shown or merely asserted that *all* first principles, all rules of reason, are negotiable? In fact, what could show that *everything* is negotiable except a foundationist theory of rationality? What else would be strong enough to make everything negotiable *in principle*?

Indeed, how strong is Fish's claim? Of course, there are literary critical arguments that challenge principles. This claim is provocative and useful. But Fish appears to imply that literary criticism is *always* putting everything up for grabs. Not only has he not shown this, but it seems to be a totalizing theory in disguise. On closer inspection this contradiction becomes clear.

If we assume that literary criticism is about first principles, what should follow from that? Fish appears to conclude that everything becomes conventional. Thus he claims that "the mechanisms of persuasion, like everything else, are context-specific" (*ITC*, 369). The "everything else" is an important and characteristic qualification. Is mathematics context-specific? Is semiotics context-specific? Is the law of gravity context-specific? Is the rule that "all rules are context-specific" itself context-specific? Fish argues as if the latter were not, in which case strong conventionism becomes a more-than-modestly foundationist theory.

For conventions to be all-powerful, all hermeneutic constraints would have to be conventional, which they are not. Ignoring the variety of hermeneutic constraints conflates disparate elements: i.e. the meaning (effect) and its constraints (causes), as well as the

demonstration model, since they include nothing less than the very conditions under which the game, in all of its moves (description, evaluation, validation, and so on), will be played" (*ITC*, 357). Indeed, the institutional structure appears to foster this foundational brinksmanship, insofar as "The greatest rewards of our profession are reserved for those who challenge the assumptions within which ordinary practices go on, not so much in order to eliminate the category of the ordinary but in order to redefine it and reshape its configuration" (*ITC*, 358). Theorists are the acknowledged legislators of the critical world.

description and what it describes. Thus Fish refers to objects constituted by the act of interpretation: "the practice of literary criticism ... is absolutely essential not only to the maintenance of, but to the very production of, the objects of its attention" (*ITC*, 368). The equivocation lies in the ambiguity of the term "object": does it distinguish between the objects referred to in texts, the meanings attributed to objects in texts, or the material conditions which produced the texts and its readings? Surely, not all of these are equally produced by literary conventions.

Here we might consider Frege's distinction between sense and reference, for instance, in order to note how in some cases invariance of reference can ground variance of sense. Consider a project that sends a group of astronauts to Mars. As the astronauts approach the planet, public debate arises over the political-military interest of the planet. A concerned Commander-in-Chief decides to follow the example of his conventionist predecessor who changed the name of the Department of War to the "Defense" Department. In response to political influence, the scientific community agrees to change the planet's name from Mars to Penelope, recalling the faithfulness and patience of the Greek heroine. Yes, the sense of the planet's name may have changed, but the reference does not, nor will the scientists have to recalculate the path of the astronauts because the sense has changed. Here lies the problem of saying that nothing is independent of thought, that everything is inside language, and that everything is negotiable. For our manipulations of sense may depend on referential constraints that are beyond our control. True, maybe we should not take "theoretical transcendence" literally; but then we should not take "rewriting history" to mean "changing the past" either.

The same problem arises in literary criticism. Consider several readings of an eighteenth century "virtue rewarded" novel where the heroine is transformed from an attractive strumpet into a well-married wife. The Platonic reading says that the title contradicts the real meaning: that in a materialistic society, everything is for sale, in which case there is little virtue indeed. A historicist could reject the Platonic assumption that virtue has an essence and maintain instead that the novel portrays only an eighteenth century ideal of virtue, and does that quite accurately. One possible feminist reading might suggest that the novel portrays a woman succeeding within a system of male exploitation by learning how to manage her assets, although she remains a victor in hostile territory. A Foucaultian genealogist could reject any residual exploitation pathos by suggesting that within the mechanistic *epistémè* of the eighteenth century everyone was complicit with the system by virtue of the shared assumptions, in which case the novel really was a *Bildungsroman* for its time. The historical materialist reading, however, might say that regardless of the value one attaches to the heroine's behavior, that behavior presupposes a society in which central moral institutions have become enmeshed in a commodity system to the point of being openly transformed by it. This, it could be argued, is a historical contingency that is not only conventionally true but objectively true as well since there are non-conventional conditions of meaning-production. How many of the constraints that determine these readings are *wholly* constituted by the interpreter and his community? Are not the conventional constraints of history enmeshed in constraints that are prediscursive?

Fish sidetracks the issue of constraints by counter-attacking those positivists who fear that anarchy will be loosed upon the world if interpretation cannot be secured by theory: "The mistake is to think of interpretation as an activity in need of constraints, when in fact interpretation is a *structure* of constraints." But the problem for conventionism is not explaining how it keeps anarchy from breaking loose, which Fish does admirably. The problem for conventionism is explaining how it accounts for a world that seems remarkably resistant to the irrational stipulations of its readers throughout the flux of conventions. If conventionism wants to be "strong," the burden of proof is on Fish to show that conventional constraints are not only necessary, but *sufficient* to account for meaning, lest we require grounds more substantive than his. For it does not follow from (a) the fact that *some* "conditions under which the [literary critical] game will be played" are up for grabs, that (b) *all* conditions are negotiable. Again, the only way to get from "some are conventional" to "all are conventional" would be to theorize the universal conditions of meaning, which is what conventionist anti-foundationism cannot do without betraying itself.

The fallacy of "some = all" leads Fish to the "total negotiability" thesis by a two-step sleight of hand. Thus Fish begins by pointing to the contingency of persuasion: "Notice that the determination of what would count as being persuasive is a function of what is understood to be at stake." But then he jumps from "some constraints are context-specific" to the implication that everything is negotiable: "That is, the mechanisms of persuasion, like everything else, are context-specific; what will be persuasive in any argument depends on what the parties have agreed to in advance" (*ITC*, 369). True, interlocutors must agree on *some* of the stakes of a debate, lest there be nothing from which to start the debate, and such agreements will include context-specific constraints. But Fish cannot claim that *all* stakes and rules are agreed upon, or that none are context-transcendent.[7] Would Fish contend, for instance, that no one argued logically before Aristotle codified the syllogism so that debaters could agree to it?

Strong conventionism cannot be maintained without its contradictions victimizing its advocates. And so if we ask how Fish can know the limits of conventionality, we find Fish the anti-totalizer in a difficult position. In a later admission of the limits of consensus, Fish himself will argue that consensus is not transparent:

[seeing through historical constraints] is the one thing a historically conditioned consciousness cannot do – scrutinize its own beliefs, conduct a rational examination of its own convictions – for in order to begin such a scrutiny, it would first have to escape the grounds of its own possibility, and it could only do that if it were not historically conditioned and were instead an acontextual or unsituated entity of the kind that is rendered unavailable by the first principle of the interpretivist or conventionist view.   (*AP*, 107)

Curiously, except for those few remaining Platonists, the victim of this point is Fish's own position. For while formal and objective conditions of meaning can be somewhat reliably recuperated by empirical science and logic, it seems that the *historical* ground of interpretation is the more self-consuming source of indeterminacy. The only grounds being mystified here are the conventional ones; unhappily, those are the only ones Fish recognizes.[8]

---

7. Syllogistic logic, for instance, is at once context-specific (it depends on its premises for content) *and* context-transcendent (it is formally structured to yield necessary conclusions), and is necessarily presupposed by critics (when they are not writing poetry). Since one cannot argue without it, one need not agree upon it in advance. Since its truth depends on its premises, it depends on context for truth. But since some of its authority is formal, it is not *reducible* to context.

8. When Fish defers to the first principle of strong conventionism, he indicates the *a priori* character of its assumptions, i.e. the false dilemma between Platonic transcendence and non-arbitrary critique, the assumption that we either hope vainly to escape practice or surrender to the unchecked sway of arbitrary local commitments. But one need not stand outside history to transcend convention – objectivity *intrudes* itself into history, and the formal grounds of meaning are always already *inside* the contingencies of history. Paradoxically, whereas conventions are sometimes too close to see except from a historical distance,

Given these daunting odds, how could Fish universalize his "nothing-but-context-specificity" thesis? Fish uses two tactics: first, he theorizes an inherently irrational psychology of belief; second, he demonstrates how anyone less strong-conventionist than himself must be Plato in disguise.

B. The prison-house of full commitment

Lacking exterior constraints, Fish's self-legitimating conventions become a self-contemplating system of local truths, an anarchy of collective self-affirmations. The truth is simply what we believe it is until a stronger belief comes along. Indeed, even communal consensus turns out to be too narrow for the irrationality of conventionism: for the arbitrariness of conventions has an individualized face as well. Being irrational at root, jumping from one arbitrary belief to the next, our experience does not constitute any sort of progress. Life is a montage of gestalt switches that have no systematic, objective, or metanarrative logic.

Fish consistently unfolds the perplexing consequences of this arbitrary model of meaning. Movement is always toward new arbitrary commitments, new apparent givens, new seeming necessities. Since there are only conventions, there is nothing to mitigate their hold on us: they must be irresistible. Even knowing that our beliefs were inadequate many times before does not lessen our vulnerability to them now: "An awareness that one's perspective is limited does not make the facts yielded by that perspective seem any less real; and when that perspective has given way to another, a new set of facts will occupy the position of the real ones" (*ITC*, 362). That we may discard facts one after another does not diminish their grip. We are belief addicts. For Fish, there is no willing or unwilling suspension of belief or disbelief.[9] Experience, for conventionism, is not a teacher, but a

objective and formal constraints can sometimes be identified more easily just because they already transcend linguistic contingency.

9. "Stephen Booth tells me that [my] formulation may be too strong, and he reminds me of an experience many of us will be able to recall, knowing while watching a horror movie that certain devices are being used to frighten us and yet being frightened nevertheless despite our knowledge. In experiences like this an analytical understanding of what is happening exists side by side with what is happening but does not affect or neutralize it ... [An] analytical perspective on a practice does not insulate one from experiencing the practice in all its fullness, that is in the same way one would experience it were the analytical perspective

taskmaster. Belief is a hermeneutic fate that cannot be resisted by the resources of reason: "one cannot, properly speaking, *be* a skeptic, and one cannot be a skeptic for the same reason that one cannot be a relativist ... The conclusion is tautological but inescapable: one believes what one believes, and one does so without reservation" (*ITC*, 361).

This conclusion, however, is a non-sequitur: the tautology only covers the first clause – one believes what one believes – it does not cover the second, given that human psychology is a bit more complicated than the syllogism.

1. Tautology as psychology

As a number of commentators have pointed out regarding the psychology of Fish's universalized reader – as early as *Surprised by sin* – the expectations of Fish's reader/believer are immune to experience. Fish's model of belief precludes getting over the surprise at being wrong. Fish's universalized naivety, however, appears to be contradicted by the massive evidence that analytic experience does interfere with feelings of certitude, of optimism, of hopefulness, of trust, of surprise, and of mystery whether one considers revolutionary fervor, the chemistry of seduction, or the differences between naive and sentimental poetry, between early and late romanticism, between classicism and postmodernism, or a host of other commonplace chronologies. Indeed, for better or worse, the more experienced we get – as the trailing clouds of glory get fainter and fainter – the more likely we are to join Wordsworth in wishing that feeling *were* as insulated from knowledge as Fish says. (Perhaps a nineteenth century specialist would have arrived at different theoretical conclusions from a Miltonist.) For Fish, however, the lack of any claim on belief beside the rule of convention insures that its authority is uncontested by anything but more historical accidents.

Fish's anti-progressivism provides an illustrative contrast to Gadamer's historicist view of the fruits of experience: "the experienced person proves to be ... someone who is radically undogmatic

unavailable" (BI, 21). But if Fish's disarming of irony by credulity were correct, then we would make no distinction between lamenting real tragedies and enjoying fictional ones. Notwithstanding certain exceptions (e.g. gladiators and Christians), obliterating the distinction is not normal because irony diminishes the fullness of credulity.

... The dialectic of experience has its own fulfilment not in definitive knowledge, but in that openness to experience that is encouraged by experience itself" (*TM*, 319). Gadamer finds that experience makes us aware of our "finitude," and therefore of the fallibility of our beliefs. Fish, however, finds no diminishing of full commitment.

If Fish's reader seems unrealistic, it is because Fish has fallen prey to a confusion of language and psychology, i.e. confusing the semantics of tautology (i.e. we believe what we believe) with the complexity of reflective attitudes (i.e. we always believe with full commitment). Feelings, however, are not reducible to tautologies, and the attitude of doubt is not simply an all-or-nothing affair. Fish's reader is like Milton's Satan, who cannot imagine that there is a dignified position between defiance and self-abasement. But that too is a false dilemma; there are a multitude of degrees and structures of commitment. One is not committed to one's friend, one's parents, one's spouse, one's profession, and one's nation in the same always-absolute way. Beliefs are no different. Fish's false dilemma of all-or-nothing, of full-commitment-or-utter-skepticism, simply misunderstands doubt. His ontogeny of perpetually full commitment is an equivocation rather than a portrait of the experienced reader.

Since Fish's psychology of feeling is based on a categorical (yes, even essentialist) logic alien to feeling, his analysis of the feeling of progress quickly becomes incoherent. Fish hopes to explain the feeling of progress as a kind of subjective illusion: "the idea of progress is inevitable, not, however, because there *is* a progress in the sense of a clearer and clearer sight of an independent object but because the *feeling* of having progressed is an inevitable consequence of the firmness with which we hold our beliefs, or, to be more precise, of the firmness with which our beliefs hold us" (*ITC*, 3). For Fish, it is the feeling of firmness that gives rise to the sense of progress: feeling is the cause, sense is the effect. But this is literally preposterous: for it is just the feeling of firmness that needs to be explained, and calling it the cause won't work.

A more careful analysis of the psychology of belief change shows something else. Feelings of progress do not follow firmness, which are effects of an achievement of understanding. If feelings were the cause of sense, and arbitrarily so, then there would be no motive for seeking a new idea other than our favorites from the past. Furthermore, not every new idea appears to us as inevitable. Rather, we attach firmness to a new belief because we believe it explains more than the old belief.

Only if we believe that we have progressed from error to something better do we reattach firmness. The feeling of progress, in other words, is not explained by claiming that full commitment is inevitable, but by the fact that we would not have moved on to a non-progressive idea.

What makes an idea progressive? Not something inherent in the idea, and not just a feeling. It is a relation to our past ideas. Later ideas are progressive, not because of absolute commitment or because of an abstract quality of those ideas, but because they explain what was previously puzzling to us. The logic of belief is an immanent logic that constrains us as believers, taking advantage of, but not reducing to, the natural structure of the world and the accidents of history.

The contingency of thought falls between the necessary and the arbitrary, and thus allows progress without requiring absolute knowledge. Conversely, ignorance of the logic of inquiry fosters confusions of necessity and contingency. For naive readers and dogmatists, judgment is an uncritical experience: belief is truth. Hermeneutic experience, however, allows us to consider judgment and belief in light of their intrinsic inadequacy to the truth. The self-reflexive structure of belief drives a wedge between belief and full commitment. Hermeneutic openness turns judgment against itself, leading to the kind of openness Gadamer associates with hermeneutic maturity, the Socratic insight that humility is the sign of wisdom. Judgment then ceases to be the tyrant Fish portrays it to be just because it is possible to insulate our feelings of rightness with experience. We do not glory in the partiality of our vision; we rather suspect its very limitation before we even know what it is. Thus, not only do our beliefs grow; our attitude toward belief can grow as well, but only by moving away from Fish's unreserved commitment.

Fish's argument betrays the suppleness of hermeneutics by collapsing questionability into a straitjacket of arbitrary but irresistible impulses. Fish's feelings about belief never learn to give up strong foundational necessity: they just disguise it as radical contingency. Thus Fish misreads his tautology in a strong epistemic sense rather than understanding it in a hermeneutic sense: what is true *a priori* is not that we believe what we believe with full commitment (an empirical falsehood), but only that we believe what we believe to be true, however provisionally we believe it.

Of course, the assumptions of strong conventionism are incompatible with progress, requiring that belief change rise no higher than to arbitrariness. But when pressed to explain the motives for belief change in the face of this arbitrariness, conventionism can only be confounded: for if conventions were truly sufficient and all powerful in shaping our meanings, and if there were no non-conventional constraints on belief, we would never have to change them. As "producers of the object of interpretation" – i.e. the world – our beliefs should always be adequate to the world. Yet we are forced to change beliefs because our conventions are not adequate. There really is something outside our beliefs.

2. There is nothing to be done

For Fish there is no real progress because there is no ground outside practice by which to judge progress. Practices have only conventional legitimacy, and conventions are historical accidents. Belief change, therefore, is arbitrary by any standards other than those we hold at a given moment. But if progress is an illusion, then what are we supposed to be teaching in class?

In response to this question – behind which lie issues of some social and pedagogical substance – Fish responds with his tautology: since we must believe what we believe, we always know just what we must teach. Indeed, since there is no choice, there is no resisting it, nothing to do about it, no improving upon it. In his view, since self-contemplation is inevitable, discovering that fact leaves everything in place: "the general or metacritical belief ... does not in any way affect the belief or set of beliefs (about the nature of literature, the proper mode of critical inquiry, the forms of literary evidence, and so on) which yields the interpretation that now seems to you (or me) to be inescapable and obvious" (*ITC*, 359). Discovering the inevitability of our beliefs has, as Fish says, no consequences.

Here we have complete critical paralysis. On the one hand, beliefs are social in origin; on the other hand, individuals are helplessly in their grip. Since we believe what we believe, there is no sense worrying about it since such analytic attitudes are impotent against full commitment. Inquiry, dialogue, pedagogy, scholarship, research are all nothing but exchanges between fully-committed-wills-to-conventional-power. There is nothing to do but dig in one's heels and wait for the next arbitrary gestalt switch.

Once again, however, a closer look reveals a theoretical incoherence in the no-consequences thesis, an utter reversal of the anti-transcendental first principle of conventionism. For the no-consequences thesis could only be true if Fish's position claimed universality, a totalization of the possibilities in the present, a transcendence of external circumstances. And indeed, that is exactly the height Fish claims to "descend" from:

> it does not follow from what I have been saying that you should go out and do literary criticism in a certain way or refrain from doing it in other ways. The reason for this is that the position I have been presenting is not one that you (or anyone else) could live by ... As soon as you *descend from theoretical reasoning about your assumptions,* you will once again inhabit them and you will inhabit them without any reservations whatsoever.
>
> (ITC, 370; my italics)

Surprise: *Fish's position is outside practice.* For only if Fish's theorizing comes from somewhere higher up could we descend from it, and only if it transcended practice would it have no consequences.

Again the anti-foundationist's paradox. It is just because Fish presumes to have reduced the constraints on reading to his interpretive conventions and to have truly represented the psychology of reading in full commitment that he can expect his model to apply to everyone and still leave everything in place. Fish believes his model has no consequences because he believes it is already universally true, i.e. *not* conventional, not optional.

How does such a fundamental contradiction arise? Fish's error follows from the conventionist's aim to reject strong foundationism with something equally strong, equally comprehensive, which then becomes equally reductive. This he attempts by focusing only on what is negotiable in our beliefs, as if the world of belief is utterly self-enclosed in a network of discardable options. But the fallacy of that view is exposed when we realize that it is precisely the *lack* of closure of our beliefs that drives it forward, a lack of closure that is structured by necessary constraints as well as conventional ones. Just because our worlds are not hermetically or hermeneutically sealed, we are *forced* to deal with those constraints that do transcend convention. We know our conventions are limited just by virtue of those constraints that are not conventional.

C. The problem of performative integrity

However thin the psychology of full commitment, it would be far less objectionable if it actually *did* have no consequences. Unfortunately, its consequences are clearly embodied in Fish's misreadings of

everyone whom he suspects of less-than-strong-conventionist
naivety. As a universalist in disguise, Fish's conventionism becomes as
dictatorial as his full commitment.

Far from having "no consequences," Fish's hermeneutics have
consequences opposite to those advocated by Rorty's and Gadamer's
hermeneutic theories. Rorty imagines hermeneutic conversation as
unconstrained, reciprocal explorations of another's coherence, and
Gadamer proclaims the open-mindedness to which hermeneutic
experience points. On the one hand, Fish's anti-essentialist anti-
foundationism likewise implies that critical inquiry inhabits a land of
floating, usage-defined boundaries with no transcendent identities, no
invariant essences, no solid ground. On the other hand, his guided
tour of that land is ruthlessly totalizing, rigorously assigning "the real
meanings" of others' words, ever demarcating the true from the false
claims. Instead of seeking understanding, Fish finds in conventionism
a stern taskmaster who strains to separate, with categorical precision,
the true contextualists from the naive crypto-essentialists. Fish's
radical hermeneutics condemns universalism, but constantly practices
it.

As the following examples show, Fish's strategic contradiction
intends to show the vanity of progressive intentions, the critical
paralysis of all emancipatory discourse, but instead reveals the critical
paralysis of Fish's own performative contradiction, his own covert
essentialism.

1. Professional fictions

In his essay "Anti-professionalism" Fish's strong conventionism
becomes strong moral relativism. The issue concerns the possible
grounds for critiquing professional behavior. Fish argues that since
professional values are institutional and practical, they reduce to what
professionals do, not to transcendent notions of professional behavior.
Professionals are accountable only to their own practices, not to
essential standards.

The problem in question is well-known: professions are sometimes
charged with self-serving practices in which "the very values for
which the enterprise supposedly exists ... are sacrificed to the special
interests that the ... profession at once represents and embodies" (AP,
90). When such complaints come from outside the profession, it is
claimed that society and client are ill-served by some practice. But Fish
notes that such complaints arise internally as well, for "the pressure of

professional life leads to the proliferation of work ... that has no justification in anything but the artificial demands of an empty and self-serving careerism" (AP, 91) until finally even the "professional ... becomes his own victim as the cynicism he practices transforms him into its image, leaving him with the base motives of an empty and self-serving careerism" (AP, 90).

Fish essentializes the issue as always necessarily a question of Plato against the Sophists, forcing the false dilemma of either claiming that the aim of curing disease is medicine's essence (which may not be so bad an idea) or admitting that curing illness is only a conventional, and therefore dispensable, aim of doctors. Thus anti-professionalism becomes a version of the ideology problem. If all positions are ideologies and none of them are essentially privileged, then one cannot accuse another of impropriety; one can only have a different ideology of propriety. Professions are merely vocational ideologies. To criticize a professional does not make him unprofessional; it merely shows that you have a different professional ideology. For Fish, then, since all standards are finally arbitrary, professions are standards-unto-themselves. Similarly, charges of professionalism misunderstand that professional values are institutional, contextual, ideological and perspectival.

To frame Fish's reading of the issue, let us note what anti-professional charges involve. In its typical form, the problem of professionalism is a relatively non-exceptional ethical problem of ends and means (although it can become complex, of course, in particular situations). Regarding the ultimate ends of the professions, the charge of anti-professionalism presupposes only the conventional fact that, as interpretive communities, professional institutions are organized in the name of certain values: e.g. preventing and curing illness, defending and prosecuting litigants, educating the young, etc. Yet given such conventional purposes, it is still possible to question in utterly pragmatic terms whether those ideals are being effectively served or whether the actual practices of the institution might be in the service of ideals less lofty.

Let us take as an example the trend in modern medical training away from general practice and toward surgery, high technology, and pharmacological treatments. An unsympathetic critic might point out that these trends have in common the high price tag and the increased dependence of the patient on the specialist – a formula for mono-polistic advantage – whereas comparable investments in preventive medicine might have (a) avoided the expensive diseases in question, although they would also have (b) made less price-intensive work for doctors. Such a critique merely depends on (a) acknowledging a multitude of values being served in a profession (e.g. public service, private success), (b) acknowledging possible conflicts between those values, and (c) the need to decide how to reconcile the priorities consistent with public professions of standards. In this case, a pragmatic critique of "heroic" medicine can be made in terms of the profession's own conventional claim to minimize, not exploit, disease.

Fish overlooks this pragmatic form of professional critique, however, in order to wage his crypto-universalist critique of progressive and emancipatory discourse.[10]

2. If Plato didn't exist, Fish would have to invent him

As in the anti-theory and full-commitment arguments, Fish's strategy harbors a totalization of the question, a hidden essentialism that categorizes in iron-clad terms the possibilities of argument. Fish assumes that a charge of unprofessionalism *must* be concerned with an essential truth rather than a conventional truth; it *must* claim to come from a position outside the convention. Thus Fish essentializes anti-professionalism as

the protection and nourishment of a set of related and finally equivalent acontextual entities. First there is a truth that exists independently of any temporal or local concern; and then there is knowledge about this truth, a knowledge that is itself dependent on no particular perspective but has as its object this same transperspectival truth; and finally, and most importantly, there is a self or knowing consciousness that is under the sway of no partial vision and is therefore free (in a very strong sense) first to identify and then to embrace the truth to which a disinterested knowledge inescapably points. On the other side, this happy eventuality is continually threatened by the

---

10. True, on highly technical matters, professional integrity may be beyond the judgment of those they serve at a distance. On a variety of technical and moral matters, however, professions are not beyond external critique. Clients do not go to doctors to find out if they feel good: they go to stop feeling bad, the success of which they can judge for themselves. Though Lyndon Johnson was elected in 1964 to keep America out of a war, he failed to do so and honorably took the political consequences rather than trying to redefine war. When the data of Cyril Burt's case for racial inferiority were discovered to be fixed, it did not take another biologist to pass judgment on the case. Professional integrity and its violation by self-service or incompetence do not require essences for critical conditions. The validity of such charges is a pragmatic question from within the conventions of the professions themselves.

contingent, the accidental, the merely fashionable, the narrowly political, the superficial, the blindly interested, the inessential, the merely historical, the rhetorical, by everything that seems to so many to be the content of professionalism once it has been divorced from or has forgotten the higher purposes and values it is supposed to serve. (AP, 93–4)

Ignore, for the moment, the theoretical position required to make this kind of *a priori* generalization. That aside, this Procrustean polarization between transcendence and convention still misses the point of the typical cases of anti-professional critique. Critics need not question the conventions of a profession from outside, because it is precisely from within those conventions that they can question how effectively they are being met. One need not challenge the curative aims of medicine to object to hospital admissions procedures, nor challenge the due processes of law to question the level of attorneys' fees, nor challenge the aims of academia to question the emphasis on publishing. Indeed, it is just those conventional values to which one appeals. Professional essences are not necessary for professional critique: consistency with conventional standards of judgment is enough.

Fish's false dilemma of transcendent or arbitrary grounds depends on a universalistic reduction Fish candidly foregrounds: "What I have tried to demonstrate is that anti-professionalism, as a set of attitudes and arguments, is indefensible no matter what form it takes" (AP, 104). Anti-professionalism can be critiqued in one shot, that is, because it is not context-specific, because it has an essence which Fish has identified and shown to be impossible. Yet if Fish's conventionism were right, then one would expect that anti-professionalism *would be* context-specific, and reflect the variety of local conventions within which the professional critics were situated. Instead, Fish's perspective invokes a Kantian transcendental deduction on anti-professional argument to discover once and for all its necessary conditions, the logical presuppositions that make anti-professional arguments possible.

Fish's universalism follows the contradictory logic of strong conventionism, which at once presumes to remove constraints on interpretation while presuming to define its limits. The heuristic value of Fish's argument is that he constantly raises it to the foundationist level, which is just where the inadequacies and contradictions of conventionism are most clear. Thus Fish's analysis becomes progressively more equivocal the more global it becomes, distorting the interpretive dynamics of the very interpretive communities he pretends to describe.

Take, for instance, Fish's acknowledgement that anti-professional critique occurs both within and without professional boundaries. Assume, furthermore, that professional values are conventional, as Fish claims. It follows that both internal and external critiques are explicable on conventional and pragmatic terms. Internal critique occurs when professionals believe that their institution is not meeting its own conventional ideals in the most efficient way, or when individual practitioners are not behaving in accordance with either the means or ends conventionally professed by the institution. External critique, on the other hand, can occur for those same reasons, as well as when the public at large believes that the profession's conventions do not serve the conventional values of the larger community. In any case, anti-professional critiques can be glossed in entirely conventionist and pragmatic terms either by comparing means and ends, or by comparing larger and narrower contexts in which the ends are to be understood. To say they are ideological is not to say they are always undecidable by commonly held values.

Having Platonized anti-professionalism, Fish's conclusion can only equivocate between a trivial tautology – i.e. that all professionals act professionally – and professional license to be unaccountable to any larger social context. Where the full-commitment argument confuses tautology and psychology at the expense of psychology, the anti-professionalism argument confuses tautology and ethics at the expense of ethics.

3. Hermeneutic freedom as critical paralysis

Whereas some have taken Fish for another deconstructor of logocentric domination, his denial of any but local and arbitrary values turns out to be resolutely anti-emancipatory. His attacks on social critique from the right and the left turn on the impossibility of meaningful progress on any level. For Fish it is not only absolute progress that depends on the much maligned Platonic essences, but all claims to progress. Because even local change is arbitrary and irrational, to suggest any hint of progress or emancipation is to invoke the ghost of Plato.

Of course, it is not so surprising that the anti-professional critics from the right (e.g. Toulmin, Bate, Levin, Crews, Bledstein) turn out to be essentialists in Fish's reading – since classicism is a kind of literary counterpart to essentialism in philosophy. The irony, according to Fish, is his discovery that those of the left are equally guilty of covert essentialism despite the left's traditional commitment to tracing social authority to historically relative grounds. Because of its pretenses to possible emancipatory progress, the historicity of the left falls fatally short of the truer, nihilistic historicity of strong conventionism, and therefore must be revealed as crypto-essentialist from the lofty perch of the True Conventionism.

a. Transcendental paralysis

In a critique of Richard Ohmann's crypto-essentialism, Fish tells of how Ohmann fell from the path of liberal humanism and the ideal of "the redemptive power of literature and the arts" whose emancipatory power lay in "their transcendence of politics" and their ideal of a world "apart from the utilitarian one where words and forms advance pragmatic interests."[11] On becoming a professional, Ohmann found that the profession did not effectively serve this emancipatory end; rather, "our scheme of professional organization is destructive of community" (Ohmann, 12). Ohmann discovered, that is, that institutional self-interests and corruption from external commercial interests interfere with the professed humanistic ideal of the free development of the individual.

When Fish finds this charge to be the "classical [sic] anti-professionalist indictment," we can assume that he has found it Platonic in its assumption of "an atemporal value capable of lifting those who embrace it to an answerable level of transcendence" (AP, 99). On Fish's reading, Ohmann wants to liberate students to acontextual freedom: "[Ohmann] falls into the trap of reserving 'real' for choices that depend on no previously instituted circumstances whatsoever, choices that would be, in some strong sense, original ... [W]hat Ohmann desires are wholly free choices, made according to standards more objective than any attached to a particular perspective or partisan vision and by persons who are themselves above faction and entirely disinterested" (AP, 101). Thus, despite Ohmann's leftist, historicizing sympathies, his anti-professionalism "turns out to be the same" as that of the essentialist right: "the goal is still the 'free

---

11. Richard Ohmann, *English in America*, New York: Oxford, 1976; 33; hereafter referred to as "Ohmann."

development' of human potential, and the barrier to that goal is still professional and institutional procedures, which are declared to be in a relation of subversion and corruption to genuine values" (AP, 99).

But does Ohmann's critique share with the right more than a belief in the possibility of some unspecified form of progress, and the belief that pseudo-professional conduct may interfere with that possibility? How can Fish critique that vacuous concept *until* it is made context-specific? Fish believes he can critique it because, for Fish, believers in progress are necessarily Platonists in essence (or in this case, it is Ohmann's "Neoplatonic sources" that Fish hears echoing in Ohmann's emancipatory rhetoric). But *does* the belief in progress have a transcendent essence shared by the left and right? How *could* it by conventionist concepts of value?

Let us look more closely at what Ohmann, not Fish, says about what Ohmann means. Does Ohmann wish to achieve theoretical transcendence in order to be, as Fish accuses, "entirely disinterested"? Hardly:

It is not just that science seeks to achieve a neutrality towards particular events; the activity of theorizing is essentially neutral ... Our activities of research and publication [in the humanities] imitate those of the sciences, whose effort is toward the abstract and impersonal. The model is a bad one for us, since our inquiries point ultimately toward the concrete and the personal. (Ohmann, 14, 17)

Fish says that theorists want to stand outside the conventions of interpretive communities. Does Ohmann, as Fish accuses, envision freedom from the interpretive community or from "previously instituted circumstances"? Not exactly: rather, he complains that "institutions often betray the ideals of the professional group" (Ohmann, 24), whereas "a prior responsibility is to our own community, our corporate identity; and it is precisely that identity that seems most threatened by our present means of conducting and presenting research" (Ohmann, 13). Fish says that anti-professional critique presupposes a professional essence with which to critique the conventional aims of the profession. Is Ohmann concerned to stand above the professed aims of the profession? Not according to Ohmann, who charges that academics abandon their own conventional aims for the aims of those with power to influence them from outside the professional conventions: "The point is that, institutionally, we perform certain services at society's behest to earn a livelihood, but these services are not the parts of our work that accord best with professional dignity or with what we think society *ought* to want from us" (Ohmann, 233). Ohmann's notion of unprofessional behavior represents a betrayal from within, not from above.

Ohmann's critical grounds are not essentialist; they pose only a conventional and pragmatic question: What is the best way to educate society according to academia's own ideals of critical thought and social responsibility? What of Ohmann's quoted pleas for transcendence? Let us put back into context the passage Fish cites as evidence of Ohmann's continuing desire for transcendence:

Perhaps some who accept the involvement of knowledge, of intellectuals, and of universities in the present crisis of politics might still wish to exempt the humanities. The academic humanities seem both well-intentioned and harmless, or, more positively, a force for decency and liberation. Certainly this has been the message of much literary theory and aesthetics in our century: the redemptive power of literature and the arts is due to their transcendence of politics and to their building <u>a world apart from the utilitarian one where words and forms advance pragmatic interests.</u> I sometimes wish this were true, *but I don't believe it to be.*

(Ohmann, 334, quoted words are underlined; my italics)

What Fish quotes as Ohmann's position is Ohmann's paraphrase of the liberal self-image he has rejected. Evidently, since Fish knows Ohmann to be an essentialist anyway, it does not matter that Fish attributes the canonical position to Ohmann and omits Ohmann's rejection of it. Against this misquotation, Ohmann is explicitly rejecting the very transcendence Fish is attributing to him.

On the one hand, Fish is right to suggest that Ohmann cannot hope for a world beyond contextual values. On the other hand, Fish is wrong to suggest that Ohmann's hoped-for progress presupposes such essentialist, acontextual values, and Ohmann's own context shows that he has no such intentions. But perhaps if Fish believes that no meanings are fixed, he also believes he can in good conscience plant his own premises on the suspect's premises to reveal the inevitable Platonism lurking beneath emancipatory rhetoric, no matter how much against the grain Fish must read to do so.

In the name of history and context, for instance, Ohmann claims that "There is just no sense in pondering the function of literature without relating it to the actual society that uses it, to the centers of power within that society, and to the institutions that mediate between literature and the people" (Ohmann, 303). To this flagrantly anti-essentialist claim Fish responds:

This all seems fine until one notices that the "it" in the sentence remains constant and is simply put to different uses by different interests ... It never seems to occur to Ohmann that not only the uses of literature change, but the items and qualities subsumed under the category can change; it never occurs to him that literature is not an essential, but a conventional category ...

(AP, 102)

But Fish is simply attributing to Ohmann's "it" an invariance that Ohmann does not intend. Indeed, Ohmann's point is that "it" means nothing in particular until it is historically contextualized.

Not surprisingly, the shoe is on the other foot; the totalizing pronoun occurs in Fish's characterization of literary criticism: "Indeed, this is the whole of critical activity, an attempt on the part of one party to alter the beliefs of another so that the evidence cited by the first will be seen *as* evidence by the second" (*ITC*, 365; my underline). Unlike Ohmann, it is Fish who has totalized criticism as always already about rationality itself. When we notice that bibliographical, historical, formalist, and other literary activities appear to be ruled out of Fish's meta-foundationist concept of literary criticism – a variety of forms of literary work which are compatible with Ohmann's more supple historicism – then the position which is the more essentialist becomes obvious.

Ironically, Ohmann's progress means the demystification of essentialism and naive individualism, both of which obscure the social character of Fish's interpretive communities. But to Fish's ears, everyone else's local claims to progress recall the transcendental impossibility of Platonic progress. The difference between Fish and Ohmann is that Fish's totalizing urge prevents him from descending into the pragmatic world where progress can be debated according to the conventions that we do happen to have. Given his own transcendental irrationalism, Fish believes that any claims to progress must immediately regress to the presupposition of a Platonic *Telos*. Not only can there be no ultimate *Telos* in Fish's world; there can be no local ones either, since that would put us on the slippery slope to the Big One.

Unlike Fish, Ohmann sees that if essentialism is an error, then to recognize the historicity of belief is itself progress, a liberation from strong foundationism. Such progress does not need essences; it only needs conventional priorities. Likewise, Ohmann can object to the profession's abandonment of its original notion of service to society, charging that today the "profession exists so that there may be a means of accreditation and advancement for people in the profession, not out of any inner necessity and certainly not out of cultural need or the need of individual teachers" (Ohmann, 40). Obliviousness to cultural and pedagogical needs is a substantive issue of professional integrity, however rooted in conventional values. But having essentialized anti-professional critique by definition, Fish presumes to dismiss, as necessarily essentialist, any suggestion that progress, liberation, and integrity are not arbitrary.

It is not Ohmann's literary "it" that is essentialist; it is Fish's categories. That is why the only alternative to essences Fish can imagine is absolute professional autonomy and self-service, which, being inevitable, cannot be objectionable. Since self-service is universal, there can be no conflict between it and any other claims upon us, and certainly no conflict with higher priorities:

> [Ohmann's claim that the profession exists for itself] seems to be the right one, but it does not seem to me as it does to Ohmann to be a matter of scandal; it is merely a recognition of the fact that needs and values do not exist independently of socially organized activities but emerge simultaneously with the institutional and conventional structures within which they are intelligible. (AP, 101)

Again the issue is missed. The point is not whether values are situated, which of course they are. The problem is the existence of multiple value contexts and their multiple claims upon us. Fish uses the red herring of contextuality to obscure the possibility that there are *conflicts of contextual interests*, in which case we must define priorities. Once priorities are defined and professed, then we are liable to inconsistency and hypocrisy, i.e. to charges that we have betrayed our professed priorities.

Pragmatism, in professions as well as in science, is all about methodically distinguishing different aims and their relative priorities, and about devising mechanisms to serve them efficiently. For instance, the rationale for why lawyers are sworn to defend clients despite personal hunches about guilt is not to employ more lawyers, but to guarantee as much impartiality as possible according to the ideal of presumed innocence. By contrast, doctors are not sworn to assume either the health or the infirmity of their patients, since that does not serve their profession's aims. The legal mechanism, however imperfect, is designed to perform a pragmatic function in its larger social and moral context.

If professional self-service were the aim of professionalism, all professional conventions would converge on the most successfully self-serving. There would only be one profession, in other words, and it would be indistinguishable from commerce. To the extent that this is not the case (i.e. to the extent that professions have different procedures and methods rooted in their ideal and contextual constraints), professional self-service is subordinated to larger and distinguishable social functions. Not only are professionalism and self-service not identical, but pragmatism requires and succeeds at making a distinction between the two.

Because Fish has misconstrued the issue of anti-professionalism as a choice between essentialist and arbitrary critique, he fosters a cure that is worse than the disease; for his reduction is equally as reductive as essentialism, only it eliminates *any* check on self-interest in the interest of removing absolute or transcendental priorities.

It is not Ohmann's historicism that turns out to be "skin deep" but Fish's anti-foundationism. Moreover, Fish's defense of professional arbitrariness instantiates the very mystification of grounds that Ohmann objects to in literary academics. Fish's anti-theoretical position, in other words, is "covertly or unconsciously" political insofar as it denies having consequences, ignores its own aggressiveness, obscures its imperial ambitions, and implicitly exempts itself from the essentialist sins it imputes to everyone else.

b. The persistence of the letter in disciplinary practice

In *Profession 89*, Fish addresses the postmodern challenge to disciplinary authority. Here again one might think that Fish would ally with those exploring the constitutive character of disciplinary boundaries. Yet Fish again seems more concerned to repudiate emancipation than to explore rigorously the ways of convention.

Fish notes that a variety of theoretically and politically inspired thinkers – such as Marxists, feminists, deconstructors, and neo-pragmatists – have attempted to combine a constructivist epistemology with a rhetoric of emancipation, but without (in his view) understanding the final incompatibility of these two threads. For example, Shoshana Felman notes that "human knowledge is by definition that which is untotalizable, that which rules out any possibility of totalizing what it knows or of eradicating its own ignorance" (BI, 18). This leads post-structuralist liberators to what Fish calls a "pedagogy of antiknowledge," negating "the hope of anything beyond [the] repeated unsettling of whatever claims us in the name of established knowledge" (BI, 18). One would think that if post-structuralism had informed us about unsuspected limits to our knowledge, its lessons should become a welcomed part of our professional self-representations. But for Fish post-structuralist decon-structors err by concluding any emancipatory significance from this debunking. The emancipatory and subversive thrusts of post-structuralism are finally incompatible, Fish argues, because eman-cipation presupposes a foundational ideal denied by the constructivist epistemology. Coming to know that we don't know is not progress for Fish because, once again, progress demands essences.

On the one hand, Fish's suspicion of post-structuralist emancipatory presumptions is well taken. (I address this issue below in the chapters on Foucault and the Frankfurt School.) On the other hand, his attempt to ground these suspicions in his strong conventionist model only leads to more strong misreadings of his interlocutors.

The post-structuralist critique of absolute origins does not rule out, as Fish claims, a more modest kind of progress regarding the significance of practices and contexts, as Jeffrey Peck indicates:

In the spirit of critical reflection meaning and values of traditional pedagogy can be scrutinized ... The intersubjectivity of meaning can be exposed, and educational institutions, the classroom, the discipline, and the university can be seen to construct and condition knowledge. In this way literary study, as the study of textuality, ... reveals the epistemological structures that organize how we know, how our knowledge gets transmitted and accepted, and why and how students receive it. (BI, 18)

Like Ohmann, Peck is indicating the literary value of hermeneutic foregrounding – the same task at which Fish is employed – a task of political consciousness-raising that "denaturalizes" the convention-ality of knowledge. As we have seen, however, Fish believes that the lack of an ultimate perspective deprives us of any emancipatory hope at all. Since no ultimate disclosure of grounds is possible, Fish concludes that critique itself must be *essentially* impossible: "The strategy of 'making visible what was hidden' can only be pursued within forms of thought that are themselves hidden ... Partiality and parochialism are not eliminated *or even diminished* by the exposure of their operations, merely relocated" (BI, 18; my italics). Not eliminated, perhaps, but why not diminished? Why is Socrates not wiser knowing his ignorance? Why? ... because critique is *essentially* impossible. Thus spake the Anti-essentialist.

Fish seems unaware of the fact that postmodernism's rejection of totalizing theory might lead it to a post-revolutionary position, as Derrida repeatedly insists. So when Fish says of post-structuralists that the "epistemological argument deprives the political argument of any possible force, because it leaves no room for a revolutionary project," it is Fish who is making critique depend on a revolutionary model of critical authority. Whereas Gadamer, Feyerabend, Derrida, Rorty, Lyotard, Foucault and others are content to make local progress of sorts, Fish's anti-Platonic paranoia refuses to allow for a post-revolutionary progress where no essences are sought.

Since Fish believes that *all* categories are conventional, he agrees that disciplinary categories must be as well. But since we are all trapped in our arbitrary beliefs anyway, for post-structuralists to deconstruct disciplinary boundaries has no emancipatory value. The truth about disciplines shall not make us free, because the artifice of disciplines is just another prison house of full commitment. Disciplinary boundaries are not profitably crossed, because boundaries either remain in force or are merely renamed, but remain ever closed in any case: the "American mind, like any other, will always be closed, and the only question is whether we find the form of closure it currently assumes answerable to our present urgencies" (BI, 21). But again, this prison-house metaphor merely begs the question, which is not whether the mind is open or closed *absolutely*. Rather, the question is how to open it more completely to its exterior challenges. Fish even implies this: for if the mind were truly closed, then the "urgencies" would not be pressing in on us. But they are, and the differences in degree of mental closure and differences of kinds of closure take on significance because of that urgency.

Fish's explanation of how interpretive conventions actually work shows that for him conventions are just more ideal readers, strong in their intractability. Thus Fish concludes that importing into one's practice "the machinery of other practices" cannot serve "to relax the constraints of one's practice" since "the imported product will always have the form of its appropriation rather than the form it exhibits 'at home'; therefore at the very moment of its introduction, it will already be marked by the discourse it supposedly 'opens'" (BI, 19). Again, Fish treats his objects as essences, as if two practices or conventions cannot combine to form a third, new item.

The constitution of new terrain would only be impossible if disciplinary boundaries were *essentially* invariant, and therefore impervious to the influence of other conventions. In fact, that is the classic notion of an essence: what remains the same through transformations. But then intertextuality would be impossible, since meanings would remain untouched, as would be conventionism itself.

For Fish's crypto-essentialism the Law of the Excluded Middle works not only for truth, but for conventions as well. But practices are not logical binaries so we need not always choose between them. As Barthes' *Mythologies* details in its introduction, meaning is not either/or, but can be layered with the interpenetrating influences of other meanings. Uniforms take on new meanings when worn by professional wrestlers and strippers. But when transplanted they change the context of wrestling, as a comparison with olympic wrestling shows. Since conventions do meld, the point is not whether a practice is marked by its confrontation with other practices, but to what effect.

Fish almost sees the true dynamism of conventions when he notes of interdisciplinary importations, "the shape they appear in will always be *relative* to the socially constructed activity that has received them and made them its own" (BI, 19; my italics). Such a concession verges on allowing for a progress of new relations out of interacting conventions. But since Fish wants revolutionary change or none at all, he rules out the possibility that mere changes in relations are a substantive part of textual practice. Ironically, for post-structuralists, for whom this relativity is all there is, it is just this intertextuality that subverts essentialism. But since Fish is fully committed to the absolute power of conventions, the disciplines remain for him untransformed by intertextual relations.

c. Consistency and integrity

Fish hopes to defuse progressive critique by requiring for it an essentialist ground. But progress requires only that someone be consistent with pragmatic ideals. Fish cannot be consistent with his, because they are theoretically contradictory: he cannot consistently call his *a priori* legislation of critical authority "anti-foundationism" and "anti-theory." His pretension to totalize the impossibility of totalization, to universalize the impossibility of universal principles, etc. renders his arguments incoherent: his case would have to be, in fact, exactly the kind of theory strong conventionism attacks. Finally, it is not the historicizing critic who is in bad faith to question social

conventions – which can always be questioned against other conventions; rather, it is the strong conventionist who is in bad faith to
dictate what everyone must mean if, as he claims, nothing *must* be
anything in particular.

D. The limits of conventionism: the mind is not just its own place

Platonist hermeneutics puts meaning beyond practice, inviting a false
dilemma between hermeneutic science and impressionism. Fish saw
through that false dilemma when he discovered that "at one stroke the
dilemma [between objective text and subjective reader] that gave rise
to the debate between the champions of the text and the champions
of the reader ... is dissolved because the competing entities are no
longer perceived as independent" (*ITC*, 14). Not quite: the problem is
dissolved when we stop believing that meaning is determined by one
factor alone. But Fish is so glad to be rid of objectivism and
subjectivism that he fails to see that conventionism is no more
adequate than the others. He rejects Plato, but not Plato's *problém-
atique*.

Fish may be right to conclude that "the subject-object dichotomy"
can be "eliminated as the only framework within which critical debate
could occur" (*ITC*, 15–16) if that means that interpretation does not
reduce to choosing between objectivity or subjectivity. But Fish does
not see the danger of another form of reduction, the form that believes
that objective and subjective constraints on meaning can be
"eliminated" by focusing only on what is conventional. The
imperative of history and context does not imply that formal
distinctions such as subject and object are *themselves conventional* in the
sense of being dispensable. Yet this is how Fish would have us
understand the mediacy of thought: "the claims of objectivity and
subjectivity can no longer be debated because the authorizing agency
... is at once both and neither" (*ITC*, 14). More precisely, it is both and
something else as well: conventional. But because it is all three, it
remains for critics to debate subjects, objects, *and* conventions. What
cannot be maintained is that any term can be *reduced* to another,
including to conventions.

Understanding critical conditions requires *not* taking literally either
the Platonic metaphor of transcendence or the formalist metaphor of
textual interiority, but requires seeing how formal and objective

constraints function within practices which are conventional. The issue of critical conditions, that is, depends on seeing that the conventional option of changing practices does not necessarily mean the option of changing the formal and objective constraints on those practices. As interpreters, we are always working within our conventions, so Fish correctly claims that *we* can never take a position outside our conventions and methods. But that does not mean that our conventions are not constrained by something else that is *outside us*. By choosing to use them or not, conventions do not efface the existence of outer and inner constraints, but rather mediate them for our understanding. Conventions, then, though necessary for understanding, can never be *sufficient* to explain understanding; rather, their function is to explain *what constrains them*, i.e. what is not already known, what is not entirely our product.[12]

Strong conventionism, lacking the non-conventional constraints of formality and objectivity, loses this balance of factors, and suffers idealism, the belief that thinking makes it so (as opposed to the realist belief that thinking *makes intelligible* what is so). Like idealism, the strong conventionist view is trapped between its inability to explain

---

12. Given the infinitude of hermeneutic questionability, what limits conventional arbitrariness and context-specificity? We should first note that context-specificity is itself a relative term in more ways than conventionists admit. Formal sciences (such as logic, mathematics, and information science) are defined in a purely abstract context, which is why there are not bourgeois, communist, and feminist versions. Literary meaning, however, is specified only in a particular context, which is where conventions lie. Criticism, that is, is context-specific in *practice*. But since the more particular contexts depend on the more general ones, meaning requires a combination of particular conditions and general conditions, i.e. two levels of context–specificity. The freedom of one depends on the constraints of the other.

Ignoring this difference in levels of abstraction leads to a confusion between (a) the option of choosing a practice and (b) the option of ignoring its conditions once you have chosen it. To keep track of this difference, one must not only insist that practices have contexts, but notice as well that different pragmatic aims may have formal conditions to which practitioners can be held accountable. One need not do literary criticism; one may do impressionistic readings or gourmet cooking. However, if one chooses argument as one's mode and claims its authority, then one is liable to its strictures. Fish takes literally Hayden White's suggestion that literary criticism is the science of rules that has no rules. But that hyperbole only appears true if one is looking at literary criticism from the outside, where its focus on novelty may appear chaotic; for when one begins to do literary criticism, at that point one becomes immersed in both conventional (local) and non-conventional (semiotic) constraints.

what is outside the text, and the impossible claim that everything inside the text is dispensable and finally arbitrary. Conventionism cannot explain history, but must pretend that it can rewrite history at will, according to conventional decisions.

As we have seen repeatedly, however, conventionism must equivocate to maintain its plausibility. When it wants to be comprehensive, everything counts as a text. So when it promotes negotiability, it considers only literature professors deciding how to read Milton, not semioticians discussing the formal grounds of meaning, or engineers building bridges that either hold up or collapse. By looking selectively at the hermeneutic element in textual understanding, conventionists appear to by-pass formal and objective constraints without explaining the objective conditions of technological success or the formal conditions of interpretation.

Whereas New Critics highlighted the interdependence of form and content, strong conventionists eliminate the content altogether, as if there were nothing besides the arbitrary form of belief. But this ignores the fact that conventions themselves have critical conditions. Conventions are but one aspect of meaning, and theory only makes sense by allowing for constraints on convention more invariant than the decisions and habits of interpretive communities. For without any theoretical substance, interpretive practice becomes unintelligible and arbitrary, uncritical and domineering. The consequences of Fish's theoretical incoherence are, ironically, to enfeeble the very notion of practice he hopes to save from theory. Theoretical incoherence, the impossibility of progress, and the social unaccountability of professions are too high a price to pay for Fish's strong conventionism.

2

Brave new words: postmodernism on epistemology

A. Beyond foundationism

In what Jean-François Lyotard has called the postmodern condition, anti-foundationism is a commonplace. Richard Rorty concludes "that the intellectual tradition [of foundationist epistemology] has not paid off, is more trouble than it is worth, has become an incubus," and that we need to displace philosophy-as-epistemology with philosophy-as-hermeneutics (*CP*, xxxvii). Similarly, Stanley Fish attacks literary theorists who seek a general hermeneutic theory to determine particular literary interpretations in comparably global terms, arguing against theory "that this substitution of the general for the local has never been and will never be achieved. [Foundationist] theory is an impossible project which will never succeed" (*AT*, 110). And Lyotard says of the future-science that it too must abandon a deterministic model of knowledge, and that even now this future-science "is producing not the known but the unknown" (*PC*, 60). In each of these cases one finds a rejection of the traditional epistemological quest for a foundation of knowledge, truth, or meaning. And in each case, one finds a movement toward a more conventionist or relativist model of cognitive or hermeneutic authority.

In each case, however, one finds a problem common to all anti-foundationist positions: a gravitation towards claims about philosophy, literary theory, and science *in general*. The problem is obvious: How does one rule out categorical theories in principle without getting categorical? How does one universalize about theory's inability to universalize? The intransigence of these problems suggests that the subversiveness of the postmodern condition is easily overstated as "the end of epistemology" rather than "the end of foundationist reduction."

Of course, to ease the revolutionary flavor of postmodern manifestos, conventionists such as Rorty and Fish assure us that the loss of transcendental criteria for philosophical authority is no loss at all, since we never had them anyway, and since we still have what we always had: our local, conventional, intersubjectively binding practices. Just as some linguists claim that all natural languages are necessarily adequate to their worlds, anti-foundationists can claim that all philosophical orthodoxies are equally adequate for distinguishing the rational from the irrational in their own terms.

More traditional philosophers, however, are not comforted by such *de facto* assurances of relative rationality. Thus Hilary Putnam claims: "There is something that makes cultural relativism a far more dangerous cultural tendency than materialism. At bottom, there is a deep irrationalism to cultural relativism, a denial of the possibility of thinking (as opposed to making noises in counterpoint or in chorus)."[1] For the conventionist, consensus is the best we can do about being right. For the rationalist, philosophy needs to distinguish more and less rational communities.

On the other hand, Putnam's remark needs to be sharpened. The question is not the reality of rationality (i.e. "the possibility of thinking"), but the rationality of reality. In their own way, conventionists grant the reality of group-think. What they do not believe is that reality prefers one group-thought to another. Likewise, the intersubjectivity of the conventionist may be real, as far as it goes, but that is not why it should trouble the rationalist. The righteous consensus of the Aztec priesthood, of the Office of the Inquisition, of the Salem Fathers, or of the House Committee on Un-American Activities were real enough, and they may have jointly sacrificed their local sinners with "rational" intentions for the good of the community. But such corporate good intentions do not commit us to the claim – which conventionism appears to imply – that globally speaking, all communities are created equal, in which case *orthodoxy is always but only locally right*. Intersubjectivity may be a fact, but the ultimate issue for rationalism is what makes one community *more* rational than another. To allow that everyone has his reasons, the realist argues, is philosophically the same as everyone having no good reasons at all. Rationality, as Rorty portrays it, has "no depth": it is what people do when they approve of what they do.

1. "Why reason can't be naturalized," reprinted in *After philosophy: end or transformation?*, eds. Baynes, Bohman, and McCarthy, Cambridge: MIT, 1987; p. 229.

Notwithstanding the problems of traditional realism, however, the strategy of conventionism fails to escape the strong foundationist ideal against which it defines itself. Conventionism conceives of the issue of rationality as a choice between (1) monology – a single rational standard which must objectively rank behavior and cultures, and (2) conventionism – an incommensurate plurality of rationalities grounded in the accidental features of a culture or sub-group. This is a false dilemma, however, insofar as communities can be rational in a variety of commensurable ways, no matter how idiosyncratic. Convention is not incompatible with universal commensurability as long as a monological reduction to an *ultimate* standard is not implied. Incommensurability, that is, is an equivocal term which conventionists, especially following Kuhn's early work, have radicalized in an incoherent way.

Cultures are incommensurable in the sense of lacking a single principle of comparison to which all would agree, and which would bring all other principles into line. Cultures, in other words, lack a reductive principle to adjudicate their differences. But should this be surprising? Members of the *same* culture do not have such principles either. That sort of commensurability is beside the point because it does not exist anywhere. On the other hand, cultures are not incommensurable if that means there are not any principles with which they could compare themselves. What anthropology shows is not that cultures are incommensurable, but that they are commensurable in ways that we cannot predict in advance.

That there always turn out to be a variety of ways in which commensurability remains possible is crucial for the issue of post-foundationist discourse insofar as its proponents tend to assume the demise of objectivity. The death of objectivity, so often the first casualty of critiques of theoretical excesses, is always a premature burial. Objectivity – the technical success of science, for instance – survives historical and cultural border crossings; it is we subjects, our language, and our meanings that change in the process.

Postmodernist philosophers misstate the problem of traditional epistemology, targeting invariant constraints instead of certainty, monology, and reductionism. Thus they prematurely rule out the possibility of a heterological epistemology of several necessary constraints on knowledge and meaning. Instead of seeking the single Philosopher's Stone, a heterological epistemology says that objectivity is a kind of constraint against which our practices work in predictable ways. Rationality changes, but not because there are not convention-transcending standards of objective and formal character. Rather, it is just because formality and objectivity do not reduce to each other that they must be mediated by historical, contextual conventions. Logic and external objectivity are not enough to yield science: we must have methodological or practical conventions that pick out and support certain ends with which we wish to be linked. The epistemic constraints of logic and objectivity are universal only in the sense that they apply cross-culturally, though our *descriptions* of these constraints and their products are *not* universal. Because of this hermeneutic dimension to language, a heterological epistemology is not universalist in the traditional sense: it does not produce universal meanings, even if it prescribes necessary constraints.

Given this reluctance to prescribe universal meanings, the conventionist might first suspect that this heterological commensurability is conventionism in disguise, but such is not the case. For by strong conventionist standards there are no transcending constraints at all. But a heterological epistemology distinguishes the linguistic mediacy of meaning (conventionism) from the semiotic mediacy of thought and experience (the necessary conditions of knowledge), a distinction that reveals the limits of conventionism. The former is wholly constitutive, the latter is not wholly so: something in physics transcends conventions. Sooner or later, the contents of conventionist explanations point to an authority that is not merely convention, not merely language, custom, or human will. As a product of the critique of strong foundationism, postmodern anti-foundationists are too radical, raising problems as troubling as the ones they intend to displace. As the examples of Rorty and Lyotard show, these bolder forays beyond all foundationist terms cannot avoid subverting their own critical force in the interests of an incoherent ideal of understanding.

B. Epistemology and/or hermeneutics: Rorty

Rorty's work is of great importance to the current situation of philosophy, both because of his considerable influence and for what his style of philosophy represents. For many, his *Philosophy and the mirror of nature* constitutes the broadest and most radical critique of foundationism within the analytic tradition: " ... dispensing with foundations is dispensing with philosophy" (*PM*, 179). In his ideal of hermeneutic pluralism, furthermore, Rorty comes very close to articulating the notion of a heterological epistemology. Unhappily, such a revisionary epistemology is blocked by Rorty's equation of epistemology with strong foundationism, which discredits the authority of non-conventional critical conditions, the sort of conditions that resist the excesses of relativism. Finally, however, Rorty himself acknowledges the impossibility of anti-foundationist skepticism in his own about-face: for after rejecting epistemological foundationism for the bulk of his argument, Rorty finally admits that epistemology must stand in a complementary relation to the hermeneutic tasks he recommends to philosophy. This is, finally, to demand revision of the foundationism he himself dismisses.

1. The failure of strong foundationism

According to Rorty, modern philosophy has misconceived its legitimacy in strong foundationist terms. Against the epistemological conception, he maintains, Wittgenstein, Heidegger, and Dewey are the disabused voices crying in the post-foundationist wilderness. Having seen through the strong foundationist myth, these pioneers advocated a revolutionary view of philosophy's task as "therapeutic rather than constructive, edifying rather than systematic" (*PM*, 5–6). Rorty's aim is to persuade us to their perspective, to move us "from epistemology to hermeneutics."

Rorty's critique begins with a memorable description of philosophy in its strong foundationist spirit:

Philosophy as a discipline thus sees itself as the attempt to underwrite or debunk claims to knowledge made by science, morality, art, or religion. It purports to do this on the basis of its special understanding of the nature of knowledge and of mind. Philosophy can be foundational in respect to the rest of culture because culture is the assemblage of claims to knowledge, and philosophy adjudicates such claims. It can do so because it understands the foundations of knowledge, and it finds these foundations in a study of man-as-knower, of the "mental processes" or the "activity of representation" which make knowledge possible. To know is to represent accurately what is outside the mind; so to understand the possibility and nature of knowledge is to understand the way in which the mind is able to construct such representations. Philosophy's central concern is to be a general theory of representations, a theory which will divide up culture into areas which represent reality well, those which represent it less well, and those which do not represent it at all (despite their pretense of doing so). (*PM*, 3)

Perhaps the most recognizable feature of this foundationism is its claim to universal adjudicatory power, the power idealized as a univocal philosophical authority. Against this ideal Rorty hopes to advance a radically different conception of philosophy.

But while Rorty's characterization appears to discover a mono-logical ideal of epistemology lurking behind the whole canon, his specifications diffuse its precision considerably. First, his model underestimates classical philosophy, which Rorty considers to predate epistemology proper. Second, his emphasis on the quest for certainty makes rationalist epistemology a disproportionately important target. Third, his version of empiricism emphasizes the limits of the representational model of thought and the hermeneutics of theory change, at the expense of the central issue of technological progress. For these reasons, Rorty's image of philosophy is even historically far too reductive, let alone theoretically adequate.

His conflation of differing foundationist theories is symptomatic of Rorty's critical strategy: he evaluates different strong foundationist theories only as they resemble the monological ideal. Thus they are only considered for the reductive form of the argument, not in terms of the potential significance of their content. But just because monology is a chimera, this heterogeneity of specific theories does not truly constitute a single target at all, and therefore should not be assessed according to its distorted self-image. Even if reduction is impossible, as I suggest it is, that still leaves the significance of epistemology's content to be accounted for. To ignore the content is to use the very practice being criticized: it reduces epistemology to what is primarily wrong with it – the reductive form of its arguments. This straw man approach condemns Rorty's analysis to a systematic partial truth that becomes another form of reduction. Whereas the history of epistemological theories reveals progressively more aspects of heterology, Rorty's narrowed approach sees only the repetition of the monological error. No wonder he is moved to reject epistemology in principle: he thinks epistemology is exactly what it never was, and never could be.[2]

2. Rorty's procrustean definition portrays his targets as more alike than they really are. Thus he mistakes Kantian formality for a kind of Lockean mechanism: "Kant did not ... free us from Locke's confusion between justification and causal explanation ... Kant's advance in the direction of a propositional rather than a perceptual view of knowledge went only half-way because it was contained within the framework of causal metaphors – 'constitution', 'making',

What is missing from Rorty's strategy is the recognition that epistemology may have a non-reductive function. Thus, while classical, rationalist and empirical philosophies may have erred in seeking strong foundations, these legacies may nonetheless discover useful theoretical dimensions of knowledge by way of their different discursive strategies. In that case, they require distinct considerations rather than categorical dismissal. Indeed, insofar as Rorty shows that epistemology is *not* monological, the strong foundational ideal is necessarily a straw man, and its limitations do not redound upon the authority of whatever insights epistemology has fostered. Only if the strong foundationist ideal were true should epistemological theories be held to its standard. Once we have rejected that standard, we then want to know what other sort of foundational status these theories might have. Rorty's preoccupation with strong foundationism, therefore, becomes an extended exercise in showing us the kind of authority that past epistemological theories do not have, while ignoring the question of the kind of authority they might have.

2. Epistemology and the Enlightenment

Rather than reforming epistemology, Rorty insists on defining epistemology monologically, tying his argument to the historical errors of the post-Cartesian strong foundation canon. This gives too much authority to Enlightenment philosophy: "We owe the notion of a 'theory of knowledge' based on an understanding of 'mental processes' to the seventeenth century, and especially to Locke"; "'the mind' as a separate entity ... to Descartes"; "philosophy as a tribunal ... to the eighteenth century and especially to Kant" (*PM*, 3–4). The consequence of this strategy is to equate epistemology with its most

'shaping', 'synthesizing', and the like" (*PM*, 161). But Kant is explaining formal causation, not a mechanistic or psychologistic causation of the Locke-Hume type. At some points, formal causation *is* "justification" (as opposed to the mechanistic causation of a psychologized epistemology). Kant's distinction between *a priori* and *a posteriori* truth moves his model sufficiently far from psychologistic causality in the direction of formal truth to warrant a post-Lockean angle of critique.

As Rorty implies when he notes that Kant's "causality" was a system of rules of thought, the problem with Kant's model is not that it is psychologistic, but that it is a closed formal system supposed to limit absolutely the function of reason. Having oversimplified strong foundationism, Rorty conflates the empiricist's claim to mechanistic truth with the rationalist's claim to formal closure, i.e. as if all strong foundational candidates are interchangeable.

reductive versions, insofar as its Enlightenment proponents were preoccupied with post-metaphysical skepticism, simplicity, and certainty.

Indeed, Rorty's insistence on the Enlightenment origins of epistemology shows how artificially constrained his notion of theory of knowledge is:

[Descartes did not] make epistemology the foundation [of philosophy] so much as to invent something new – epistemology – to bear the name "philosophy." The picture of ancient and medieval philosophy as concerned with *things*, the philosophy of the [Enlightenment] with *ideas*, and the enlightened contemporary philosophical scene with *words* has considerable plausibility. But this sequence should not be thought of as offering three contrasting views about what is primary, or what is foundational. It is not that Aristotle thought that one could best explain ideas and words in terms of things, whereas Descartes and Russell rearranged the order of explanation. It would be more correct to say that Aristotle did not have – did not feel the need of – a theory of knowledge, and that Descartes and Locke did not have a theory of meaning. (*PM*, 262–3)

One must disagree. Aristotle quite explicitly *was* offering what he thought was the best explanation of knowledge, i.e. in terms of its ontological ground. He does not have an epistemology in the modern sense because it is scattered between his *Organon*, his *Psychology*, and his *Metaphysics*. Indeed, Aristotle's epistemology, while reductive in some ways, is not reductive in Rorty's modern sense. Rorty is being led by his notion of epistemology rather than by a historically informed reading of Aristotle.[3]

If Rorty were true to his hermeneutic principles rather than to his epistemological straw man, he would see that the order of explanation should be historicized in exactly the sense he rejects here. The crux of philosophical hermeneutics is that self-evidence has a history, and that Aristotle's givens led him to a different form of epistemology from the modern one. This means that epistemology, as theory of knowledge, has no essence, no proper form. Ironically, only on strong foundationist assumptions could epistemology be properly limited to what Descartes, Locke, or Kant think it must be – that is, only if

---

3. With Aristotle historically contextualized, we see not only a theory of knowledge, but centrality of that interest for breaking with Platonism: he complained that transcendental dualism explained a lesser mystery (experience) with a greater one (transcendental ideas). Aristotle wanted the priorities of explanation adjusted. However metaphysical Aristotle's results, only a narrower epistemology could exclude his from qualifying.

epistemology has a privileged form could it be legislated in advance. This point is especially significant for Rorty's argument insofar as it shows how his conception of epistemology is complicit with strong foundationist assumptions, rather than with a hermeneutic approach to the conditions and limits of knowledge.

Rorty's definition of epistemology is essentialist and historicist in precisely the wrong ways: it privileges Enlightenment epistemology because it is the most extreme, turns it into an essence, and thus betrays the relativity-of-the-given he should be arguing for. True, Descartes would have accused Aristotle of not having an epistemology, but only because Descartes was even more reductive than Aristotle. By taking such claims too seriously, Rorty reduces the history of philosophy to its greatest error.

Thus Rorty's argument equivocates on a key issue: it pretends to be an argument against foundationism *in principle*, yet it is structured as an *historical* argument against particular attempts at strong foundationism, attempts we know to be misconceived. His insistence on the Enlightenment legacy takes epistemology at its most excessively narrow moment. Likewise, the historical narrowness of his targets underdetermines the theoretical depth of his anti-foundationist conclusion, which purports to hold in principle. The foundationist issue, finally, cannot be decided historically, but only by the nature of theoretical authority and the critical conditions of argument.

3. Epistemology as foundations

Rorty's insistence on the Enlightenment legacy guarantees that epistemology will appear totalitarian. He sets up the characteristic anti-foundationist false dilemma of monology and conventionism, foreshadowing his "constraint-free" model of hermeneutic midwifing:

> It is the notion that human activity ... takes place within a framework which can be isolated prior to the conclusion of inquiry – a set of presuppositions discoverable *a priori* – which links contemporary philosophy to the Descartes-Locke-Kant tradition ... The notion that there could be such a thing as "foundations of knowledge" (*all* knowledge – in every field, past, present, and future) or a "theory of representation" (*all* representation, in familiar vocabularies and those not yet dreamed of) depends on the assumption that there is some such *a priori* constraint. (*PM*, 8–9)

If one is still concerned to defeat strong foundationism, this analysis is persuasive. But if one has already granted Rorty the impossibility of a monological theory of knowledge, one finds that a host of foundational questions are left untouched by Rorty's analysis. Are semiotics, logic, and mathematics prior to, or results of, inquiry? Are phenomenology and all forms of observation empirical or only experimental ones? Need formal sciences (i.e. mathematics) be fallible in theory or only in practice? Does the displacement of the quest for certainty by fallibilism mean that mathematics is not in some sense a foundation of engineering and that semiotics is not in some sense a foundation of literary theory? If we grant Rorty and Kuhn that facticity does not provide the positivist with an unambiguous standard for all philosophical problems, does this mean that technological progress is as insecure as the translatability of scientific terms across theory changes?

It is not clear, finally, that Rorty has dissolved the possibility of foundations, constraints, and theories of representation so much as the possibility that all these problems could be solved by a single principle of epistemic authority. That is, he can only conclude that epistemic reduction appears to be impossible. He cannot conclude that the plurality of theoretical factors theorized by Aristotle, Kant, and Peirce do not point toward a heterological epistemology that unites products of other sciences in a non-reductive theory of knowledge.

4. Epistemology as an autonomous theory

Rorty's closest approximation to a heterological foundationism occurs in his critique of epistemology as an autonomous discipline. This aspect of epistemology is indeed a part of its Enlightenment heritage. Whereas Aristotle's epistemology was an "interfield theory" uniting several disciplines,[4] the Enlightenment version assumed the need to discover a new methodology which would ground all the other sciences. "Kant ... managed to transform the old notion of philosophy – metaphysics as 'queen of the sciences' – into the notion of a 'most basic' discipline – a foundational discipline" (*PM*, 132). This historical destiny suggests to Rorty that epistemology depends on the Enlightenment's horizon of questionability: "If [thinking of knowledge as a foundation problem] is optional, then so is epistemology, and so

---

4. That is, Aristotle thought that he had demonstrated how epistemology could be both composed of different sciences and subject to systemic interconnections.

is philosophy as it has understood itself since the middle of the last century" (*PM*, 137). History conditioned the need for strong foundationism, therefore we can discursively detoxify ourselves of the need.

On closer inspection, this argument begs the question of post-strong-foundational legitimacy. Assuming the conventionism he is arguing for, Rorty's rebuttal assumes that *being convinced* of the strong foundation ideal is the issue, in which case, only therapy is required to cure our anxiety over pseudo-deep questions: if one is historically disposed to ignore a pseudo-deep question, it will go away. Yet no scientist would believe that merely believing in his predictions will make them succeed. Rorty has merely assumed that historical context is not only a necessary factor in epistemological foundations but a *sufficient* explanation of their validity.

The issue is this: given the demise of the belief that philosophical foundations are determined incorrigibly by a single, ultimate theory, is the questionability that gave rise to that hope assuaged or dissolved? Is the dissolution of yesterday's epistemological property (e.g. apriority, apodeicticity, analyticity, etc.) into today's specialized sciences (e.g. set theory, neurocircuitry, diachrony, etc.) tantamount to the demise of epistemology as an autonomous discipline? According to the Enlightenment ideal, epistemology was monologous or nothing, and Rorty accepts that implication.

But there are numerous counterexamples to the notion that a discipline must be monological rather than an interfield theory. For instance, *interfield* disciplines – such as biochemistry, political economy, physical anthropology, etc. – seek relationships, principles, and laws that do not appear elsewhere. But they are not monological: they do not reduce to exclusively mathematical, experimental, or hermeneutic paradigms of truth. In fact, one might conclude from Rorty's (Quinean or Sellarsean) holism that *no* discipline is autonomous anyway since they all must depend on each other. In that case, why should epistemology be held to a standard that other disciplines are not? A discipline only needs an identifiable focus, not complete autonomy, in which case autonomy is a false issue for the legitimacy of epistemology.

If epistemology is an interfield theory – linking logic, semiotics, phenomenology, psychology, and methodology – then it will not merely dissolve into those several disciplines on whose work it depends and whose results it helps to interpret. Rather, by virtue of its generality, and by virtue of the theoretical holism that links those specialized sciences to each other through epistemological theory, epistemology will constitute a perspective of some theoretical weight, just as Aristotle's revision of Platonic metaphysics, Kant's revision of ontological epistemology, and Peirce's revision of traditional logic and empiricism were all driven by epistemological considerations but yielded consequences for more specific disciplines.

5. Epistemology as social discourse

For Rorty's anti-foundationism as for Kuhn's history of science, the primary conditions of critique worth talking about are the conventions of social history. Foundations are contextual insofar as "nothing counts as justification unless by reference to what we already accept, and [insofar as] there is no way to get outside our beliefs and our language so as to find some test other than coherence" (*PM*, 178). The explanation of knowledge is, on this view, sociological: "justification is not a matter of a special relation between ideas ... and objects, but of conversation, of social practice" (*PM*, 170). In this view, the traditional epistemological aim of explanation in terms of meta-practices and underlying causes appears in its true irrelevance: "If we see knowledge as a matter of conversation and of social practice rather than as an attempt to mirror nature, we will not be likely to envisage a metapractice which will be the critique of all possible forms of practice" (*PM*, 171); "if assertions are justified by society rather than by the character of the inner representations they express, then there is no point in attempting to isolate *privileged* representations" (*PM*, 174). This new perspective, which Rorty calls "epistemological behaviorism," explains "rationality and epistemic authority by reference to what society lets us say, rather than the latter by the former" (*PM*, 174). Yet it is precisely this *reversal* of explanatory priority that shows where the anti-foundationist's privileged paradigm arises: now sociological explanations are ultimate.

This would-be-revolutionary inversion goes the epistemic crux of postmodern anti-foundationism: it questions the notion of what counts as explanation. We may have noticed that Rorty is still hoping to explain things. What might trouble us in this is his inconsistency about what explains what. In the bad, old days, epistemology told us the terms in which to explain everything. Rorty suggests that that should not happen again. But Rorty seems not completely decided whether that means that social conventions explain everything, or whether to allow that "explanatory power is where we find it" (*PM*, 209). The first is sociologism, the second methodological anarchy. And what is worse, Rorty cannot be faithful to either of these alternatives.

On the one hand, if Rorty sides with sociologism, he must rule out in principle traditional formalist and objectivist explanations, both of which bracket social conventions. That is, if social conventions are supposed to explain everything that traditional epistemology took as foundations, then we simply have a new hierarchy, an inversion of the old priority of epistemology over history. On the other hand, if Rorty embraces methodological anarchy, then he cannot rule out a heterological analysis of necessary conditions in advance, depriving him of his anti-epistemological stance.

This ambivalence is decided, like his definition of epistemology, by his basic anti-foundationist stance. Thus, since Rorty's anti-foundationism excludes certain theoretical methods in principle, he cannot accept explanations where he finds them and instead argues broadly for contingency. Rorty becomes trapped, finally, by the contradiction of legislating against foundationism, a trap which takes the form of privileging what is seen to be the alternative to the traditional products of epistemology. The impossibility of doing this consistently arises because Rorty, like everyone else, cannot do without priorities, constraints, and conditions that transcend whatever we happen to decide.

6. The end of epistemology

Given his conflation of Enlightenment strong foundationism with epistemology in general, it follows that Rorty is, at first, emphatic about his rejection of epistemology. Nothing, we are told, "still remains for epistemology to be" (*PM*, 210). The more moderate Quine, who shares Rorty's rejection of the strong foundationist ideal, believes that epistemology needs to be continued though "in a new setting and a clarified status ... in order to see how evidence relates to theory, and in what ways one's theory of nature transcends the available evidence" (*PM*, 221). But Rorty insists that "understanding modern philosophy requires a more radical break with the tradition than Quine wants to make" (*PM*, 223). Furthermore, "the attempt to render all discourses commensurate by translating them into a preferred set of terms ... is unlikely to be a useful strategy. The reason is ... that the Whiggish assumption that we have got such a language blocks the road of inquiry" (*PM*, 349).

Rorty's well-known solution to the decline of epistemology is its displacement by a hermeneutic model of philosophizing. Of course, his hermeneutics is not a better version of epistemology:

I am *not* putting hermeneutics forward as a "successor subject" to epistemology ... Hermeneutics is not the name of a discipline, nor for a method of achieving the sort of results which epistemology failed to achieve, nor for a program of research ... [rather, it is] the expression of a hope that ... the demand for constraint and confrontation is no longer felt.

(*PM*, 315–16)

This disillusioned philosophy-to-come is conveyed in an extended contrast to the epistemologist as neo-Platonic "cultural overseer who knows everyone's common ground":

[the new philosopher will be an] informed dilettante, the polypragmatic, Socratic intermediary between various discourses ... [whose interlocutors are] charmed out of their self-enclosed practices ... [D]isagreements between disciplines and discourses are compromised or transcended in the course of conversation ... [He] sees the relations between various discourses as those of strands in a possible conversation, a conversation which presupposes no disciplinary matrix which unites the speakers, but where the hope of agreement is never lost so long as the conversation lasts. This hope is not the hope for the discovery of an antecedently existing common ground, but simply hope for agreement ... For [him] to be rational is to be willing to refrain from epistemology – from thinking there is a special set of terms in which all contributions to the conversation should be put – and to be willing to pick up the jargon of the interlocutor rather than translating it into one's own ... For [him], inquiry is routine conversation ... [He views interlocutors] as united in what he calls a *societas* – persons whose paths through life have fallen together, united by civility rather than by a common goal, much less by a common ground.   (*PM*, 318)

The problem with Rorty's dichotomy is that, while it is clear that the strong foundationist is the bad guy, it is not clear that the midwife is doing much philosophy of *any* sort. Let us assume for a moment that Rorty has described the future-philosopher as a translator between two interlocutors from vastly different cultures. Does he literally do no more than translate their languages for each other? If so, should philosophers be no more than conduits of the intentions and judgments of others? Did Rorty's vaunted Socrates do no more than that, or did he too have an agenda? And why aren't translators *constrained* by logic and facts that transcend social convention? How does one know what constraints are commensurable and which ones aren't?

If one puts a bit of pressure on Rorty's dichotomy, it appears that he has given us another false dilemma: the choice between philosopher-as-strong-foundationist and midwife-as-translator-without-constraints, without facts, without hope of an antecedent common goal or a common ground. For if one considers what happens in dialogues, one finds that neither of those two options works. Dialogue is neither a machine nor a free-for-all. Rather, the ideal dialogue is a hybrid of epistemological judgment and hermeneutic openness. One cannot dialogue with a tyrant, but one cannot dialogue without antecedent or objective common ground either. Science is not the only antecedent common goal or ground: Rorty's vaunted *societas* and communication are as well. Just as the strong foundationist choice between absolute foundations and anarchy is a false dilemma, so is the anti-foundationist choice between discursive tyranny and no constraints. It is a choice even Rorty cannot live with for the duration of the chapter.

The need for epistemology in novel hermeneutic contexts is codified in the "principle of charity" to which Rorty sometimes refers. This means that when one's reading of someone else's discourse appears perplexing, one puts the most cogent construal on it one can. What is involved here is not mere politeness. Rather, it makes sense to hypothesize and impute the most universal truths as far as possible; any other assumption is simply a bad risk. But this means that we must proceed with epistemological hypotheses about common grounds and common goals. Indeed, Rorty admits that "nothing is so valuable for the hermeneutic inquirer into an exotic culture as the discovery of an epistemology written within that culture" (*PM*, 346). But that is just because dialogue is as much a search for common constraints as it is an articulation of differences.

When understood in this context, epistemology neither resembles the ideals of Descartes, Locke, and Kant, nor does it disappear into mere translation of different languages. Rather, it simply means, as it should, theory of knowledge. In such an activity some constraints will be formal, some will be objective, and some will be conventional. To bring out the hermeneutic dimension of epistemology does not make its particular interests go away, but instead shows (1) that epistemology is an hypothesis, and (2) that hermeneutics presupposes it, not as final, but at least as a starting point. For hermeneutics, epistemology is the pragmatic *a priori*, the logic of justification and the condition of critique.

7. Complementarity as modality

Rorty's global gambit of identifying epistemology with strong foundationism hopes to displace epistemological practice with hermeneutic practice. Presumably, this would displace all questions of knowledge with questions of understanding others' meanings. The irony is that he obscures that form of discourse which he himself is practicing: post-strong-foundationist epistemology. As we saw in his highjacking of Aristotle, his argument is not in the hermeneutic mode; it is not merely a struggle to understand Aristotle, Kant, Wittgenstein, Heidegger, or Dewey. Rorty hopes to critique strong foundationism and make it go away. He has a global agenda. His argument is a judgment against the cogency and possibility of a kind of theory; it is, in other words, an epistemological argument. Because of its confusion over discursive modes, however, it advances on the basis of partial truths that serve to obscure their own authority.

But as already glimpsed, Rorty finally recognizes the need of hermeneutics for critical conditions – i.e. for theories of what first to attribute to the understanding of another – and the end of his argument attempts to revise the relation between epistemic and hermeneutic modes of discourse. "If we draw the line between epistemology and hermeneutics as I have been drawing it – as a contrast between discourse about normal and about abnormal discourse – then it seems clear that the two do not compete, but rather help each other out" (*PM*, 346). Of course, by making epistemology a mode of discourse, he repudiates his earlier reduction of it to Enlightenment strong foundationism. He now admits, not only that epistemology may be possible, but even "the possibility that hermeneutics is always parasitic upon the possibility (and actuality) of epistemology" (*PM*, 366). Rorty thus repudiates his earlier anti-foundationism with an inchoate recognition of the need for a revisionary foundationism, a foundationism no longer idealized as reducing to a single ultimate principle, but able to provide critical conditions as heterological and irreducible.

C. Standing science on its head: Lyotard

For many, the term "postmodern" recalls Jean-François Lyotard's *The postmodern condition: a report on knowledge*, which situated postmodernism in the technocratic character of the age, thereby bringing into relief the link between postmodernism's sociological and epistemological interests. From within the legacy of Enlightenment optimism, Lyotard recognizes a cultural crisis resulting from the loss of the *metanarratives* – especially that of positivistic progress – that legitimated Western culture in the past. For Lyotard, the only possibility for a credible and humane future lies in those sciences which no longer seek legitimation through consensus and monology, but which recognize as primary the dissent and paralogy (logical discontinuities) that motivate scientific progress. Reminiscent of Feyerabend's empiricist anarchism, Lyotard seeks "a form of legitimation based solely on paralogy" (*PC*, 61).

Lyotard's reaction against the positivist tradition of reductive theorizing leads him, as it does Rorty and Fish, to underestimate the need for theoretical unity as the final state of scientific process, however temporary and open-ended that process may be. So Lyotard, by assuming a too-reductive notion of theory, is also seduced by the false dilemma between the ideals of strong foundationist theorizing and theoretical anarchy.

1. The politics of science

Like Rorty, Lyotard shows an interest in the institutional dimension of the foundationist issue. Indeed, Lyotard's political motivations are perhaps even more decisive than Rorty's in shaping his conclusions. Concerned with the imperial thrust of traditional epistemology, Lyotard claims that ever since Plato's philosopher-king, "the question of the legitimacy of science has been indissociably linked to the legitimation of the legislator" (*PC*, 8). And for the postmodern condition and "the computer age, the question of knowledge is now more than ever a question of government" (*PC*, 9). The connection between monology and repression is no doubt one of the blind spots of Enlightenment scientism that Lyotard does well to challenge. For monology suggests that there is a privileged point of critique from which everything and everyone can be judged with scientific precision, and that that vantage point belongs to the technocrats. But it remains to be seen if Lyotard's politics are best served in terms of his epistemological argument.

The bulk of Lyotard's case rests on two sociological premises: the failure of the Enlightenment myth of progress, and the methodological error of consensus and monology. On the first point, Lyotard finds the metanarrative of positivist progress – the monology of scientific reason – belied by postmodern social fragmentation. On the second point, his analysis is sociological in the sense that, like Feyerabend, he condemns positivism for obscuring the role of dissent and paralogy (i.e. the agon and discontinuity of theory) in the institutional realities of science.

Insofar as he rejects the traditional epistemological goals of consensus and monology (i.e. the final coherence of theory), the question for Lyotard is whether or not he can make sense of a science that *seeks* dissent. According to the following analysis, Lyotard does not and cannot remain faithful to this ideal, a failure which leads to several paralogies of the unproductive kind. Like other anti-foundationists, Lyotard's equivocation hopes to discredit the foundational thrust of theory while making his own categorical generalizations about the nature of society, science and theory. But he, too, throws away more of theoretical coherence than he can afford to lose.

2. The critique of positivism

According to Lyotard's analysis of monology, the positivist "philosophy of efficiency" is legitimated by a too ambitious, mechanistic concept of determinism applied universally. Such reductivism is false both to nature and to science.

Against the positivist metanarrative of a universal, monologous determinism, Lyotard displaces the totalizing field-theory ideal of science with the emergence of a plurality of local determinisms (a powerful and convincing image of heterological foundations) and the quasi-autonomy of fields. Reminiscent of Feyerabend's claim that the plurality of sciences demand a plurality of methodologies that cannot be constrained *a priori*, Lyotard charges that the legacy of positivist methodology is false to the heterogeneous nature of determinacy itself, which can only be described locally and discontinuously. Unlike other postmodern skeptics, however, Lyotard defends heterology in objective terms, if I read him correctly, rather than suggesting that it is the conventional nature of language that accounts for the local character of truth.

Thus Lyotard's critique of monology leads him to heterology. But what about the relation between heterology and consensus? The problem arises when Lyotard considers the optimum relation between heterology and scientific method, and the kind of demands heterology makes on method. Lyotard fails to see that if monology is untrue to knowledge and needs to be replaced by a heterological model, that does not say anything particular about the way to *discover* heterology. In particular, it does not mean that the way to correct the positivist reduction is to invert the priority of consensus over dissent, and coherence over contradiction; but that is the conclusion Lyotard draws.

In the name of deterministic discontinuity, Lyotard (echoing Popper's falsificationism) maintains that science cannot advance except by challenging the adequacy of received models with new paradoxes, new anomalies, i.e. by "producing the unknown." This is supposed to correct the positivist's mechanistic model of institutional efficiency: "since performativity is defined by an input/output ratio, there is a [positivist] presupposition that the system into which the input is entered is stable; that the system must follow a regular path" (*PC*, 54). But as Lyotard notes: "Science does not expand by means of the mechanism of efficiency. The opposite is true: working on a proof means searching for and 'inventing' counterexamples, in other words, the unintelligible; supporting an argument means looking for a 'paradox' and legitimating it with new rules in the games of reasoning" (*PC*, 54). Because positivism had a prejudice in favor of coherence, Lyotard decides in favor of discontinuity.

But like positivism, this still confuses method and result, only in the reverse order from the positivists. Whereas positivism made the error of privileging the goal of science – consensus and coherence – at the expense of the freedom of discovery and theory-production, Lyotard wants to invert the hierarchy to privilege the cause of theorizing – dissent and contradiction – as if they were its goal. Against the ideal of theoretical monology, Lyotard poses the logic of dissent, and demands "a form of legitimation based solely on paralogy [i.e. the logic of discontinuity]" (*PC*, 61). Science should not seek consensus and monology, but rather dissent and the unknown. Already, Lyotard approves, postmodern science is in the process of "theorizing its own

evolution as discontinuous, catastrophic, nonrectifiable, and paradoxical" (*PC*, 60). This postmodern science "is producing not the
known, but the unknown" (*PC*, 60). So Lyotard concludes: "Consensus is only a particular state of discussion, not [the] end" of science
as such; "Its end, on the contrary, is paralogy" (*PC*, 65–6).

3. The revenge of coherence

Like Feyerabend's methodological anarchy, Lyotard's valorizing of
paralogy leads to a confusion between the context of theory
production and the final authority of theory, or in Reichenbach's
terms, between the contexts of discovery and justification. This
confusion is based on the half truth that positivist reductivism is the
result of the tyranny of coherence (the hegemonic, monological
context of justification) over the pluralism of conflicting beliefs (the
agonistic, paralogical context of discovery). But this misplaces the
error of positivism in its desire for coherence rather than in its desire
for a reductive, monological coherence. Finding no ground between
monology and anarchy, Lyotard chooses anarchy – but at the expense
of argument and the heterological foundations he implies.

The heterology of grounds Lyotard implies need not sacrifice coherence, as evidenced by the fact that Lyotard's critique of monology
is more coherent than positivism. And why is Lyotard's model more
coherent? Because the positivist reduction of science to a single
method contradicts the heterology of scientific constraints and
methods, the very contradiction Lyotard's argument seeks to rectify
by theorizing heterology. Heterology offers coherence without
reduction, which is what neither monology nor anarchy can provide.
The problem with positivism, then, is not that it wants coherence, but
that it wants only one coherence, which yields an incoherent result.

Unfortunately, however, rather than correcting the positivist error,
the dissent-paralogy strategy merely inverts it. Whereas the positivists
had overemphasized the ideal of theoretical coherence in the name of
the logic of justification, Lyotard underemphasizes theoretical coherence in the name of the logic of discovery, the dissent-motivated
inquiry that pushes the search for coherence further. But this
perversion of the motive of science can quickly become pernicious: for
instrumental intervention becomes its own justification (where Bacon's
vexing of nature becomes an end in itself) and the larger end of science
becomes obscured in the name of the local cause. In the long view, the

point of science is not to find more dissent, agon, and incoherence. That comes uninvited. Indeed, it is just because dissent and contradiction keep returning that we keep having to seek its coherence.

Through his inversion of positivist reduction, Lyotard's idealization of dissent obscures its status as much as the positivists' did (though for a different agenda): for if cognitive dissonance were the end of science, then science would begin with understanding and end in confusion. Obviously, not even Lyotard believes this is the case, nor do his examples suggest that he does. If we were to take Lyotard's analysis at face value, we would believe that theorists of catastrophe, fractals, discontinuity, quantum leaps, and random decay are busy producing dissent and the unknown. But this is not the case. If we take quantum theory, whose concepts of random behavior and discontinuous action embody the novelties Lyotard speaks of, we find that, in the words of Paul Davies, they still fulfill standard epistemological functions:

Quantum mechanics is not merely a speculative theory of the subatomic world, but an elaborate mathematical framework which holds together most of modern physics. Without quantum mechanics, our detailed and extensive understanding of atoms, nuclei, molecules, crystals, light, electricity, sub-atomic particles, lasers, transistors and much else would disintegrate. No scientist seriously doubts that the basic ideas of quantum mechanics are correct.[5]

Despite all the counter-intuitive elements in quantum theory, it still takes its value from its explanatory power (i.e. its problem-solving success), the fruits of which are consensus and theoretical coherence. The fact that it posits more discontinuity of physical behavior than the Newtonian model does not disturb the broader epistemological point: we need not confuse physical coherence with epistemological coherence. The more an empirical model approximates the chaos of nature, the more epistemologically coherent it is.

The same point can be made with all of Lyotard's examples. Fractals, for instance, are patterns generated by mathematical formulae that are open to random factors. Does its openness to randomness mean that fractal science "produces the unknown"? Only by the standards of a mechanistic determinism for which the not- totally- predictable is the unknown. For everyone else, the unknown does a fine job of producing itself. If we accept the premise that reality might be determined by non-mechanical patterns, then fractal science

5. *Other worlds*, New York: Simon and Schuster, 1980; pp. 17–18.

represents a reclamation of the unknown into new forms of the known. Thus for the cartographer, fractal formulas allow for unprecedented approximations of the lengths of coastlines – with their random curvatures – which cannot be measured, but which can be simulated by fractal-generating formulae. This is an example of a quite traditional virtue of theory: to approximate reality by formalization. In this case, however, it accounts for an irreducible heterology of determinisms rather than forcing the monological determinism of the mechanists. The fact that the formalization is probabilistic or partially randomized does not change the fact that the problem is the unknown and the answer is the known. The teleology of theory is not thereby inverted. The suggestion that if the end of science is not mechanical determinism, it must be dissent and the unknown is the very false dilemma characteristic of strong foundationism.

Like other postmodern critics of strong foundationism, Lyotard wants to invert the priority of coherence and conflict, and make dissent, which is the *motive* and context of theorizing, into the *aim* of science. To do so, Lyotard must interpret out of context such novelties as fractal theory and chaos theory when he says that postmodern science "is producing not the known, but the unknown" (*PC*, 60). Such claims distract us from noting that fractal theory, like traditional theory, provides approximately accurate descriptions where none was possible before. Such theories still move us from lesser to greater conditions of intelligibility. It does not follow, therefore, that "consensus is only a particular state of discussion, not its end" (*PC*, 65–6) unless one disallows tentative ends, in which case *neither* dissent nor consensus are ends.

4. Toward non-reductive theory

Insofar as Lyotard's critique of epistemological reductionism is sound, it points in the direction, not of dissent and the unknown as the products of science, but of a heterological, interfield epistemology. But Lyotard fails to see the coherence of such a neo-foundational thesis, and instead rejects the theoretical ideal in principle though, like Rorty, he cannot be faithful to such revolutionary conclusions.

Let us grant that Lyotard's local determinisms refute the possibility of science as reducible into a single method or paradigm. But is the proliferation of local determinisms ultimately generative of dissent? For even if these determinisms are heterological and unreducible, are they still not determinisms, in which case they are theorizable as separate domains with implications for each other? Is this not what Lyotard is doing himself, and does he not want our consent in this project? The heterological or interfield model of scientific theory offers, by contrast to the monological ideal, the proliferation of local determinisms about which one hopes we will agree.

Not only does Lyotard seek consent in his critique; he has his own strong claims about science and truth that sound suspiciously like global truth and interfield coherence. Like Kuhn, Lyotard is not afraid to state that "Science develops – and no one will deny that it develops – by developing [the questions, 'What is your argument worth, what is your proof worth?']" (*PC*, 54). The reason why this question of legitimation cannot *finally* be answered in positivist terms is that it can only be answered in epistemological terms, i.e. heterologically. And Lyotard himself sees the epistemological thrust of this claim: "And this question, as it develops, leads to the following question, that is to say, metaquestion, the question of legitimacy: 'What is your "what is it worth" worth?'" (*PC*, 54). Having rejected positivist standards, the problem for Lyotard is that this question cannot be legitimated on the basis of dissent either, but must rely on the power of theory to discover coherence – however heterological and meta-theoretical – and compel consent.

Not surprisingly, Lyotard's inversion of the process of theory-production cannot survive his own analysis. Thus he quotes P. B. Medawar as saying that "having ideas is the scientist's highest accomplishment" (*PC*, 60). It is just in this epistemological sense of "highest" that theory and consensus *are* the end of discussion, and it is in that sense that Lyotard still looks forward to postmodern science "theorizing its own evolution as discontinuous, catastrophic, non-rectifiable, and paradoxical" (*PC*, 60). If one considers this hope carefully, one sees that it is still the hope of theoretical coherence, however heterological. Hence, though post-positivist science seeks a *less closed coherence* than that of the positivist legacy, Lyotard himself wants from it the guiding, unifying, high accomplishment of theory that a critique of positivism needs for its own critical legitimacy.

Thus we need to discriminate productive and unproductive paralogies, a discrimination that will lead to more *complex* forms of coherence. Tension between two contradictory beliefs whose tension provokes the discovery of a higher non-reductive unity is productive. On the contrary, the tension between Lyotard's ideal of dissent and his implicit legitimation of science on the consensus of progress which "*no one will deny*" is not a productive tension, but a misleading one insofar as it induces us to be complacent with the contradictions we have, and uninterested in more adequate coherence. In both scientific and epistemological modes of inquiry, the aim of legitimation is that of consensus and coherence. If it is true that finding anomalies leads to better theories, those theories are better only because they provide a wider coherence of explanatory power. What Lyotard overlooks is the fact that epistemological consensus need not demand monology. Rather, theoretical coherence can be as one finds it: a loose association of disparate theories whose connection is not *a priori* determined, but which remains to be established as an inter-theoretical task of theory.

D. Discursive necessities

The examples of Rorty and Lyotard illustrate several of the contemporary strategies by which the heterological nature of foundations is either misrepresented or reduced in the name of anti-foundationism. In each case their strategies overlook some aspect of the heterological constraints required for their own critical discourse, constraints more invariant than can be accounted for by their arguments. In contrast to such decentering agendas, the heterological nature of foundations repudiates *both* the strong foundationist reductions *and* the denial of foundational constraints altogether. For all critical discourse depends both on the discursive necessities of those constraints and on their irreducible nature.

3

Theory and/or deconstruction: Derrida's slippage

A. Theory against itself

> The necessary decentering cannot be a philosophic or scientific act as such, since it is a question of dislocating, through access to another system linking speech and writing, the founding categories of language and the grammar of the *epistémè*. The natural tendency of *theory* – what unites philosophy and science in the *epistémè* – will push rather toward filling in the breach than toward forcing the closure.
> (*OG*, 92)

Within the theoretical discourse of our time, one of the most provocative challenges to the philosophical foundations of our tradition comes from a collection of rigorously subversive textual practices referred to as "deconstruction." As the opening quotation indicates, Derrida's challenge to traditional philosophy seems to oppose the philosophical ideal of coherence – the ideal to which theory gravitates – with the effect of deconstruction, which is to discover the heterogeneity of the discursive or textual conditions of theory, the fissures and ambiguities in the conceptual structure of the *epistémè* (the fabric of signs and texts that constitute the historical present). At times, as in the above passage, the relation between theory and deconstruction seems to be one of antagonism. When philosophy proposes an ideal order capable of appropriation by theoretical discourse, deconstructive critique shows the discourse to be already contaminated by the same impurities philosophy is trying to escape. For many, the significance of this theory-subverting power is to spell the fundamental antagonism between theory and deconstruction. Yet, even among the advocates of deconstruction, the precise relation of theory to deconstruction is not so clear.

For some practitioners of deconstruction, its putative significance is the final end of the traditional foundational hegemony of theory over practice. For others, however, grammatology and deconstruction depend on what Derrida refers to as "the general system of [the] economy" of which deconstruction is the practice. In this case, deconstruction depends on a yet more profound coherence that subverts earlier epistemological and hermeneutic theories by finding a deeper ground, a ground as rigorous as the most traditional theory if more remote than the systems of traditional theory. As Rodolphe Gasché puts it, "Deconstruction is concerned ... with determining the limits (the conditions of impossibility) of the possibility of systematicity and system-formation."[1] In this latter view, deconstructive practice does not deny systematic ground as much as displace it beyond the appropriations of representation.

But if deconstruction depends so fundamentally on a systematic ground, then how can deconstruction subvert in principle the means (i.e. theory) by which such grounds are appropriated? How can both views of deconstruction be correct? The tension between these two views of deconstruction raises a fundamental question regarding the relation of theory to deconstruction: just how far is theory supposed to be subverted and discredited by the possibility of deconstructive practice? The answer to this question largely determines the status of deconstruction either within or without the practices of philosophy.

B. Self-occulting totalities: deconstruction from within

The relation of theory to deconstruction has problematized deconstruction's influence even among its defenders. Indeed, this difficulty begins with the question of the very identity of deconstruction, a problem captured best by Derrida in his characterization of the displacement of the science of language and Western metaphysics by grammatology and the deconstructive significance of writing:

today something lets [the deconstruction of logocentrism] appear as such, allows it a kind of takeover without our being able to translate this novelty into clear cut notions of mutation, explicitation, accumulation, revolution, or tradition ... such a science of writing [grammatology] runs the risk of never being established as such and with that name. Of never being able to define the unity of its project or its object. Of not being able either to write its discourse on method or to describe the limits of its field. For essential reasons: the unity of all that allows itself to be attempted today through the most diverse concepts of science and of writing, is, in principle, more or less covertly yet always, determined by an historico-metaphysical epoch of which we merely glimpse the *closure*. I do not say the *end*.   (*OG*, 4)

1. *Deconstruction and philosophy*, John Sallis (ed.), Chicago: Univ. of Chicago, 1987; p. 7; hereafter referred to as "Sallis."

Deconstruction's relentless questioning of the authority of perception and thought discovers the heterogeneous conditions of significance, the conditions of both theoretical coherence and deconstructive play. This twofold character of discursive conditions is always available to subvert the "tendency of theory ... toward filling the breach rather than towards forcing the closure" of the *epistémè*. Thus the significance of deconstruction seems to be found in this work of decentering the center, this practical heterogeneity that works, so it is said, in opposition to the logical homogeneity of theory, the tendency of theory to fill the gaps in the discursive field. Systemically and historically, it would appear, deconstruction is the undoing of theory.

Not surprisingly, deconstruction's subversion of theory-as-ground is thought to be its most subversive trait. But here emerges a paradox: the more fundamental and comprehensive is its critique of the totalizing systematicity of Western metaphysics, the more deconstruction necessarily remains within the kind of totalizing terms that resemble the very theoretical thought meant to be deconstructed. Thus deconstruction claims as its vocation "the de-construction of *the greatest totality* – the concept of the *epistémè* and logocentric metaphysics" (*OG*, 46). The more complete the deconstruction of logocentrism, the more total the scope of the critique itself, whose inscription or "trace" must articulate "its possibility in the entire field" of signification (*OG*, 47). Just insofar as deconstruction becomes fundamental, it gravitates toward a paradoxical relationship with the totalizing thrust of theory, appearing to assume and deny at once the authority of the foundations of signification in general.

By a necessary irony which Derrida often notes, it is not just incidentally or heuristically that deconstructive discourse often seems to resemble its theoretical targets. But this fact destabilizes the distinction between theory and deconstructive practice, reflexively questioning deconstructive authority in the same gesture that questions theory. For instance, Derrida says that one does not leave the epoch one closes (*OG*, 12), implying one's confinement to the terms being deconstructed; and that deconstruction always "in a certain way falls prey to its own work" (*OG*, 24), implying that deconstruction cannot finally escape its own opening movement; while Gasché claims that Derrida "recognizes philosophy's demand for systematicity and system-formation as an unsurpassable and indispensable demand to which antisystematic thought ... remains profoundly committed" (Sallis, 6).

Deconstructors themselves claim a kind of rigorous economic necessity and accountability of their own that can sound quite theoretical and total. Thus deconstruction discovers a logocentric "movement of *economy*" which is "absolutely necessary" (*OG*, 7). This necessity imputes an essential integrity to the ground of signification such that grammatology may "stop receiving its guiding concepts from other human sciences" (*OG*, 83) – and that before all oppositions, the trace is "*a priori* written, whether inscribed or not, in a 'sensible' and 'spatial' element that is called 'exterior'" (*OG*, 70). Likewise, in his extensive analysis of deconstructive logic, Gasché claims that "deconstruction accounts for ... constitutive 'contradictions' through the construction of arche-syntheses, or infrastructures" (Sallis, 5), suggesting a notion of "accounting" with something like the systemic force of theory. There is, finally, throughout the deconstructive pas-de-deux with theory, a curious play of distances and tensions between theory and the deconstructive movement itself which the notion of accountability will not allow to be reduced to a merely enigmatic difference, for mere enigma could not warrant the necessity attributed to the general system on which deconstruction relies.

At this point, deconstruction's tendency to approximate theoretical accountability may confound the subversion of theoretical authority and the ubiquity of play, insofar as this questioning becomes a self-questioning of the limits of its own critical force. The deconstruction of theory, finally, questions deconstructive authority both from within and from without its own movement. Deconstruction is not merely a problem for theory; theory is also a problem for deconstruction.

Likewise, along with this ambivalence towards theory goes a fundamental ambiguity: it is not fortuitous that the meditation on grammatology verges toward its theoretical impossibility and that the deconstruction of presence relentlessly resembles a new theory of conditions, foundations, origins, and necessities. The conflation of these two aims – grammatology and deconstruction – may be symptomatic of a need to distinguish better the kind of theory that needs deconstructing and the kind of theoretical authority deconstruction requires. For Derrida has conceived of his project from within the heart of foundational theory, though he has not yet distinguished between the theories he is deconstructing and the one he needs. His discourse must therefore seem to resemble theory in the questioning of it, and to flee theory in the very practice of it.

From within the pragmatic perspective, however, the antagonism between theory and deconstruction does not exist, though the Derridean discourse sometimes suggests otherwise. Ironically, one finds that rather than constituting a subversion of theory, Derrida's *Of grammatology* involves a highly theoretical and figurative post-foundationist revision of theoretical authority, which reinscribes the legitimacy of its own theoretical ground as a part of its critique of strong foundationist theory.

C. Kant turned inside out: strong systematicity/radical mediacy

The lack of a clear relation between deconstruction and theory is due in part to deconstruction's frequent appearance as a postmodern questioning of particular texts. On the other hand, Gasché insists that Derrida's method is not fragmentary. Whereas the post-Nietzschean avoidance of system construction has led many to fragmentary criticism, Gasché claims that Derrida rejects the inability of such approaches to subvert radically their own complicity with the systematic tradition. A radical deconstruction of philosophy does not abandon systematicity by forgetting, but subverts by questioning, "operating necessarily from the inside, borrowing all the strategic and economic resources of subversion from the old structure, borrowing them structurally" (Sallis, 24). Hence, Derrida's most radical significance comes from his perversion of systematicity against its traditional forms. Systematicity, therefore, is fundamentally ambiguous in the deconstructive view, which likewise remains ambivalent about theory.

On the other hand, when deconstructors sound most far-reaching, most epochal, most anti-foundational, and most untraditional, they tend not to distinguish carefully between possible epistemological targets, conferring upon theory the same imperial integrity which their critique ultimately denies. Conversely, there emerges from this elision of theoretical distinctions a strong anti-theoretical stance that, when taken for granted and over-generalized, obscures deconstruction's own theoretical commitments. Indeed, such epochal demarcations betray the heterogeneity of theory in Western philosophy in the interest of epochal revolution. But consistency with their own insights into discursive heterogeneity would require that postmodern discussions of theory distinguish forms of foundationism and theoretical authority; otherwise, the rhetorical strategy of totalizing logocentrism or Western metaphysics or epistemology reifies and therefore authorizes the very conceptual integrity that is suspect.

For instance, by over-extending the critique of essences, most post-structuralist critics overlook the fact that the critique of presence is already implied by the first premise of the Kantian revolution in epistemology, i.e. by Kant's nominalist denial that thoughts represent things-in-themselves. Whereas classical epistemology grounds theory in immediate intuitions of being (i.e. the myth of presence), Kant's notion of theory is discursive, grounding itself in the inferred conditions of its structural mediacy rather than in its correspondence to an object in itself. As Hegel's *Phenomenology* and Heidegger's *Kant and the problem of metaphysics* make clear, the major post-Kantian foundational theories from Hegel to Derrida evolve by radicalizing the temporality of thought's mediacy, though their appeals to thought's conditions show that they are still within the concept of the mediacy of thought. No matter how historical the conditions, or even if one seeks "the conditions of impossibility ... of the possibility of systematicity," arguments from systematicity to conditions still presuppose a systemic – albeit post-Kantian – theoretical authority. Thus the genealogy of the critique of presence is not without an equivocal relation to theory, even by the age of Kant.

Through the influence of Hegel and Heidegger, on the one hand, the deconstructive project remains within the first premise of Kant's revolution in epistemology, the reorientation toward the mediating conditions of thought rather than to the mechanisms of corre-spondence of thought to thing. This legacy of theorized conditions allows a departure from the classical myth of presence.

On the other hand, however, it is the post-Kantian heritage of systematicity which gives Derrida his theoretical foundation, the totalizing terms of the epistemological question – the question of "what produces transcendentality itself" (*OG*, 23) – for these are the totalizing terms in which he finds the vulnerability of logocentrism always already there, the necessarily available terms of arche-writing, differance, and the trace. As the heart of Kant's displacement of classical epistemological authority, the terms of strong systematicity are an offspring of Enlightenment formalism and the philosophy of reflection.

Of course, we must distinguish between the excesses of Kant and the modesty of his offspring. For Kant's notion of strong systematicity

– i.e. the rational closure of thought's mediacy – presupposes the perfect unity of pure reason, a notion wherein formal conditions define not merely the initial possibility of experience but its boundaries as well. For Kant, in other words, it is the comprehensive necessity of the foundational system as a final limit that guarantees its authority as a warrant against hypothetical uncertainty: "For pure speculative reason has a structure wherein everything is an *organ*, the whole being for the sake of every part, and every part for the sake of all the others, so that even the smallest imperfection, be it a fault (error) or a deficiency, must inevitably betray itself in use."[2] For Kant the ultimate theoretical authority is this strong systematicity. Likewise, the Kantian conception of epistemology is constituted by this uniquely rational totality and its conditions, the latter being the logically necessary presuppositions which can be deduced from the structure of knowledge with the assumption of a unique and self-evident foundation.

The crucial break between Kant and those who radicalized his premise of mediacy occurs with their rejection of the uniqueness and closure of the foundational system that mediates thought. Though they agree that thought is necessarily mediated by concepts or language, they deny that the structure of this mediation is unique and ahistorical. Rather, semioticians, pragmatists and hermeneuticists alike can preserve the notion that thought is mediated systematically while exploring the historical and pragmatic contingency of this mediation. Thus, these theorists may still seek the foundations, conditions, and origins of thought; but these Kantian terms are now open to the rationality of contexts and the different formalities of semiotics. Through the projects of Husserl, Heidegger, and Derrida, this Kantian perspective on foundations remains evident, giving Derrida's notion of theory and deconstruction a distinctly Kantian orientation toward mediacy, formal conditions, necessities, and generalities of application.

In the work of two of Derrida's most theoretically sensitive commentators, his debt to Kantian theory is noted. Thus Irene Harvey calls deconstruction a "critique of critique in the Kantian sense." Harvey's phrase is perfectly ambiguous, catching both senses in which Derrida is anti-Kantian and neo-Kantian: a critique of Kantian (strong foundational) critique vs a Kantian (establishing the conditions)

2. *Critique of pure reason*, Trans. Norman Kemp Smith. New York: St. Martin's, 1965; p. 33.

critique of critique. To its discredit, the Kantian project was an attempt to define absolutely the limits of pure reason, to set the definitive categorical boundaries of philosophical authority in order to keep philosophy uncontaminated by everything "which bears any manner of resemblance to an hypothesis."[3] Deconstruction, on the other hand, discovers the impossibility of this ideal, as Harvey notes:

Rather than seeking to limit this contamination, which Kant had revealed to a certain extent in spite of himself, Derrida shows the essential necessity of such contamination. In the process Derrida too is aiming to curtail the unbounded use of our Reason – logocentrism – but not in order to ground metaphysics and Reason in the service of an absolute certainty, as Kant sought to do. Rather, deconstruction of the metaphysical tradition shows the limits of rational, metaphysical, and speculative control with respect to discourse, writing, the sign, language, and, in more general terms, textuality itself.[4]

While Harvey indicates the subversive thrust of deconstruction's relation to Kantian foundationism, she also indicates another effort of curtailment, another demonstration of limits, another discovery of an "essential necessity." She shows, that is, just in what way Derrida is still within the Kantian practice of analysis to conditions, even as a critique of Kantian critique.[5]

Another case for the systematicity of Derrida's thought is made by Rodolphe Gasché, for whom deconstruction "reveals to even a superficial examination, a well-ordered procedure, a step-by-step type of argumentation based on an acute awareness of level-distinctions, a marked thoroughness and regularity" (Sallis, 3). This rigor, furthermore, is moving toward distinctly neo-Kantian aims: "the specific displacements of traditional philosophical issues by deconstruction amount not to an abandonment of philosophical thought as such, but rather to an attempt at positively recasting philosophy's necessity and possibility in view of its inevitable inconsistencies" (Sallis, 2). This is

---

3. *Critique of pure reason*, 11.
4. "The wellsprings of deconstruction" in *Tracing literary theory*, ed. Joseph Natoli, Urbana: University of Illinois, 1987; p. 129.
5. Harvey's reference to an essential necessity discovered by Derrida threatens to sneak *a priori* foundational necessity in the back door with a certainty that has merely been displaced one level of abstraction from categories to limits on categories. We need, therefore, a much fuller articulation of the difference between Kantian and Derridean perspectives on foundationism. As Harvey indicates further on, this difference is developed in the direction of contextualization, though the Kantian terms still hover around these more radical strategies.

not just pure practice; rather "deconstruction yields to the philosophical demand of accounting for such heterogeneous manifoldness by means of quasi-synthetic constructions" that still function as an "accounting." That is, deconstruction "accounts for [the] constitutive 'contradictions' through the construction of arche-syntheses, or infrastructures ... These infrastructures represent laws of distribution and disposition, economically minimal clusters of concepts, predicates, or possibilities of these 'conflicting' concepts, levels of argumentation, or heterogeneous instances of discourse" (Sallis, 5).

Like Harvey, Gasché finds in Derrida a neo-foundational systematicity that suggests an attenuated Kant. Thus Derrida's writing "displays a subtle economy that recognizes the essential requirements of philosophical thought while questioning the limits of the possibility of these requirements. Deconstruction ... is engaged in the construction of the 'quasi-synthetic concepts' which account for the economy of the conditions of possibility and impossibility of the basic philosophemes" (Sallis, 7). The question, finally, raised by Harvey's and Gasché's postulation of ultimate deconstructive limits is the question leveled by Hegel against Kant: can one define limits without transgressing them? Does deconstruction allow for the kind of systematicity that Harvey and Gasché find? And if this systematicity does underlie deconstruction's authority, how completely can deconstruction oppose theory's filling of the breach opened by deconstruction?

In *Of grammatology*, this tension between system and non-system, theory and deconstruction, plays a major role in structuring Derrida's argument. Derrida's answer to this problem determines whether Harvey and Gasché are right to cast deconstruction in such powerful – albeit revisionary – Kantian terms.

D. The shadow on the ground: the semiotic basis of deconstructive disclosure

Regarding the role of theory for deconstruction, Derrida relies on a double strategy of negation and acceptance: (1) critiquing the theoretical "incompetence" of science, e.g. Saussure's and other linguistic models; and (2) recalling Peirce's theory of signification. The two flanks of this strategy are closely related, although their implications for theory are somewhat obscured by a lack of metatheoretical clarification.

The Peircean observations about signification reveal the Kantian linkage insofar as Peirce's semiotic, a "quasi-necessary, or formal doctrine of signs," proposes the universal structure of thought as a sign process (*OG*, 48). While constituting a theory of universal conditions, Peirce's semiotic is qualified by his pragmatic critique of Kantian apriorism: semiotic categories are understood as hypothetical. Moreover, given Peirce's thesis of the ubiquity of interpretation and hypothesis, rationality cannot *reduce* to a single categorical structure. Rather, that structure shows how thought is dynamically open to the influx of its various grounds, and therefore must be subject to the systemic variations that such influences require.

This is a balance of system and history which Derrida appreciates: Peirce complies with two apparently incompatible exigencies, either of which it would be a mistake to sacrifice. On the one hand, the symbolic (Peirce's sense of the arbitrariness of the sign) is rooted in the nonsymbolic, in a transcendent world to which signs can relate by such representational relations as iconicity: "Symbols grow. They come into being by development out of other signs, particularly from icons, or from mixed signs." On the other hand, these representational roots do not compromise the autonomy of the field of symbols, an autonomous domain of production and play. There is no presymbolic origin that can be *immediately* appropriated: "So it is only out of symbols that a new symbol can grow. *Omne symbolum de symbolo*" (*OG*, 48).

Crediting Peirce with having semiotically mediated the transcendental signified, Derrida fixes on a suggestive paradox structured by Peirce's theory of the sign. Reading Peirce against Kantian closure, Derrida finds the *lack* of closure of semiosis to be the systematic condition of thought, its *differance*: "*What broaches the movement of signification is what makes its interruption impossible. The thing itself is a sign*" (*OG*, 49). It is the openness of semiosis that makes it an infinite condition of world-constitution. For thought, everything is a sign without a final determination.

This infinitude implies that the historicity of thought is the necessary condition of semiosis *as mediacy*, just insofar as it continually ruptures the border between the interior (abstractly formal) and exterior (objective) constraints upon the self-constitution of thought. It is not that thought does not have these transcendental grounds of pure formality and a real world: but rather that these two transcendental kinds of constraint always require interpretation or representation for the mind. Thus, on the one hand, all objects of thought are rendered as signs, mediating the exteriority of thought. On the other hand, the process of thought is always interpretively specifying grounds or conditions of thought that are not *wholly* constituted. Semiosis thereby intermediates the exterior and interior constraints of thought in the uniqueness of the moment.

Thus the formality of semiosis and its infinitude coincide. As Derrida notes later in his discussion, "a signifier is from the very beginning the possibility of its own repetition, of its own image or resemblance. It is the condition of its ideality, what identifies it as signifier, and what makes it function as such, relating it to a signified which, for the same reasons, could never be a 'unique and singular reality'" (*OG*, 91). As a theory of mediacy (i.e. the thought-constituting process) Peircean semiosis gives philosophical hermeneutics a logical model that can include its key features: (1) temporality; (2) the formal origin of understanding, interpretation, and application; and (3) infinite mediacy.

Peirce's balance of formality and temporality suggests a critique of linguistic foundationism, such as Saussure's phonocentrism, a line of critique that post-structuralist theory has made commonplace. According to Derrida's critique, Saussurean phonocentrism typifies the problem of attempting to close off the semiotic openness suggested by the Peircean model. Derrida charges this strategy with "limiting the internal system of language in general by a bad abstraction" (*OG*, 43), i.e. by an abstraction to an inadequate determinacy. In the shadow of traditional expectations about scientific foundations, Saussure was too quick to assume that "the scientificity of [linguistics] ... [rested on] its *phonological* foundations" (*OG*, 29). This privileging of the voice structures a hierarchy between speech and writing, a subordination of grammatology to linguistics. But in light of the Peircean model of semiosis, and of the Derridean analysis of the relation between speech and writing, this hierarchy cannot be maintained: there is no point at which the phonocentric model can constitute a foundation for signification that is not already structured by arche-writing, or systematicity in general, the condition of any linguistic model.

Here is where Derrida's thought turns transcendentally critical, i.e. to the question of the critical priority of logical grounds. Regarding the foundational character of linguistics, Derrida wants to ask, what do the limits and presuppositions of arche-writing imply? Against Saussure's phonocentrism grammatology suggests that linguistics cannot predetermine meaning as long as it defines its outside and inside in terms of a determined linguistic form (voice vs writing). Such formal specificity renders linguistics subordinate to *systematicity in general*, which, being more original, leaves linguistics open to the play of these prior rules. Thus linguistics cannot precede grammatology as long as linguistics remains open to rewriting from without and within according to the rules of the general system:

The system of writing in general is not exterior to the system of language in general, unless it is granted that the division between exterior and interior passes through the interior of the interior or the exterior of the exterior, to the point where the immanence of language is essentially exposed to the intervention of forces that are apparently alien to its system.   (*OG*, 43)

In the terms of Peircean semiosis, this critique of Saussure's hierarchy of speech and writing shows the failure of speech to be original: for phonocentrism to be foundational would require that there be a significance in speech that is semiotically prior to that of writing. Yet the movement of semiosis itself – of thought, from one sign to another – involves an inscription that is perhaps less a speech than a writing. For what is a sign?: "Anything which determines something else (its interpretant) to refer to an object to which itself refers (its object) in the same way, this becoming in turn a sign, and so on ad infinitum" (Peirce, quoted by Derrida, *OG*, 50). Saussure's acceptance of phonocentrism fails as a foundation on account of its bad abstraction, its erroneous privileging of speech within the context of a more original and infinite semiotic movement of thought.

According to Derrida's view of the *epistémè* of logocentrism, its epochal myth of presence structures a semiotic repression of writing by a privileging of speech. Now, however, the semiotic subversion of Saussure's phonocentric linguistics points Derrida "beyond the field of the *epistémè*" (*OG*, 93). Derrida merely begins with phonocentrism because its failure is paradigmatic for the "incompetence" of scientificity to yield a strong exclusion of the irrational: "the condition for the scientificity of linguistics is that the field ... [have] hard and fast frontiers, that it be a system regulated by an *internal* necessity, and that in a certain way its structure be closed" (*OG*, 33). Against such closure, Peirce's semiosis and Derrida's hermeneutics describe a process in which both formal necessity and objectification are theorized from within as constraints on an infinite interpretation. Theory never finally reaches the ideal of closure because the boundaries are never wholly contextualized and are therefore always being reinterpreted, a gap that opens the system in the very act of closing it: "there is a short-of and a beyond of transcendental criticism. To see to it that the beyond does not return to the within is to recognize in the contortion the necessity of a pathway. That pathway must leave a track in the text" (*OG*, 61).

E. From theory to the general system

By virtue of semiotic mediacy – whose historical structure is the logocentric *epistémè* – semiosis is the theoretical condition of logocentric metaphysics and Western rationality. By necessity, then, deconstruction begins within the metaphysical field in order to question the field, a point that determines both the sense and limit of anti-foundationism. Finally, deconstruction is not the renunciation of rationality, but the work of a rationality "which governs a writing thus enlarged and radicalized, no longer [issuing] from a logos" (*OG*, 10). Like Heidegger before him, Derrida intends to rethink "the roots of scientificity" and "the origin of historicity" (*OG*, 27). And to do this takes him back in the direction of the Kantian discovery of the conditions of thought in order to rewrite epistemology from within.

This movement is still Kantian because like Kant the Heideggerean-Derridean move puts *mediacy* before being – for us. Derrida's arche-writing recalls Heidegger's reminder that "the sense of being is neither the word 'being' nor the concept of being ... [but is] ... tied, if not to a particular word or to a particular system of language ..., at least to the possibility of the word in general" (*OG*, 21). This "possibility of the word," as with semiotic infinitude, disrupts the traditional unity attributed to the logos and being: "In examining the state just before all determinations of being, destroying the securities of onto-theology, such a mediation contributes, quite as much as the most contemporary linguistics, to the dislocation of the unity of the sense of being, that is, in the last instance, the unity of the word" (*OG*, 22).

And yet here is where anti-foundationism must be ambivalent: for the *necessity* of hermeneutic instability is not locally warranted: rather, it follows from systematicity itself. Likewise, the discovery of the conditions of the word and being points to an *original* dis-unity. Again in semiotic terms: "It is not the question of a constituted difference *here*, but rather, before *all* determination of the content, of the *pure movement* which produces difference. The (pure) trace is differance. It does not depend on any sensible plenitude, audible or visible, phonic or graphic. It is, on the contrary, the *condition* of such a plenitude" (*OG*, 62; my italics). Unlike the closed systematicity of Kantian foundations, deconstruction discovers an original indeterminacy that is the condition of ordering, the "pure movement which produces difference" in both being and meaning. Yet, in this originality its necessity can only be discovered theoretically, however much its consequences lie in a practical instability.

Being more original than any form of language, this trace, this arche-writing, is the "ultimate foundation" of experience and intelligibility, but it cannot succumb to scientificity: "arche-writing, movement of differance, irreducible arche-synthesis, opening in one and the same possibility, temporalization as well as relationship with the other and language, cannot, as the condition of all linguistic systems, form a part of the linguistic system itself and be situated as an object in its field" (*OG*, 60). The conditions of deconstruction, therefore, cannot constitute the object of a science – at least on the monological model of science.

This final "enlarging and radicalizing" of rationality, this exhaustion of the Kantian ideal of systematicity leads, finally, to the turning of Kant inside out. For Kant's purpose was to "deprive metaphysics, once and for all, of its injurious influence, by attacking its errors at their very source" (*Critique*, 30). This aim required of epistemology a systemic closing of theory over itself to constitute a wholly determinate origin of philosophical authority: a "sphere of logic ... quite precisely delimited; its sole concern is to give an exhaustive exposition and a strict proof of the formal rules of all thought, whether it be *a priori* or empirical, whatever be its origin or its object" (*Critique*, 18). It is precisely such a strong theoretical closure, however, that deconstruction and radical semiosis render impossible. Rather, deconstruction discovers that the unrecuperable condition of experience and signification – the trace, arche-writing, differance – is always cutting a path through the boundaries of sense, a rift whose work can only be traced in hermeneutic and deconstructive reflection, which, being itself an infinite task, can never finally be comprehended or represented.

In this infolding of the conditions of science beyond the representability of science, Derrida is sometimes said to have turned the discourse of origins against the authority of theory. Thus Derrida concludes Part One of *Of grammatology* with what seems like a practical displacement of theoretical authority, a deferral of theory by deconstruction:

the necessary decentering cannot be a philosophic or scientific act as such, since it is a question of dislocating, through access to another system linking speech and writing, the founding categories of language and the grammar of the *epistémè*. The natural tendency of theory – of what unites philosophy and science in the *epistémè* – *will push rather toward filling in the breach than toward forcing the closure.* (*OG*, 92; my emphasis)

This displacement of theory seems to be the subversive conclusion to the enlarging and radicalization of rationality beyond the hegemony of the logos, beyond the traditional theoretical conditions of scientificity. Just as the subversion of the phonocentric hierarchy of speech and writing troubles the ability of scientific theory to insure its "hard and fast frontiers" and its closed structure, so the infinitude of semiosis will allow, and deconstruction will discover, a pathway from the exterior to the interior of theory.

On the other hand, though this privileging of deconstruction over theory in the critique of logocentrism seems to follow from the problems of traditional theory, a number of questions remain regarding the relation of theory to deconstruction. If not theory, for instance, then what discovers "another system linking speech and writing," a system which presumably has its own economy, i.e. that of the origin of writing, the "formation of form," which formation "conceals and erases itself in its own production" (*OG*, 7)? What, in other words, points to this new post-Kantian condition of indeterminate systematicity and indicates its economy if not theory? And what, finally, would differentiate between the work of theory – as in Peirce's semiotic displacement of Kant – and the work of deconstruction? Is Derrida's discourse of transcendental scientificity only a bridge to some more essential ludic condition which is beyond deconstructing itself as theory? Is the transcendental character of grammatology, then, only a figurative illusion for a pragmatic effect? These questions of the relation of theory to deconstruction quickly turn into problems which Derrida's terms often only exacerbate (as he was the first to recognize).[6]

6. Indeed, it is Derrida's residual sympathy with theoretical depth that Rorty objects to in *Consequences of pragmatism.*

F. The ambiguity of theory: the topology of transgression

What, then, should be the status and role of theory in a deconstructive discourse that approximates the claims of theory, only to analyze these claims in the original sense of loosening? As I noted above, Derrida's dialectic of theory and deconstruction culminates in the final contrast between theoretical breach-filling and deconstructive de-centering. But is this oppositional characterization of theory and deconstruction in fact the role of theory in Derrida's text?

That theory must be put aside seems to presuppose a doubtful dichotomy when we look at the fate of writing after deconstruction. Why, that is, should *writing* undergo a deconstructive transformation of meaning but not *theory*, even as theory yields the Peircean semiotic model that subverts linguistic foundationism? This exploitation of theory is both relied upon and occulted by Derrida's anti-theoretical figurations. Nor could this ambivalence about theory help but follow from the ambiguous scope of the term itself, a scope that stretches from the most imperial ambitions of epistemology to the most modest empirical predictions. Of course, the deconstruction of metaphysics depends on revealing the disclosure of reason, yet theory's positive role in that disclosure remains unaccounted for by anti-theoretical anti-foundationism.[7]

The occulting of theory in *Of grammatology* follows Derrida's equivocation between the inferential sense of theory – implied by Peirce's semiotics – and the Kantian *a priori* sense of theory as the strong foundational system. This equivocation is made explicit when

7. In fact, Derrida acknowledges that this local sense of theory must be specifically excluded from his deconstructive subversion when he insists that "these original significations [of conceptuality] must not be confused within the orbit of the system where they are opposed" (*OG*, 85). Derrida knows he must preserve the local authority of theory, which indeed plays a significant role in Derrida's semiotic thought, though its relation to a transcendental phenomenology and to the epochal critique is obscured by his anti-foundationist drift. Nor is this obscurity inconsequential, for it is Derrida's self-occulting use of theory which leads to its final ambiguity for the deconstruction of logocentrism. Both the foundational and the local senses of theory, however, are illuminated by attention to an even more fundamental ambiguity which pertains to theory as indifferently referring to a particular premise or to the logical context that is constituted by that premise (i.e. as logic itself or the product of particular sciences). This ambiguity has significant implications for the scope of theory and leads to the conflation of its local and foundational senses.

Derrida defines the grapheme within the grammatological system, an equivocation that fails to distinguish between epistemologies of presence and those of mediacy: "... the *gramme* – or the *graphème* – would thus name the element. An element without simplicity. An element, whether it is understood as the medium or as the irreducible atom, of the arche-synthesis in general, of what one must forbid oneself to define within the system of oppositions of metaphysics" (*OG*, 9). Derrida allows the fundamentality of the grapheme either as medium or atom. But insofar as "atom" implies presence and "medium" allows for semiotic indeterminacy and hermeneutic instability, these alternatives are hardly indifferent to what requires deconstruction. Only a strong epistemological theory seeks to reduce the grapheme to the irreducible, immediate element, whereas the grapheme as a medium – just because it rules out irreducible atoms – implies the semiotic indeterminacy that Derrida wants. Such an element cannot be immediate just because it is an element *in* mediacy. To elide that difference in theoretical elements obscures the kind of constitutive theoreticity that is Derrida's own critical condition.

This obscuring of the difference between essentialist and mediate epistemologies reveals a totalizing flaw typical of anti-foundationism. For by repudiating foundational theory in general, Derrida obscures the kind of theory which informs the possibility of deconstruction itself.

Returning to Derrida's critique of linguistic theory, we see the consequences of his ambiguous rendering of theory. He begins by acknowledging that the sign "must be the unity of a heterogeneity" (*OG*, 18), the unity that represents a juncture of different kinds of elements. For the purposes of deconstructive universality, Derrida wants to posit the *sign* as that which "escapes the instituting question of philosophy: 'what is ... ?'" (*OG*, 19). And yet, as Derrida's own analysis of semiosis shows, this unity in heterogeneity is not *seen*, but rather discovered by theory. Furthermore, it is the point of the Kantian revolution in epistemology that theory need not be ontological or metaphysical to discover such a unity. Theory, too, can escape the question of "what is" without ceasing to be epistemology.

To say that deconstruction begins with the necessary indeterminacy of semiotic conditions is, in its own way, originary. And what is this originary signifying condition but the constitution of a field for understanding, an ordering synthesis that must be projective as well as referential? These analogous implications of theory and signification are considerable: for if they are equally originary for meaning, then theory is coextensive with signification itself (as Peirce has suggested in his logic). This is not a feature of theory for which Derrida's distinction between theory and deconstruction accounts or for which critiques of strong foundationism hold.[8]

This Derridean ambivalence about theory issues in the final ambiguity about the relation between grammatology as theory and deconstruction as practice. For finally the question of the status of grammatology as science raises the question of whether *Of grammatology* is a critique of theory or a critical theory of theory. Answering this question depends on one's understanding of the roles of grammatology and deconstruction as theory and as practice. There is good reason, nevertheless, to conclude that Derrida aims at a reversal of the traditional epistemological hierarchy of theory and practice. We are told that the deconstruction of logocentric metaphysics must work "by inhabiting those structures" (*OG*, 24); that grammatology does not yet have its own concepts; that the deconstruction of logocentrism must avoid theory's tendency to fill the breach in the *epistémè*; and that theory cannot reach its traditionally sought closure. Under the sign of deconstruction, such indications suggest, theory seems less on the mend than on the run.

Yet, when we have distinguished between the rigorous closure of classical presence and Kantian systematicity on the one hand, and hermeneutic or pragmatic indeterminacy on the other, then it is doubtful that Derrida has surpassed theory in principle *except* in the strong foundational sense. On the contrary, we find numerous crucial points where a theoretical coherence seems the critical point of Derrida's analysis.

8. Yet there are indications that such a broad interpretation of theory is implied by Derrida's analysis of the theoretical structure of language (e.g. intertextuality). The theoretical constitution of the semiotic field, for instance, is suggested by Derrida himself when he insists on the arbitrary ground of the sign, for this semiotic ground is nothing other than a theoretical – i.e. constituted – ordering: "from the moment that one considers the totality of determined signs, spoken, and *a fortiori* written, as unmotivated institutions, one must exclude any relationship of natural subordination, any natural hierarchy among signifiers or orders of signifiers" (*OG*, 44). Derrida's critique of semiotic economy displaces phenomenological priority (as given) with semiotic self-constitution (as the theoretically possible).

G. Theory in deconstruction: the critical condition

We have discovered two distinct strains in *Of grammatology* whose relation to theory is far from clear.

There is, for instance, (1) a universalistic, aprioristic, grammatological rhetoric of the trace, of arche-writing, and of differance. These tropes constitute various rhetorical or figurative moves that are supposed to resist referential or conceptual identity. This discourse thus functions as a kind of allegory of the Origin of Sense, an allegory of discursivity that revises the generality of traditional discourse about metaphysics and epistemology by reducing it to an autonomous figuration rather than to a true origin.

But there is also (2) a discourse which is implicitly theoretical in the traditional way, a theory of the sign that serves both to critique weaker theories and to posit a more open paradigm (e.g. Peirce's). Given Derrida's suspicions about theory, one might at first assume that his self-conscious figurations are an attempt to subvert the possibility of theory, except that the semiotic-theoretical critique functions in a complementary fashion to the allegory of (non)origins. The heterogeneity of Derrida's discourse, then, may finally serve a single purpose in a way that redeems theory: the deconstruction of strong foundationism through a revision of theoretical coherence. Theory, that is, provides the constitutive force that weaves together critique and figurations of inconceivable origins.

But even if, allowing him to blur the distinction between theory and figuration, we allow Derrida this (de)constructively discursive heterogeneity, his discourse not only lacks an account of his theoretical presuppositions, but even seems to obscure their interest by virtue of the inverted theoretical-practical hierarchy. Isn't theory, after all, the filler of breaches whose work we intend to undo? But here is where the coextension of deconstructive figurations and theoretical-critical work subverts that choice as a choice. There is, in this revisionary sense, no ultimate antagonism between theory and deconstruction, nor can there be.

Derrida's theoretical difficulty is highlighted by the question of the authority of his key terms. When we examine the notion of the trace or differance, for instance, we find that Derrida has rehearsed some of the same theoretical difficulties as Kant's totalizing theory by resorting to some of the same rhetorical solutions.

There is, for instance, the problem of accounting for the constitution of unity in heterogeneity. Before Derrida, Kant had asked the question of the origin of the synthetic unity of apperception and of the unity between the structures of the understanding and sensibility. The problem was to explain how the unity is achieved by thought since pure conceptions of the understanding and sensuous intuitions appear to be quite heterogeneous. How then is the subsumption of the senses under the categories of understanding possible? Kant concluded that "there must be some third thing, which is homogeneous on the one hand with the category, and on the other hand with the appearance."[9] This is the origin of the infamous transcendental schemata, which mediate the heterogeneous media of sense and concept. Of course, as Kant's critics have noted, this explains nothing of how this mediation is done; it merely names the faculty that must be there to do it, threatening the kind of infinite regress of semiotic functions that it was Kant's hope to close off.

Derrida's originary terms fulfil a similar function to Kant's schemata in his discourse: they provide the "third thing" that accounts for the unity in heterogeneity, the ground of all dualities, the (non)origin of all identities, etc. Of course, Derrida's third things are not quite so transcendental: they are neither atemporal nor nonempirical in the Kantian senses. In fact, they have no distinctions in themselves, being only negatively indicated by their transcendence of categories. Thus Derrida's (non)principles are even more radically universal than Kant's in their mediacy of categories (which is why deconstruction is the radicalized semiotic extension of Kantian mediacy). And as such they give rise to the same theoretical problems as Kant's schemata: by what authority are they inferred?

For instance, whereas it is clear in what sense Kant's categories of the understanding (e.g. causality, possibility, necessity, etc.) might mediate our understanding of phenomena, in what sense is differance a condition of sense? Indeed, in what sense is differance a condition? Even if categories are more contingent than Kant thought, surely they or something like them are presupposed by the logic of our discourse. *Their* traces are not so hard to find.

But is differance logically or semiotically presupposed by our discourse? If it has no self-identity, how could anything depend on it? It is certainly not obviously implied by the modest degree of systematicity implied in ordinary language. Rather, the inference to

---

9. *Critique of pure reason*, 181.

differance comes from the presupposition of an extraordinarily strong systematicity, i.e. of a necessary systemic dependence on semiotic conditions. For even if systematicity is temporalized in Hegelian, Heideggerean, or hermeneutic fashion, nothing short of strong systematicity could underwrite Derrida's claims that the theory of the sign controls "metaphysics in its totality" (*OG*, 13); that "history and knowledge ... have always been determined (and not only etymologically or philosophically) as detours *for the purpose of* the reappropriation of presence" (*OG*, 10); and that the trace "articulates its possibility through the entire field of the entity which metaphysics has defined as the being-present starting before the entity" (*OG*, 47). This is not postmodern localism.

How could such terms be implied except within a framework of strong systematicity, and how, except for the semiotic indeterminacy we have already theorized, is such a systematicity different from the ground of the "greatest totality" being deconstructed?

To make the ground of signification and being a "pure" indeterminacy (Derrida) rather than a pure intelligibility (Kant) does not subvert theory, but rather reappropriates it in a transcendental theoretical self-critique. Derrida could consistently (1) presuppose the strong systematicity he attributes to logocentrism, which gives him his (non)concepts, and (2) still deconstruct the traditional foundational ideal that philosophy has held up as its mirror; but only by either reforming Kantian mediacy into an indeterminacy of necessary conditions or by giving up his grammatological project. The problem is his avoidance of this choice. If the trace, differance, and arche-writing become new theoretical grounds, even figuratively, then they raise all the difficulties of their theoretical status, allowing little philosophical wood to be cut, and rightly appear to a neo-pragmatist such as Rorty to recall the presuppositions and liabilities of idealism.

Furthermore, even if differance is the condition of semiotic play, it cannot be the ground on which logocentrism's closure can be glimpsed because deconstructive practice does not glimpse closure, it dis-closes. Through a revisionary theory, however, such closure can be glimpsed *as the condition of theory*. Thus to have *both* grammatology and the critique of traditional theory, Derrida needs a new theory of theory, a critical ground continuous with differance as a limiting condition of that ground. Happily, Peirce's semiotic revision of theory saves *Of grammatology* from its theoretical ambivalence and confusion of practices by distinguishing between the grammatological reliance on theory and deconstructive critique of it.

H. The pharmacy of theory

That Derrida destabilizes theoretical closure into ambiguity is now one of the truisms of post-structuralism. And yet *Of grammatology* remains unproductively ambiguous on this point insofar as deconstruction wants critical force as much as it does skeptical breadth, and it is not clear that it can have both without theory. The project of grammatology points toward the possibility of a most general science of writing, and yet the heart of the text seems to gesture toward arche-writing, which "cannot and never can be recognized as the object of a science," (which, though it cannot be situated in the field of linguistics, "does not mean it has a real field *elsewhere, another* assignable *site*") (*OG*, 60). Does Derrida mean to raise the possibility of grammatology, a science more fundamental than linguistics, only to diffuse its hopes with the corrosions of deconstructive loosening?

If it were not for his use of Peircean semiotic theory, we might conclude that Derrida's deconstructive discourse escapes the authority of theory. But the centrality of semiosis shows that he has not surpassed theory, even if his attempts to oppose it to deconstruction suggest that he has. Rather, the adequacy of the Peircean semiotic theory to Derrida's deconstructive purposes shows that deconstruction is not "outside" theory as something that has been surpassed. Rather, theory is at most outside deconstruction in the way that grammatology and semiotics are outside the scope of linguistics, which is to say, not *practically* outside at all.

Derrida, in the interests of deconstructive difference from traditional theory, neglects how close to his grammatological ideal semiotic theory already is. The place of theory in *Of grammatology* is not merely that of historical or discursive precedence to the deconstructive act of decentering, for the very genealogy of deconstructive practice implies a revision of theory. The place of theory is finally circumscribed by a different discursive purpose, that of exploring the border of interiority and exteriority of particular theories. Whereas the aim of theory is to fix such borders, the decentering aim is to explore their instability, to "make enigmatic" the consciousness that takes for granted its given borders, to "designate the crevice through which the yet unnameable glimmer beyond the closure [of logocentrism] can be glimpsed" (*OG*, 14), and to explore the significance of this instability as "play." This is not the aim of theory, for whereas theory aims at a hypothetical unity in heterogeneity, the deconstructive aim seeks to find and delineate fissures, gaps, ruptures, and such. The aims are quite simply different, as are the appropriate methods and standards of success.

Yet, the differences in discursive aims of theory and deconstruction do not reduce to a categorical exteriority or a categorical incompatibility. They are *pragmatically* different. When Derrida's deconstruction of Western metaphysics appears anti-theoretical it misleads: for, despite the distinguishable aims of theory and deconstruction, the scope of deconstruction implies a revisionary foundationism in spite of itself. It gravitates into the same transcendental theoretical mode that it critiques, positing a quasi-transcendental figuration of grounds no less general than traditional metaphysics.

The only way out of this dilemma is to allow that if every theory allows for its own critique, the authority of critique is itself theoretical. Though practically different, theory remains the critical condition of deconstruction. Derrida's turn from the fulfilling effect of theory to the breaching effect of deconstruction is, in fact, a pseudo-choice. Derrida does not displace theory, he refines it.

The mistargeting of theory as the motivation behind the totalizing sins of traditional philosophy misleads, therefore, in two significant ways: it distracts us (1) from Derrida's own theoretical commitments, and (2) from his own totalizing force, as required by his deconstructive aims. Whereas Derrida's rhetoric, with its figurations of (non)origins, may serve the deconstructive purpose of familiarizing the instability of discursive limits, it also tends to obscure the deeper legitimacy of his work as systematic critique. To note the interdependence, on the other hand, of Derrida's foundational-theoretical work and his deconstructive-theoretical play allows a more precise accounting of the relations between theory and the heterology of foundations.

4

Gadamer's universalism: the limits of hermeneutic authority

A. Hermeneutics and the end of modernism

Today's academy is a compromise between classical-medieval forms of authority and the ideals of modern science, Enlightenment rationalism, and democratic liberalism. Recently, however, these older conceptions of authority have suffered a concurrence of heterodox assaults: (1) on philosophy by the hermeneutics of suspicion, (2) on natural science by sociologists of knowledge, (3) on literary criticism by political and gender critique, and (4) on empirical social science by genealogists of power. This new counter-orthodoxy hopes to add to the quarrel of ancients and moderns a third antagonistic perspective, one whose resistance to traditional and modern universalisms seeks to give a more radical emphasis to historical uniqueness, freedom of identity, and the contextual limits of theoretical claims to social authority.

One common theme among these challenges concerns the inadequacy of philosophical and scientific methods to the problems of meaning and truth, with consequent doubts about the human sciences as sciences. Whereas the nineteenth century had witnessed Dilthey's defense of the autonomy of historical sciences against positivism, some postmoderns are less concerned to insulate the human sciences from physics than to turn the problems of language and interpretation against the very possibility of an objectivist science. As a final reversal of philosophy's struggle to ground language in theory, radical postmoderns seek to undermine theory with the instability of meaning.[1]

---

1. Traditionally, theory has played the conservative role of isolating the principles by which disciplinary orthodoxy is grounded. Theory provided the categories of content and of judgment, the procedures of decision, the criteria of authority that organized culture and society. In classical culture, it was metaphysical theory, the

Some of the irrational aspects of postmodern critique have lent to its emergence a distinctly radical flavor, an appearance that has not been lost on recent academic politics and its media presentations. But despite these radical appearances, which at times do match the claims of postmodernists, counter-assaults on postmodernism have often over simplified the relation between theory and ideology. For instance, some counter-critiques have implied that the problems raised by postmodernists can be ascribed to certain radical theoretical and political agendas, i.e. as if postmodern attacks on the canon, on humanism, and on the universality of liberal ideals were not serious responses to real problems, but figments of ideological motives.

On the other hand, when we look more closely at the implications of language for theory and critique, we find a situation that is both theoretically and ideologically more complex than either the defenders or critics of postmodernism allow. In fact, the problems that underlie the extremities of postmodern critique have been found as congenial to conservative critiques of liberalism as they are to radical critiques. Thus, the recent history of theories of interpretation can be ideologized only at great risk to a deep political ambiguity in hermeneutic theory.

1. The postmodern flight from foundations

In literary criticism, the arrival of hermeneutic skepticism could hardly have been less expected. For decades prominent literary critics had urged that criticism establish its foundations. Thus R. S. Crane observed of the Chicago critics that:

What they thought most needed was a more critical approach to criticism itself, in something like the Kantian sense of "critical": a consideration of criticism, as a mode of inquiry, that would go behind the doctrines of different schools and try to uncover the basic assumptions about literature and literary study on which these are founded. The sort of thing they had in mind [concerns] the "grounds of criticism" ... the conditions that determine the cogency or adequacy of statements and the appropriateness or workability of methods.[2]

decline of which led to modern epistemological theories of justification, and finally the empirical theories of today's scientific establishment.

2. *Critics and criticism*, R. S. Crane (ed.), Chicago, 1952, abridged edition; introduction, p. v-vi.

Northrop Frye, literary criticism's encyclopedist, hoped that criticism would become a central force for the humanities in general, such that "the ancillary disciplines may be related to a central expanding pattern of systematic comprehension."[3] Toward this ideal, Frye wrote that critics needed to become more rigorous: "to recognize and get rid of meaningless criticism: that is, talking about literature in a way that cannot help to build up a systematic structure of knowledge ... [for] a systematic study can only progress" (Staton, 112–13). To approach the ideal of natural science Frye concluded "that what is missing from literary criticism is a coordinating principle, a central hypothesis which, like the theory of evolution in biology, will see the phenomena it deals with as parts of a whole" because the "first postulate of [literary criticism's] hypothesis is the same as that of any science: the assumption of total coherence" (Staton, 113). Accepting the modern scientific view that science is defined by its method, Frye inferred that the way for critics to become scientific is to do what scientists do: find the central theoretical assumptions that would define the literary method.

Within a decade, however, post-analytic philosophy and post-structuralist theory were challenging the prospects of foundations for the human sciences. Such classic post-positivist works as Wittgenstein's *Philosophical investigations*, Kuhn's *The structure of scientific revolutions*, and Derrida's "Structure, sign and play" all shared the view that the inability of theory to escape contamination by its linguistic-pragmatic context discredited the traditional ideals of scientific objectivity, neutrality, and finality.

In Rorty's version of the rise of postmodern philosophy, Wittgenstein's repudiation of his own picture-theory of language for a meaning-as-use notion of language is the landmark conversion of linguistic philosophy to interpretive relativity, the beginning of the end for strong foundationist analytic philosophy, and thus the end of the last great revolution in strong foundationism itself. According to Rorty, "it is by following Wittgenstein's lead that analytic philosophy has progressed toward the 'post-positivistic' stance it presently occupies" (*PM*, 12). Furthermore, the fallout of the new pragmatism has gone beyond analytic philosophy to include the interpretive turn

---

3. *Fables of identity*, New York: Harcourt, Brace and World, 1963; reprinted in Shirley Staton (ed.), *Literary theories in praxis*, Philadelphia: University of Pennsylvania, 1987; p. 112 (hereafter referred to as 'Staton').

in the social sciences,[4] as well as the proliferation of ideological criticism and theory, and the shift of literary critical interest from formalism to history, reader-reception, and the dynamics of interpretive communities. In each of these cases, the meaning-as-use perspective on language implies the loss of the privileged hermeneutic constraints of the classical, formal, or modern empiricist sorts.

Gadamer has extended the anti-foundationist claims of hermeneutic theory beyond method to the "universal scope of hermeneutic reflection" with its infinite questioning of truth and meaning. In light of Gadamer's claim to hermeneutic "universality," however, the hermeneutic turn bears comparison to the earlier foundational revolutions Rorty referred to, including epistemology's challenge to metaphysics, and empiricism's challenge to metaphysics and rationalist epistemology. For while both science and hermeneutics arise as challenges to the authority of traditional philosophy, hermeneutics wants to bury foundationism, not fulfil it.[5]

At first glance, hermeneutics coincides with science in repudiating epistemology-as-pure-theory for theory-as-*practice*: science through experiment and hermeneutics through the applied character of textual interpretation. Thus Gadamer aligns hermeneutics with rhetoric against the traditional epistemological stance: "In both rhetoric and hermeneutics ... theory is subsequent to that out of which it is abstracted; that is, to praxis" (*PH*, 21). In hermeneutics, as in science, theory does not so much precede as emerge from application: like the

---

4. "Now the time seems ripe, even overdue, to announce that there is not going to be an age of paradigm in the social sciences ... The interpretive turn refocuses attention on the concrete varieties of cultural meaning, in their particularity and complex texture" (4). Rabinow and Sullivan, (eds.), *Interpretive social science: a reader*, Berkeley: University of California Press; 1979.

5. Despite the technological successes of modern scientific practice, however, science has not succeeded in demarcating a single scientific method, a development that led some philosophers of science into an unexpected collusion with literary critics and hermeneutic theorists against the very progressivist ideal that Frye sought for criticism. Thus Feyerabend claims that methodological anarchy is the key to scientific discovery, and the sociologists of science claim that scientific progress is relative to the historical, social, and pragmatic context in which science is practiced. Meanwhile, some sociological approaches to science explain the rise of theories in terms of discursive consensus formation rather than in terms of their correspondence to a presupposed reality. Thus the pragmatic and sociological conceptions of the philosophy of science often capitalize on the interpretive elements in science, eroding the distance between natural and human sciences in the direction of cultural relativity.

extrapolation of scientific theories through prediction, hermeneutics applies its theorized patterns of significance to particular texts and contexts in order to make its way into new territories of meaning. For Gadamer, this practice of application, not theory, is the ground of interpretation.

Still, a shared pragmatic character has not meant a coincidence of scientific and hermeneutic perspectives. Their divergence is largely due to science's attachment to methodological privileges, which Gadamer finds philosophically narrow: "science always stands under definite conditions of methodological abstraction and ... the successes of modern sciences rest on the fact that other possibilities for questioning are concealed by abstraction" (*PH*, 11). Science, hermeneutically viewed, begins when we stop asking questions about the questions, and suppose a method to be sufficient to determine an answer. Science is deprived of ultimate foundational force insofar as it requires a methodological exclusion of the most fundamental theoretical questions, i.e. just those original theoretical possibilities hermeneutic reflection on "original questionability" is intended to open up. For Gadamer's philosophical hermeneutics believes that the regress of philosophical questions has no end: "No assertion is possible that cannot be understood as an answer to a question" (*PH*, 11). Likewise, whereas science is characterized by the positivity of its answers, "[t]he real power of hermeneutical consciousness is our ability to see what is questionable" (*PH*, 13).

Whereas philosophical and empirical foundationisms sought the bottom line of critical authority, hermeneutics argues that bottom lines can always be erased or moved back with further questions. From Heidegger through Gadamer to Derrida, philosophical hermeneutics has increasingly resisted reduction to epistemic principles or to a scientific method. So despite its interest in the *practice* of application, philosophical hermeneutics' rejection of methodological or theoretical privilege distinguishes it equally from epistemology and science.

In literary criticism, the spate of post-structuralist explorations of the indeterminacy of meaning has daunted some of the more ambitious foundationist hopes. Few literary critics are left who would claim to have identified the correct meaning of *Hamlet*. Rather than denials of the indeterminacy of meaning, some critics settle for strategies of damage-control. Hirsch now makes the argument for the validity of authorial intentions a moral debt we owe to the author, not a claim about what meaning "really" is. Instead of conjuring ideal readers, affective critics figure blanks into the text as Iser does, or confer the power of interpretation, as Fish does, on the shifting fortunes of the interpretive community. Marxist critics such as Eagleton and Jameson discover ideological contradiction or utopian possibility rather than moral-economic univocity. Semiologists discover in punk culture the resistance to form rather than the form of resistance. Feminist critics discover the nothing that is not there as well as the nothing that is. Short of setting up living quarters in the funhouse, much post-structuralist critical theory appears content merely to describe the slippage of meaning and prevent it from becoming a torrent. The tenuousness of such restraint, however, has failed to assure more traditional thinkers that hermeneutic indeterminacy has not challenged the very possibility of critical authority.

As would be expected, the resistance to post-structuralist de-centerings has been energetic both from more traditional critics as well as from certain politically oriented critics who are reluctant to allow the brute facts of power to be dissolved into an arbitrary play of the sign. Thus some contemporary critics have experienced the standard foundationist fear-of-nihilism through which canonical philosophy traditionally viewed skepticism and relativism. Anxiously, such critics wonder: What force has criticism, finally, if it reduces merely to self-expression? What is left of criticism's institutional authority, for instance, when critic Norman Holland claims that, "I don't just improve *Hamlet*, I create it ... [since] each person has his own *Hamlet*"?[6] What is to prevent criticism from reducing to either class hegemony or private fantasy? Does extra-personal critical authority disappear with the hope of privileged criteria for validity in interpretation?

The tension between infinite hermeneutic openness and critical closure is the crux of the hostility between foundationist and hermeneutic theory, although the problem cannot be confined to theoretical debates. As literary critics have been forced to reflect on content, method, grounds, and aims of teaching and grading, the issue of critical conditions descends from the empyrean heights of theory into the classroom and onto the margins of student papers. As recent debates over the canon, multi-culturalism, and political correctness have shown, these questions are at once theoretical, pragmatic, and social.

6. "Hamlet – my greatest creation," reprinted in Donald Keesey's *Contexts for criticism*, Mountain View, California: Mayfield, 1987; pp. 171–2.

2. From theory to practice and back

Whereas an earlier generation of literary critics turned to theory to ground practice, the post-structuralist trend has been toward the belief that practice is ungroundable in theory. But the consequences of this trend have been more than theoretical: they have served to disrupt the ideological compromise of academia's traditional and liberal commitments. In fact, what is novel about post-structuralist academic politics is not that they suggest that academia is political, but that they suggest that the traditional-liberal compromise does not work.

The problem is complicated by the Enlightenment legacy of self-evident truth whose foundations are supposed to be beyond question. Liberalism has sometimes assumed its own objectivity and universality on the grounds of the appearance of pluralism and free speech. The very existence of the traditional-liberal compromise seems to warrant the truth of liberal pluralism. But where modernists may tend to see their views as beyond ideology, traditionalists tend to view such modern egalitarian beliefs as merely a recent ideology that is naive enough not to realize its truth or its consequences. Especially in literary studies, where the cult of genius is anything but dead, there are not a few defenders of hierarchy for whom the truth of pluralism means at most a plurality of hierarchies.

On the other hand, postmodern critics of liberalism hold that it has not delivered in fact what it idealizes in theory, believing that liberal Western culture ended its revolution before it really started. The more radical egalitarians see liberal democratic pluralism as a juridical exercise in word-play, a view of society that glosses the still-hierarchical substance of power with a mere surface pluralism. Liberals, on this view, indulge a celebration of free ideas whose impotence only proves the rule of power: tolerate only that, but all of that, which does not threaten the structure of power.

What is perhaps most surprising about the post-structuralist challenge to humanist foundations is its demonstration of how fragile the traditional-liberal compromise is, and how vulnerable to further questioning. Moreover, such questioning does not merely open up more radical social possibilities, but makes the hegemony of liberal ideas vulnerable to reactionary as well as radical challenges. For the liabilities of language seem to have the ambivalent effect of fostering both conservative and more radical swerves away from the liberal center.

Indeed, whatever pretensions to political neutrality the literary profession had maintained prior to post-structuralism, contemporary hermeneutic theory has made that assumption a dream of the past. Thus Gadamer concurs with the historicizing sociologists of knowledge to suggest that critical thought has only traditional prejudices with which to ground itself. Objectivity being impossible, one can only hope to serve the best prejudices one's horizon allows. Finally, the philosopher and the critic can claim a role no more transcendent than Rorty's horizon-mediating midwives, or Fish's promoters of local conventions, or the Marxist and feminist analysts of class and gender strategies of resistance, or the genealogists of power and technologies of the self. The once stratospherically theoretical flights of post-structuralism have come home to roost as decisions about the kind of society the literary profession is fostering, whether *de facto* or *de jure*, by virtue of its professional commitments and its notion of critical authority.

In the wake of the hermeneutic turn and the collapse of the strong foundationist legacy, historicist and conventionist arguments have gained prestige. Lacking privileged grounds, anti-foundationists can maintain that the only source of critical authority is our linguistic conventions, the contingent confluence of historical forces upon the language of belief. Thus Rorty touts consensus and the coherence theory of truth: "nothing counts as justification unless by reference to what we already accept ... there is no way to get outside our beliefs and our language so as to find some test other than coherence" (*PM*, 178). A practice, on this view, is bounded by what we believe it to be bounded by, and nothing else in particular. Likewise, Stanley Fish says of literary critical disputes:

Notice that the determination of what would count as being persuasive is a function of what is understood to be at stake. That is, the mechanisms of persuasion, like everything else, are context-specific; what will be persuasive in any argument depends on what the parties have agreed to in advance ...
(*ITC*, 369)

For Fish, the grounds of interpretation are conventional, i.e. only what the parties have agreed to in advance, as if there is no critical limit to what is acceptable *beyond* what happens to be decided. Similarly, Charles Taylor draws attention to the constitutive character of social practices which, unlike the pre-existent objectivity of the heavens, do not pre-exist language, but constitute their rationality *contextually*:

[social] realities ... are practices; and these cannot be identified in abstraction from the language we use to describe them, or invoke them, or carry them out ... We can speak of mutual dependence [between social reality and language] if we like, but really what this points up is the artificiality of the distinction between social reality and the language of description of that social reality.[7]

Though Taylor is careful to refer the purely constitutive model of meaning to social realities, when pushed to its post-strong-foundationist extreme the hermeneutic turn appears to invite a new generality: the radical contingency of understanding.

As Gadamer puts it: "All self-knowledge proceeds from what is historically pre-given, what we call, with Hegel, 'substance', because it is the basis of all subjective meaning and attitude and hence both prescribes and limits every possibility of understanding any tradition whatsoever in terms of its unique historical quality" (*TM*, 269). When historicism and context are radicalized, "foundations" can mean no more than the proliferation of local determinacies, insofar as knowledge and truth are always historically constituted in fact and value by the contextual specificity of our language.

This linguistic enclosure of truth, with its suggestions of critical relativism, appears to repudiate the possibility of rational social critique that inspired the modernist project. About science's ideal of philosophical objectivity "which stands or falls with the principle of being unbiased and prejudiceless" (*PH*, 10), Gadamer is explicit: "there is undoubtedly no understanding that is free of all prejudices, however much the will of our knowledge must be directed towards escaping their thrall" (*TM*, 446). Traditional authority and prejudice, therefore, cannot be escaped, but only revised from within. Contrary to the rationalist ideal – which seeks a tradition-transcending ground by which tradition can be critiqued rationally – no critical ground can claim to transcend the enabling prejudices of tradition's conventions.

The challenge of hermeneutic theory to critical conditions has not gone unanswered. For Habermas and Apel, for instance, linguistics does not rule out critical grounds, but merely raises a new set of questions about the character of foundational constraints. In their neo-universalist views, the openness of communication takes place within specifiable pragmatic conditions. True, we may now see communi-

---

7. "Interpretation and the sciences of man," in *Interpretive social science: a reader*, eds. Paul Rabinow and William M. Sullivan, Berkeley: University of California Press, 1979; p. 45.

cation and inquiry more as a kind of linguistic *practice* than as an abstract structure. But that practice has its own minimal formal conditions that specify the possibility of discursive success. The hermeneutic turn still allows epistemology the task of discovering rational preconditions for communication and social action. To discover such necessary pragmatic conditions is to determine the transcendental grounds of critique.

This question of the foundational authority of hermeneutics inspired the debate between hermeneutics and critical theory as defended by Gadamer and Habermas, a debate over whether universality more properly belongs to an indeterminate hermeneutic questionability or to the rational preconditions of understanding. Modern critical theory was born in the hope of changing the world rather than merely interpreting it, and doing so on rational rather than merely historical grounds. Critical theory, that is, requires critical constraints independent of tradition, non-arbitrary grounds to which tradition can be held accountable. Critical theory requires conditions of discourse that are not merely constituted out of historical accidents.

Echoing his critique of scientific narrowness, Gadamer finds Habermas guilty of the desire to abstract reason from history, whereas change – no matter how progressive – is always historically bound. Interpreting the world *is* changing it on the only grounds there could be: traditional and linguistic grounds. All progress takes place *within* the prospective horizon of the past: "There is no such thing, in fact, as a point outside history from which the identity of a problem can be conceived within the vicissitudes of the various attempts to solve it" (*TM*, 338). Interpretation is a practice whose ground is necessarily continuous with tradition – the origin of all our values – in which case there is no ground more rational than tradition.

The universality of interpretation thus appears to attack the heart of modernist progressivism by challenging the opposition between tradition and something more rational. Against critical theory, philosophical hermeneutics appeals to the radical location of philosophical authority in history and language (Gadamer: "Language is the fundamental mode of operation of our being-in-the-world and the all-embracing form of the constitution of the world"; Derrida: nothing "outside the text"; Rorty: "there is no way to get outside our beliefs and our language so as to find some test other than coherence"; Fish: "what will be persuasive in any argument depends on what the parties have agreed to in advance"). For Gadamer's hermeneutics, the only critical force that can be intelligible is that which is interior to the horizon of understanding. Since philosophical hermeneutics absorbs all authority into the historical horizon of language, there are no transcending critical conditions.

Ironically, whereas post-structuralist theory was first greeted by traditionally minded critics as the end of all civilized thought, it also appears to threaten the end of progressivist thought in the name of a profound conservatism, a world in which tradition is the only authority there is.

B. Gadamer: from foundations to horizons

Gadamer's monumental *Truth and method* marks a major challenge to the strong foundational claims of epistemology and science, particularly to the former's claims to the formal authority of pure reason, and the latter's objectivist claims for the empirical method. Furthermore, his critiques of these earlier foundationist positions shape his own view of the nature of hermeneutic authority.

1. The myths of reflexive self-presence and objective neutrality

Gadamer's critique of epistemology targets the myth of an omnipotent reflective consciousness, a myth sustained by the seemingly infinite power of the mind to rationalize its contents. In fact, it is just the apparent closure of consciousness that unsuits it as a starting point for the critique of rational reflection:

Polemics against an absolute thinker has itself no starting point. The Archimedean point from where Hegel's philosophy could be toppled can never be found through reflection. This is precisely the formal quality of reflective philosophy, that there cannot be a position that is not drawn into the reflective movement of consciousness coming to itself.　　(*TM*, 308)

Instead, the critique of reflective reason must attack the notion of immediacy, the notion which prevents even Hegel's historicism from fully discovering the radically historical nature of understanding: "The appeal to immediacy ... has always been self-refuting, in that it is not itself an immediate attitude, but a reflective activity" (*TM*, 308).

Philosophy's traditional fascination with certainty distracted it from seeing its involvement in a historical substance which is never fully present to consciousness. This historical substance constitutes a sense of what is beyond question, of what must yield certainty and the full presence of reason, whether as Platonic participation, Aristotelian intuitions, Cartesian clear and distinct ideas, Kantian transcendental deduction, or empirical verificationism.

Historical knowledge as self-reflection, by contrast, reveals a different notion of knowledge, a knowledge of consciousness' imperfection and openness to a historical unconsciousness. "By dissolving the hard edge of positivity" the historical attitude becomes "reconciled to itself" in its openness and in its partiality: "the historical attitude of the mind is neither self-reflection nor the mere formal dialectical abolition of the self-alienation that it has undergone, but an experience which experiences reality and is itself real" (*TM*, 310).

We discover in history the ontological openness of human reality: "The nature of experience is conceived in terms of that which goes beyond it; for experience can never be science … The truth of experience always contains an orientation towards new experience … The dialectic of experience has its own fulfilment not in definitive knowledge, but in that openness to experience that is encouraged by experience itself" (*TM*, 319). But given the reductive tendencies of science and epistemology, the difficulty for the philosopher is keeping it open *from this side*: "the essence of the question is the opening up, and keeping open, of possibilities" (*TM*, 266). It is not experience, but we who would secure the limits of truth.

But while Gadamer's critique of epistemology turns experience against the myth of cognitive immediacy, he is equally critical of the positivism of science.

Especially in light of the influence of scientific thought on modern society and culture, one of Gadamer's primary concerns is to critique the ideals of objectivity and neutrality. Gadamer finds their pretensions to disinterestedness a misleading abstraction from the context of understanding, which is always interested, always shaped by the values or prejudices of past experience. Indeed, Gadamer notes that prejudices are the condition of any judgment at all: "To exist historically means that self-knowledge proceeds from what is historically pre-given … [which] both prescribes and limits every possibility of understanding any tradition whatsoever in terms of its unique historical quality" (*TM*, 269). It is the commitments, prejudices, or conventions of tradition – "the transcendent expectations of meaning" (*TM*, 262) – that guide understanding by structuring our openness to meaning.

If in the scientific age we believe that one can have objective understanding, this impression is itself a prejudice – although an illusory one – shaped by what seems unquestionable in our cultural moment. Conversely, hermeneutics notes that understanding does not begin by overcoming history; rather, it is only through our retrospective appropriation of history that we can gain self-knowledge of our foundational assumptions and their implications: "temporal distance is not something to be overcome ... In fact the important thing is to recognize the distance in time as a positive and productive possibility of understanding ... [Time] not only lets those prejudices that are of particular and limited nature die away, but causes those that bring about genuine understanding to emerge clearly as such" (*TM*, 264–6). Indeed, Gadamer's hermeneutics, through his notion of the "fore-conceptions" of meaning, appears to make prejudice the condition of progress in understanding: "It is not so much our judgments as it is our prejudices that constitute our being ... Prejudices are not necessarily unjustified and erroneous, so that they inevitably distort the truth. In fact, the historicity of our existence entails that prejudices, in the literal sense of the word, constitute the initial directedness of our whole ability to experience" (*PH*, 9).

Given the centrality of prejudice to the hermeneutic model of understanding, it follows that empiricism's ideal of objectivity and the abstraction of its method only obscures the contextuality of science's questions and answers: "A person who imagines that he is free of prejudices, basing his knowledge on the objectivity of his procedures and denying that he is himself influenced by historical circumstances, experiences the power of the prejudices that unconsciously dominate him" (*TM*, 324). The ideal of scientific objectivity is a historically specific epistemic prejudice that obscures its own historical ground.

Though Hegel is one target of Gadamer's critique of reflection, Gadamer acknowledges that he too belongs in the Hegelian legacy. Continuing Heidegger's revision of that legacy, Gadamer has done much to bring out the philosophical implications of the hermeneutic circle, highlighting the circular movement of interpretations by which coherence is produced in the act of understanding:

the anticipation of meaning in which the whole is envisaged becomes explicit understanding in that the parts, that are determined by the whole, themselves also determine this whole.

... Our task is to extend in concentric circles the unity of the understood meaning. The harmony of all the details with the whole is the criterion of correct understanding. The failure to achieve this understanding means that understanding has failed.   (*TM*, 259)

As this passage shows, Gadamer believes that validity is a constraint on interpretation, and that global coherence defines validity. By focusing on the hermeneutic circle, Gadamer introduces the issue of validity into the terminology of hermeneutic authority precisely at the point where epistemic theory opens up into the aesthetic constitution of interpretive wholes.

Thus the grounds of Gadamer's hermeneutics appear to differ from those of epistemology (an appearance to be qualified below): where epistemic conditions are finally formal, hermeneutical foregrounding involves tracing to its historical roots the inherent anticipation of meaning, thus uncovering the historical specificity of questionability and commitment. Whereas epistemology seeks a formal clarity, Gadamer's project of philosophical hermeneutics has a curious *doubleness* of concern with hermeneutic freedom and historical foundations, a doubleness that discovers openness and limitation at the same time: "The asking of [the question] implies openness, but also limitation. It implies the explicit establishing of presupposition, in terms of which can be seen what still remains open" (*TM*, 327).

Likewise, Gadamer's view of philosophical hermeneutics radically changes the notion of philosophical foundations: "the task of hermeneutics, seen philosophically, consists in asking what kind of understanding, what kind of science it is, that is itself changed by historical change" (*TM*, 276); as well as the notion of foundational universality: "It is clear that the structure of the question is implicit in all experience ... The openness that is part of experience is, from a logical point of view, precisely the openness of being this or that" (*TM*, 325). And so hermeneutics brings with it a new conception of philosophical virtue: "the experienced person proves to be ... someone who is radically undogmatic ... The dialectic of experience has its own fulfilment not in definitive knowledge, but in that openness to experience that is encouraged by experience itself" (*TM*, 319).

2. Hermeneutic universality and interiority

For Gadamer, what is universal is not the formal conditions epistemology seeks, but the historicity of all such theorizations: "it is a hermeneutical necessity always to go beyond mere [foundationist] reconstruction. We cannot avoid thinking about that which was unquestionably accepted, and hence not thought about" (*TM*, 337). Gadamer reverses traditional philosophical priorities by insisting on transcending epistemology with history. Whereas traditional foundationist universalisms had erred in seeking universality in fixed principles, Gadamer finds the freedom of hermeneutic questionability and the necessity of historical contexts to be the twofold universality of human being that is the hallmark of the Hegelian legacy. "Philosophical hermeneutics takes as its task the opening up of the hermeneutical dimension in its full scope, showing its fundamental significance for our entire understanding of the world and thus for all the various forms in which this understanding manifests itself: from interhuman communication to the manipulation of society" (*PH*, 18).

The linguistic mediacy of the world accounts for this "universality of the hermeneutical problem": "Language is the fundamental mode of operation of our being-in-the-world and the all-embracing form of the constitution of the world" (*PH*, 3); "What I am describing is the mode of the whole human experience of the whole world" (*PH*, 15); "the 'linguistic constitution of the world'...provides the initial schematization for all our possibilities of knowing" (*PH*, 13). This mediation of experience provides a fundamental unity out of which all difference emerges. Subjective otherness, for instance, is already accompanied by deeper unity, the reciprocality characteristic of the pronoun link between I and thou: "I may say 'thou' and I may refer to myself over against a thou, but a common understanding always precedes these situations. We all know that to say 'thou' to someone presupposes a deep common accord. Something enduring is already present when this word is spoken" (*PH*, 7).

Nor is this structure of community-in-difference exclusively a feature of intersubjectivity; for in fact it constitutes all experience: "There is always a world already interpreted, already organized in its basic relations, into which our experience steps as something new, upsetting what has led our expectations and undergoing re-organization itself in the upheaval ... Only the support of familiar and common understanding makes possible the venture into the alien" (*PH*, 15). Indeed, Gadamer's case for the universality of hermeneutic reflection depends on his interiorization of the world within language: "The phenomenon of understanding ... shows the universality of human linguisticality as a limitless medium that carries *everything* within it – not only the 'culture' that has been handed down to us through language, but absolutely everything – because everything (in the world and out of it) is included in the realm of 'understandings' and understandability in which we move" (*PH*, 25). And thus, this *interiority* "is what I meant by the sentence: 'Being that can be understood is language' ... [T]he mirror of language is reflecting everything that is. In language, and only in it, can we meet what we never 'encounter' in the world, because we are ourselves in it (and not merely what we mean or what we know of ourselves)" (*PH*, 31–2).

Gadamer's absorption of the world into language is a central issue in contemporary foundationist debate. For partisans of radical hermeneutics, on the one hand, doubting the ubiquity of language invites the putatively devastating charge that one wants to "stand outside" the practice of his discourse. For realist theorists, on the other hand, the rhetoric of linguistic interiority provokes wonder at what it is that language is mediating if not a language-transcending reality. But Gadamer denies that he suffers the problems of solipsism or perspectival relativity, as charged by those who want language constrained by something that transcends it:

Understanding is language-bound. But this assertion does not lead us into any kind of linguistic relativism ... While we live wholly within a language, the fact that we do so does not constitute linguistic relativism because there is absolutely no captivity within a language – not even within our native language ... Any language in which we live is infinite in this sense ... Precisely through our finitude, the particularity of language, the infinite dialogue is opened in the direction of the truth that we are.   (*PH*, 15–16)

Predictably, this issue of linguistic universality was one of the points of contention between Habermas and Gadamer in their well known debate. For Habermas, Gadamer's view claims too much for language:

An interpretive sociology that hypostatizes language to the subject of forms of life and of tradition ties itself to the idealist presupposition that linguistically articulated consciousness determines the material practice of life. But the objective framework of social action is not exhausted by the dimension of intersubjectivity intended and symbolically transmitted meaning.[8]

According to Habermas, the interiorization of the world within language leaves no way to explain the pressure from the objective

---

8. "A review of Gadamer's *Truth and method*", reprinted in *Hermeneutics and modern philosophy*, ed. Brice R. Wachterhauser, Albany: State University of New York Press, 1986; p. 273; hereafter referred to as "Review."

world to change our beliefs, if indeed everything is already included in our language. This loss of grounding cripples hermeneutics for the purposes of critical theory, which wants to realize the potential reality tradition lacks:

The linguistic infrastructure of a society is also constituted by the constraint of reality – by the constraint of outer nature that enters into procedures for technical mastery and by the constraint of inner nature reflected in the repressive character of social power relations. These two categories of constraint are not only the object of interpretations; behind the back of language, they also affect the very grammatical rules according to which we interpret the world. *Social actions can be comprehended only in an objective framework that is constituted conjointly by language, labor and domination.*

(Review, 273)

For Habermas, Gadamer is still too close to the Hegelian idealist philosophy of reflection: he is too willing to collapse material reality into the ideal character of thought.

Still, Gadamer stubbornly adheres to his metaphor of interiority, insisting that Habermas has not shown him anything that does not fall within the scope of hermeneutics:

Who says these concrete, so-called real factors are outside the realm of hermeneutics? From the hermeneutical standpoint, rightly understood, it is absolutely absurd to regard the concrete factors of work and politics as outside the scope of hermeneutics. What about the vital issue of prejudices with which hermeneutical reflection deals? Where do they come from? Merely out of "cultural tradition"? Surely they do, in part, but what is tradition formed from? It would be true when Habermas asserts that "hermeneutics bangs helplessly, so to speak, from within against the walls of tradition," if we understand this "within" as opposite to an "outside" that *does not enter* our world – our to-be-understood, understandable, or non-understandable world – but remains the mere observation of external alterations (instead of human action). With this area of what lies outside the realm of human understanding and human understandings (our world) hermeneutics is not concerned ... The principle of hermeneutics simply means that we should try to understand everything that can be understood.

(PH, 31)

According to this retort, the universality of hermeneutics is unshaken by Habermas' appeal to the material conditions in which linguistic practices find themselves, because these too are involved in the interests or prejudices of language that hermeneutics addresses.

To sharpen the point, Gadamer focuses on the moment of critique itself, hoping to show that critique is always located with the tradition being critiqued: "The real question is whether one sees the function of reflection as bringing something to awareness in order to confront what is in fact accepted with other possibilities – so that one can either throw it out or reject the other possibilities and accept what the tradition *de facto* is presenting – or whether bringing something to awareness *always dissolves what one has previously accepted*" (PH, 34). Only if tradition is in principle defeated by what is brought before it could Habermas claim that critique must originate from behind the back of language. But against that view Gadamer argues that language always originates the new from out of the resources of tradition, mediating change and novelty from within – even in paradigm revolutions. No exteriority to language is required.

Or is it? When Gadamer refers to "something new, upsetting what has led our expectations," it is fair to ask where the new comes from if it was already *in* language. Indeed, when the dimension of time is considered more closely, we may find that Gadamer equivocates on the interiority he takes as authoritative, vacillating between what is interior to language now and later. Gadamer reveals this temporal equivocation by (a) repudiating what is *now* exterior to language: "With this area of what *lies outside* the realm of human understanding and human understandings (our world) hermeneutics is not concerned"; while (b) also referring to the potential inclusion of *as yet unknown* reality: "The principle of hermeneutics simply means that we should try to understand everything that *can* be understood" (PH, 31; my emphasis). "Can" transcends interiority precisely because of its openness to things not yet in language.

The coherence of Gadamer's interiority thesis, and his denial that anything meaningful is outside language, depends on the propriety of saying that all future truth is somehow already within language – although it is not very clear what such a claim means, or how it answers Habermas' claim that something works behind the back of language as we now know it. In fact, this equivocation strains coherence from within. On the one hand, insofar as the universal scope of language is historical, it reduces intelligibility to the already known, the historical horizon of language; on the other hand, by speaking of infinite openness to the future, Gadamer expands the scope of language to include everything that is potentially *knowable* or "to-be-understood." It is this current absence of understandings not yet in language that Habermas wants to characterize as exterior in order to acknowledge that such an exteriority drives knowledge forward.

Hence Gadamer's equivocation between the current and potential domains of language raises some serious difficulties for Gadamer's interiority thesis.

It appears that for all his historicity, Gadamer is effacing the phenomenology of time in his metaphor of linguistic interiority. For if the interiority of language is already universal, everything is already in language whether we know it or not. Ironically, this implies that language rises above the temporality of our understanding as when Gadamer suggests that it is not language but we that change when we learn something: "Reality does not happen 'behind the back' of language; it happens rather behind the backs of those who live in the subjective opinion that they have understood 'the world' (or can no longer understand it); that is, reality happens precisely *within* language" (*PH*, 35). In this phrasing, it is we, not language, that are historical. The point of learning, therefore, is not to bring more of the world into language, but into consciousness; "[h]ermeneutical reflection fulfils the function that is accomplished in all bringing of something to a conscious awareness" (*PH*, 38). For Habermas, by contrast, language is a function of human horizons, outside of which many things may happen. But if, as Gadamer suggests, everything is always already included in language as potential understanding, then language-as-ground is no longer a historical concept, but a theological one, in which case its relevance for critical theory or the hermeneutic task of historicizing belief reduces to zero.

When Habermas speaks of things taking place behind the back of language, he is not talking about the back of absolute reason, but of understood linguistic practice. Not everything is understood or is entailed by the current state of language. That is why form and usage, as well as consciousness, change in time. Language does not only mediate the abstract, unchanging formality of mathematics and logic: it mediates experience and nature as well. How can language entail a history that has not yet happened, or a nature that is not yet created? When a scientist gathers apparently contradictory data, in what sense is the world to which his confusing data refer *inside our* language? Don't we suspect that part of that world hasn't quite made it inside language yet? If that part of the world were already inside, wouldn't it be already understandable without further experimentation or modifications of our scientific practice and language? If Gadamer wants to say that the future is inside language alongside our conscious knowledge, wouldn't the resources of analytic philosophy be adequate to all inquiry? Gadamer's interiority thesis threatens to subvert the explanatory power of language by implying that language both is and is not historical at once. Having theologized language, linguistic being is not only intelligible being, but all other being as well, and therefore necessarily transcends our understanding by working, as Gadamer's critics say, "behind our backs."[9]

Wary of transcendence, Gadamer tries to forestall the problem of the Kantian thing-in-itself by stipulating: "With this area of what lies outside the realm of human understanding and human understandings (our world) hermeneutics is not concerned" (*PH*, 31). But this tactic dispenses with too much: science is not concerned with the unknowable, but it *is* concerned with what is not yet in our understanding. For Habermas and scientific realists, if language had all of reality already in it, then speculative philosophy would have been enough to yield science; but it was not enough to account for the nature that draws us beyond our current horizons. Only the inclination of understanding to what is beyond our current language can account for what Gadamer calls the "prospective" character of language: "history is only present to us in light of our futurity" (*PH*, 9). On the other hand, if we allow that objective reality both transcends *and* inhabits our language, we can understand objectivity as something that is both inside and outside language, inside insofar as we already know something about it, and outside insofar as our understanding is "prospective" toward what is still beyond our understanding.

At times, in fact, Gadamer himself seems to be committed to a notion of objectivity that is more impervious to hermeneutic practice than his notion of interiority would suggest. On the one hand, it is evident that Gadamer rejects "the dogmatism of asserting an opposition and separation between the ongoing, natural 'tradition' and the reflective appropriation of it" (*PH*, 28). The modern priority of

---

9. Regarding the interiority of language, Gadamer needs to distinguish the formal and objective poles of linguistic mediation, rather than conflating them as modern philosophy often does. Indeed, transcendence is a poor metaphor for either, since both are mediated, though if we must press the metaphor, objectivity constitutes an exterior constraint to language while formality constitutes an interior constraint. The work of the *formal* conditions of experience take place within the horizon of language whether consciously or not – as both Gadamer and Habermas suggest – because formal systems are self-contained, i.e. already *within* themselves (speaking metaphorically, since form isn't *really* anywhere). But objectivity transcends language as an external constraint even though our experience is constituted by its intrusion into the appearing.

objective knowledge falsely separates subjective and objective knowledge, implying of the knower that "his own understanding does not enter into the event" (*PH*, 28). And yet, when Gadamer considers the project of hermeneutic questioning, he admits that science "will continue along its own path with an inner necessity beyond its control, and it will produce more and more breathtaking knowledge and controlling power" (*PH*, 10). The question therefore is this: why call this necessity "inner," given its relation to human practice? Quite simply, it is hard *not* to see the practice of empiricism as mediating the exterior necessity of nature and the inner resources of traditional philosophy. The traditional notion of objectivity as "true independently of thought" does not require that we stand outside language, but only that objectivity enter into language to the point of our understanding, while still exceeding the horizon of understanding and language.[10]

Gadamer wants notions of science, epistemology, and hermeneutics where all are in the universal horizon of hermeneutic practice, and yet he also wants to distinguish science's inner logic from the thrust of hermeneutics. If everything is within the universal scope of hermeneutics, why doesn't hermeneutics control the course of science? How can science be contained and autonomous at once? We must conclude that the metaphor of interiority simply fails to articulate the kind of complexity that structures different modes of knowledge. Rather than hermeneutics simply including the authority of science and formal science, we must allow to science, philosophy, and hermeneutics a degree of autonomous authority. Yet we must also allow that the constraints of knowledge – whether formal, objective, or interpretive – *intermediate* each other without reducing to pure formality, brute objectivity, or historical contingency. Only such an understanding of the heterogeneous foundations of thought can reconcile the universality of hermeneutics with that "inner necessity" of science which transcends the control of hermeneutic inquiry.

Lacking such distinctions, Gadamer's strategy raises two unfortunate problems. First, his notion of language courts a theological concept of historical reason. Being beyond reflective control, language

---

10. This allows language an outer constraint. The inner necessity of thought, on the other hand, pertains to whatever theories (e.g. mathematics, semiotics, transcendental pragmatics) discover the limits of practice as *formal* constraints, not as exterior constraints.

works "as something that has a teleology operating within it ... a process that works as if guided" (*PH*, 13). We can only guess what is guiding it. Second, it is also theological insofar as it includes everything within it. But as long as Gadamer is going to make language *that* universal, it would seem that the concept of interiority – which is understood in opposition to exteriority – is entirely out of place. Whereas interiority makes sense as a property of space and consciousness, it only mystifies Gadamer's theological notion of language.

C. Hermeneutics and transcendental pragmatics

Gadamer's claim for the universal scope of hermeneutics is a clear challenge to epistemology and science, its antecedent contenders for foundational privilege. The novelty of his universalism lies in the new concept of foundations: hermeneutic universality contradicts the foundational closure sought by formal systematics and objectivist empiricism, proposing instead a historical opening of meaning, the discovering of understanding's contingent historical substance. And yet the modesty of the hermeneutic version of universality does not spare it from foundational problems of its own.

As the inadequacy of the interiority metaphor shows, hermeneutic universality problematizes its own critical authority. When Gadamer says that it is a "hermeneutic necessity" to go beyond the rational reconstructors of foundations to their historical assumptions, he implies a contest of priority between the epistemic demands of science, epistemology, and hermeneutics, yet his rhetoric cannot explain in what sense this is a contest. For merely by pointing to the necessarily historical conditions of thought, he cannot dismiss the appeals of epistemology and science to formal or objective constraints as his deference to the inner necessity of science allows. Even if Gadamer makes a case for the universal scope of hermeneutic reflection, that does not vitiate the authority of formal or objective constraints: it only requires that historical context be accounted as well. What that involves remains to be seen.

1. The grounds of hermeneutic universality

In this brief introduction to Gadamer's philosophical hermeneutics, a cluster of problems emerge. On the one hand, Gadamer seems to be arguing for a kind of post-foundational historicism. On the other hand, he claims (1) the universal scope of hermeneutics, (2) the autonomy of hermeneutic reflection from rational reconstructions, and (3) the autonomy of hermeneutic reflection from empiricist methodology. These three points raise a number of questions. To begin with, how can Gadamer defend the "universal scope" of hermeneutic "necessity" without a foundationist theory of his own? On what authority does he critique formal reconstruction and objective science as in principle inadequate to knowledge? What kind of inference concludes that what is not reducible to epistemology and science is *still truth*?

Returning to the interiority question, we note that by collapsing the world into language Gadamer has not really answered the problem of critical grounds posed by empiricists and rational reconstructors – he has only swallowed it whole. When put under a bit of pressure, his claim to universality shows that he has only nominally solved the issue of grounds: "While we live wholly within a language, the fact that we do so does not constitute linguistic relativism because there is absolutely no captivity within a language ... Any language in which we live is infinite" (*PH*, 16). This infinitude or universal scope of hermeneutic reflection, the realist would say, is beside the epistemic point. The problem is not that the solipsist does not have infinite resources at his disposal; the problem is that without a rational ground of critique Gadamer's openness to the future cannot distinguish between fact and fancy, progress and regression. The issue for critical theory is not finitude or infinitude, but direction of movement. Gadamer's infinitude may be either the counsel of despair or of faith, but it is useless for critique.

Unless it can disclose its transcending ground, philosophical hermeneutics' traditionalism does not merely historicize; it totalizes indifferently: whatever happens to be traditional gets the imprimatur of history. True, this historicism is more broad-minded than positivism, but it is just as universalist as positivism and inherently uncritical. As Richard Bernstein has noted: "It is not *sufficient* to give a justification that directs us to tradition. What is required is a form of argumentation that seeks to *warrant* what is valid in this tradition."[11] If the infinitude of language suggests that the seeds of the future are in the past, it does not explain why certain parts of the past should prevail over others.

Furthermore, hermeneutic universality would not be so perplexing

---

11. "From hermeneutics to praxis" in Wachterhauser, *Hermeneutics*, p. 100; subsequently referred to as "Praxis."

a problem if Gadamer's philosophical hermeneutics were content with the verdict of history, i.e. if it did not have a metahistorical agenda of its own — but it does have such an agenda. For Gadamer is not happy about the way our tradition has treated the universal scope of hermeneutic questionability. Unfortunately, this puts Gadamer in the contradictory position of requiring something besides history and tradition by which to critique the present.

2. The three modes of inquiry

Recalling the critiques of instrumental reason by the Frankfurt School, Gadamer makes broad claims against the rise of empirical or methodological conceptions of knowledge in modern culture. Gadamer rejects our culture's "domination of technology based on science," "the false idolatry of the expert," and the "scientific mystification of the modern society of specialization." For Gadamer, the negative influence of science on modern culture is a question of misapplication. Science too often displaces moral, practical, or aesthetic judgment with technological fixes:

In a scientific culture such as ours the fields of *technē* and art are much more expanded. Thus the fields of mastering means to pre-given ends have been rendered even more monological and controllable. The crucial change is that practical wisdom can no longer be promoted by personal contact and the mutual exchange of views among citizens. Not only has craftsmanship been replaced by industrial work; many forms of our daily life are technologically organized so that they no longer require personal decision. In modern technological society public opinion itself has in a new and really decisive way become the object of very complicated techniques — and this, I think, is the main problem facing our civilization.[12]

This metacritical position involves more than the asking of a historical question of the origins of science: it is posing a philosophical *answer* to science. But to wield that much critical force — i.e. to question history itself — Gadamer's vision of philosophical hermeneutics must have non-historical authority lest it reduce to *his* historically bound prejudices. Indeed, insofar as it is history he is resisting, he cannot (and does not) appeal to history, but to some unspecified authority.

Gadamer's case against instrumental reason depends on two points: (1) that there are pragmatic and formal distinctions between the

---

12. "Hermeneutics and social science," *Cultural Hermeneutics*, 2 (1975): 313. Quoted by Bernstein in Praxis, 94.

scientific, rationalist and hermeneutic modes of inquiry and judgment; and (2) that given the dynamic relations between these modes, it is possible for the scope and authority of one to interfere with another. In particular, Gadamer's critique of instrumental reason depends on Aristotle's threefold conception of knowledge: *technē* (craft, skill, control, technology, functionalism, etc.), *epistēmē* (systematicity, formality, theory, etc.), and *phronēsis* (practical judgment, application, ethical judgment, aesthetic judgment, interpretation, etc.). By suggesting that each kind of judgment has its own questions, he can argue that technological and scientific questions cannot truly dispel what are genuinely political and moral questions, which remain perpetual possibilities of intelligible being. But this is not an appeal to history.

The immediate issue for Gadamer's model is the critical authority for this framework: how can such an obviously theoretical structure resist the historicity of knowledge? How can one claim that history and tradition are the ultimate horizon and still complain that tradition is eclipsing hermeneutic questionability itself? As Richard Bernstein has aptly put it: "on the one hand, he acutely analyzes the deformation of *praxis* in the contemporary world and shows how the main problem facing our civilization is one in which the very possibility for the exercise of *phronēsis* is undermined; and yet on the other hand he seems to suggest that, regardless of the type of community in which we live, *phronēsis* is always a real possibility" (Praxis, 101–2). What sort of authority guarantees such perpetual possibilities? This authority sounds suspiciously trans-historical, suspiciously like the kind of transcendental pragmatics that Habermas seeks as the formal conditions of reason. Is it enough to say that these distinctions are already in our tradition – via Aristotle – or is that not a way of avoiding the possibility that these distinctions, though *in* our tradition, have some sort of ahistorical or formal authority to which history and tradition are necessarily subject as Habermas suggests?

Here Gadamer encounters a problem that radical historicist and conventionist theories frequently encounter: how can one object to the trends of history and the prevailing convention if convention and history are the only or primary ground of authority? Unwittingly, the ghost of critical transcendence haunts Gadamer's own desire to critique epistemology and science: Gadamer needs constraints more invariant than tradition itself, constraints invariant enough to define the perpetual possibility of questionability.

Here once again we see the inadequacy of the interiority metaphor for linguistic universality. If science has its own inner logic and hermeneutics has its, is it not misleading to suggest that one is inside the other? Unless one is willing to say as well that hermeneutic reflection is as much inside the universality of technological and formal significance as the reverse. Or still, it would be more precise to say that science, epistemology and hermeneutics *intermediate* each other: though distinguishable abstractly, their pragmatic effects are involved in the work of each other. The practice of human knowledge can always finally be analyzed for its technological dimension, its moral-practical dimension, or for its formal conditions; that is the sense in which they are *all* universal, though not exclusively so. To privilege absolutely any of these modes is to perform the kind of abstractive narrowing of which Gadamer rightly accuses positivism; yet one must be careful not to reduce knowledge to the terms of *any* one mode. Gadamer's return to the three Aristotelian modes, therefore, gives him three universalities at once.[13]

Thus – without a more precise notion of the relation between formal, objective, and historical constraints – the combination of Gadamer's interiority and universality doctrines threatens to become a universalism incapable of consistently defending itself. If, however, we take him at his pluralist moments, as when he grants science its own inner logic, we can allow the necessity of several critical conditions, one of which is history, others of which are formality and objectivity. At this point philosophical hermeneutics does not *succeed* epistemology, but completes it, showing the fundamental epistemic openness that passes over into hermeneutics in the direction of meaning, and into empiricism in the direction of technical power. In such a context, epistemology must concede its hermeneutic question-

13. What does this modal intermediacy, this mutual universality, mean? The interpenetration of foundational modes suggests that the critique of instrumental reason would have empirical, epistemological, and hermeneutic consequences – as indeed it does whether one looks at Adorno's, Habermas' or Gadamer's versions of it. Gadamer and Habermas point to the fact that practical judgment is effaced from the positing and solution of tasks. All questions of management are taken as questions of efficient means rather than as questions of alternative ends being served. But this imbalance has an empirical consequence as well. The Taylorized deskilling of labor in industrial societies represents both an exclusion of labor from the decision making processes and a routinization of effort that excludes the exercise of craft, the use of aesthetic or intellectual judgment. Thus the heterological universality of foundational modes always involves at least three kinds of consequences at once.

ability at the moment of foundational theorizing, yet it is epistemology or rational reconstruction which discovers the formal conditions of epistemic practices, the critical conditions that allow Gadamer to argue against empiricist reductions of knowledge to instrumental reason.

D. Hermeneutics and critique

Gadamer's case against science and epistemology attacks the partiality of their methodical abstractions to form and method, their blindness to their historical and contextual limits of their questions. And yet there is this unresolved contradiction: Gadamer wants transcendental status for the universality of historicism. The authority of this critique cannot rest on the momentum of history – whose course is critiqued – but rather depends on the formal scheme of *technē*, *epistēmē*, and *phronēsis*. The universality of hermeneutics cannot be both necessary and historical, if by the latter we mean contingent and conventional.

Though history may explain the *origin* of Gadamer's critique of science and epistemology, it fails to explain its *critical* authority, which must be warranted by epistemological theorizing. So if one were to ask why Gadamer's Aristotelian modes must be assumed, the fact that Aristotle wrote what he did would only explain *how* we came by those categories, but not *why* we should believe Aristotle rather than positivism. When historicism and conventionism go beyond historicization to the claim that there is nothing but history, they commit the fallacy of origins, i.e. confusing the *origin* of a belief with its critical *validity*. Radical historicism mistakes (a) the half-truth that all understanding occurs through history and thus shapes all understanding for (b) the supposed sufficiency of history to explain the formal and objective conditions of knowledge, even as presupposed by Gadamer's critique of positivism. While explanations of origins are significant, they are significant for valid and invalid beliefs alike. Though historical explanations may be sufficient to hermeneutic understanding, they are not sufficient to epistemic critique, including Gadamer's own critique of science.

The well-known Gadamer-Habermas debate – posed as it is between the defense of rational critical grounds and hermeneutic universality – finally fails to frame the proper relation between epistemology and hermeneutics. For Gadamer's defense of universal hermeneutic openness and Habermas' defense of rational reconstruction are both legitimate: the error lies in thinking that they are mutually exclusive, an error that arises from the term "universal", whose validity tends to be taken in the traditional exclusivist and reductive sense, rather than in the sense of multiple epistemic constraints and practices.

The apparent conflict of epistemology and hermeneutics arises from their respectively centripetal and centrifugal aims, the former aiming at the formal conditions of intelligibility, the latter at the under-standing of particular textual differences. Epistemology seeks the generality of conditions and possibilities, while hermeneutics explores the particular determinacy of interpretations in context. So their proper relation is pragmatic complementarity, not opposition. This must be: hermeneutics cannot discover a world that is merely open (i.e. without formal conditions), and formal conditions do not constitute total theoretical closure (i.e. without an indeterminacy of interpretation). Experience necessarily has some formal conditions, some objective grounds, and some historical-conventional particulari-ties. Both practices are not only possible, but necessarily possible: i.e. they are *possible* because they are practical options, but they are *necessarily* so because their possibility is guaranteed by the formal conditions of thought. Textuality, finally, presupposes formal con-ditions (semiotics) and textual interpretation (reading) as two levels on which meaning is constituted.

Because Gadamer and Habermas each give a partial view of the possibilities of critique, their debate obscures their complementary relation to each other,[14] as well as obscuring the authority and limits of hermeneutic and rational reflection. Whereas Gadamer misleads by denying that epistemology can discover invariant constraints that constitute even hermeneutic contextuality, Habermas misleads by suggesting that the results of transcendental critique can dissolve the problems of hermeneutic relativity. The irony of the Gadamer-Habermas debate is that each needs what he critiques in the other's

14. Paul Ricoeur explores the complementary relation between Gadamer's and Habermas' critiques of each other, and notes that each tended to converge toward the other's position as the exchange proceeded (Wachterhauser, 1987). I suggest that the explanation for that convergence lies in their emerging recognition of the complementary characters of their projects, rather than their convergence on a single foundational paradigm. Furthermore, neither Gadamer, Habermas, nor Ricoeur brings out the *modal* character of their differences as much as one might, nor do they tie these limitations to Gadamer's equivocal use of the notion of interiority.

project: Gadamer's universality is guaranteed by the transcendental conditions of discourse, while Habermas' dialogism follows from Gadamer's opening of epistemology to pragmatic-hermeneutic contextuality, not from a categorical imperative.

Moreover, because of the intermediating character of cognitive modes, Habermas and Gadamer are each unwittingly *doing* what the other one is idealizing, securing *both* openness and formal conditions at the same time. Thus Gadamer is defining the universal conditions of hermeneutics as understanding (grounding interpretation), and Habermas seeks to define formally, or in his terms "ideally," the conventional openness of communication (opening up epistemology). By appealing to the transcendental formality of Aristotle's three forms of judgment, Gadamer shows that the discovery of the universal conditions of meaning guarantees hermeneutic openness, not an algorithm of interpretive validity, thereby rationalizing the hermeneutic dialogue that is the ideal of Habermas' emancipatory authority.

Indeed, to seek universal validity, Gadamer's philosophical hermeneutics becomes an extension of epistemology – i.e. formally defining the conditions of understanding – unlike hermeneutics in the narrowly historical sense. For just as epistemology aims at foundations that are not historical, Gadamer wants hermeneutic universality to be perpetual, not subject to eclipse by instrumental reason. Thus to do *philosophical* hermeneutics is to articulate the conditions of this perpetual openness of experience. As Gadamer's philosophical hermeneutics aspires to universality, it is a phenomenology of understanding in general, not an understanding of a historical text or moment.[15]

15. On the other hand, Habermas underestimates the practical consequences of the three modes for the formality of his ideal conditions of communication. His own version of the distinction between technological, epistemic, and practical modes indicates the heterology of foundations, the irreducible variety of discursive values. As Gadamer suggests, this implies the pragmatic and historical contextuality of communication, not the exclusive universality of its idealized conditions as the necessary pragmatic ideal.

The limits of formality for social critique are necessarily implied by the universality of hermeneutics. It may be necessarily true that when one wants to do epistemology or science one must meet certain formal conditions, or that in certain contexts of democratic and public discourse some ideal conditions (of noncoercion, reciprocity, and commitment to truth and justification) may be ideally implied. Still, the question of when one *should* be doing science or epistemology or democratic communication as opposed to something else is itself a practical-hermeneutic question of context, i.e. it is a question whose answer fails to be determined either by formal or objective conditions. (See chapter 7.)

Philosophical hermeneutics depends on epistemology, but just so that it can exceed it in its own way.

In their mutual critiques Habermas and Gadamer embody the complementary relation between epistemic and hermeneutic modes, a relation that yields two equally possible descriptions of the same territory. The confusion arises because each is focusing on the virtues of one mode of inquiry without acknowledging its limits. Habermas can hold that solely on the basis of historical hermeneutic conditions Gadamer cannot defend against epistemic relativism, thereby forfeiting his grounds for critiquing the historical hegemony of science. Yet Gadamer can object that Habermas' search for the paradigmatic practice of a free society confuses the formal necessity of one practice – free public inquiry – with the need to determine the appropriate situation of that practice. Gadamer obscures the formal authority Habermas appeals to, while Habermas obscures the practical con-textuality that Gadamer insists is always an issue. Thus the Gadamer-Habermas debate is an imperfectly defined dialogue over the critical limitations of hermeneutics and the interpretive limitations of epistemology.

In this regard, and perhaps ironically, philosophical hermeneutics resembles the universality of epistemology more than the con-textuality of hermeneutic practice, revealing – against strong con-ventionist conceptions of hermeneutics – the interpenetration of epistemological and hermeneutic authorities, but also revealing – against transcendental critics – the openness that indefinitely post-pones the securing of an absolute critical ground. Despite his focus on historicity rather than on invariance, Gadamer needs necessary conditions in order to warrant hermeneutic openness, and calls upon them when they suit his argument. For the universality of epistemic categories does not rule out hermeneutic freedom, but rather constitutes alternative interpretive possibilities.

Gadamer's defense of the universal scope of hermeneutic reflection captures much that is generous, far-sighted, and powerful in the hermeneutic turn of postmodern philosophy. Yet his strategy must finally be understood in its complementary relationship to the other cognitive interests. In the interest of greater precision, the absorption of the world into language is a risky rhetorical ploy that finally betrays the historical specificity of hermeneutics. The mediacy of our understanding of the world is historical; but it is also more than historical, a difference that is too often lost in the rush by postmodernists to leave foundationism behind. Rorty's ideal of constraint-free inquiry, Lyotard's attack on consensus in science, Fish's reduction of interpretation to conventional constraints – these are all symptoms of the belief that interpretive freedom is incompatible with the necessity of epistemic conditions.[16] Just by virtue of the depth of Gadamer's thinking on this topic, however, one sees beyond the limitations of his metaphors to the necessary complementarity of epistemic, empirical, and hermeneutic practices.

16. Given the currency of the Derrida's attack on essentialist theories of meaning, the instability of the sign has often excessively overshadowed the theoretical grounds of this slippage. Fascination with free-play has distracted many from the host of questions about the conditions and consequences of this hermeneutic aporia. But the theoretical grounds of deconstruction, which include the formal constraints that allow and even make *necessary* that slippage, are finally of as much significance for foundationism as the slippage itself. For it is only due to such theoretical constraints that Derrida's "general system" of signs makes always already available the deconstructive possibility. This is a question of more than an absence: it is the necessary and generative absence in which deconstruction takes place. For an extended discussion of the legacy of this sort of rigor, see Rodolphe Gasché's *The tain of the mirror*, Cambridge: Harvard, 1986.

5

Critical politics: deconstruction for Americans

A. Professional investigations: searching the premises

During the 1950s, among such prominent literary critics as Crane, Frye, Wellek, and Warren, one heard statements to the effect that criticism had exhausted its self-imposed tutelage, and therefore was in need of theoretical foundations. By the mid-sixties, various American critics had responded to that need, while structuralism was getting considerable attention in a variety of human sciences. On the very occasion, however, when structuralism was being officially imported to America, critical optimism about foundations was challenged by Derrida's seminal "Structure, sign, and play," whose hermeneutics of suspicion doubted whether the human sciences could be sciences. Theoretical attempts to domesticate meaning, according to Derrida, always proceed by closing off some alternative interpretations, while ignoring or repressing the new alternatives they open up. Derrida suggested, furthermore, that philosophical valor was the better part of discretion, dismissing even the hope of finding metaphysical comfort in the human sciences.

Derrida's debut in Baltimore was a landmark step in the emergence of what came to be known as deconstructive practice, an activity in which criticism's theoretical methods are no more decisive of meaning than the circumstances and habits of social and historical contexts. In fact, post-structuralists argued, not only does theory not give us the tools by which to determine the validity of interpretation, it tells us why such expectations are misleading and impossible of fulfilment. All interpretation is perpetually subject to dislocation.

This deconstructive turn of events has had startling consequences for the profession of criticism, challenging many of its premises about critical authority. Following this critical import, one could say that the academic ranks have been repeatedly polarized, except for the inaccurate suggestion that there is a single axis of professional principles that divides the defenders and accusers of deconstruction.[1]

Nor is the urgency of this issue a merely theoretical interest. The issues of the canon, of pedagogy, of the interdisciplinary nature of criticism, have quickly become quite practical questions for administrative purposes, influencing departmental curricula, structure, hiring and membership, funding, research, and other policy issues of the profession. These issues are as immediate as today's department meetings, but also as far-reaching as the presuppositions that shape the critical classics, or even the possibility of classics, of tomorrow. Given the divisiveness to which post-structuralist thought has led, the question of its professional implications becomes indistinguishable from the question of its theoretical significance in general.

Not surprisingly, therefore, there has been a variety of stimulating discussion by way of defense and critique of deconstruction. This essay will not attempt to add another yet-more-subtle, or yet-more-epochal, or yet-more-final salvo in the dialogue. Rather, I attempt here to avoid some of the difficulties of importing deconstruction by way of the Platonic-Cartesian-Husserlian tradition of Continental philosophy. Unfortunately, this derivation has surrounded the theoretical stakes of deconstruction with an exotic and numinous air that is often exaggerated by practitioners and critics alike. As a countermeasure, I would like to address the still-too-current impression that deconstruction is new, abstrusely theoretical, French, irresponsible, and resistable. Conversely, I argue that deconstruction is old, inherently practical, international, disciplined, and inevitable.

I hope to make these points indirectly by making another point. I would like to address the charge that deconstruction represents a threat to the profession of literature as it has been practiced in

---

1. Rather, post-structuralism has divided critics between theoretical and anti-theoretical camps, theoretical and historical camps, formalist and anti-formalist camps, aesthetic and ideological camps, and between various ideological camps themselves. Nor are these divisions free from crosscuts. Feminist criticism, for example, has been markedly ambivalent about how to incorporate the lessons of post-structuralist theory: should feminists develop rival theories to the hegemonic legacy of the patriarchal canon? Or should they rather inhabit those inherited theoretical structures to transform them from within? Is theory an escape from historical conditions or a tool for discovering the subtler influences of historical structures? Is the uniqueness of artistic creativity the proper focus of interpretive attention or the social context in which such genius becomes meaningful?

America, a belief which results from a false contrast between already standard critical practices and what is now called "deconstruction." Against this illusion of novelty, terminal theoreticity, and Gallicism that surround deconstruction, I will follow up what a number of critics have already noted: that deconstruction is merely "close reading" laced with insights that the New Critics would have discovered had they understood their own practices with greater rigor. Deconstruction, in other words, is not the result of new methods, but of more thorough uses of old methods. Furthermore, where deconstruction has its theoretical, rhetorical, and interpretive aspects, there is another happy coincidence with New Criticism. Since Cleanth Brooks and Robert Penn Warren together authored works in the areas of critique, theory, and rhetoric, their interdisciplinary work allows the illustration of several key deconstructive principles within a small compass of American critical classics.[2]

B. The myth of textual autonomy

My argument follows three steps. (1) Brooks and Warren practiced and incompletely theorized a proto-deconstructive practice under the rubric of "close-reading." This practice was thought to demonstrate

2. This discussion uses material from the following essays: "The language of paradox" by Cleanth Brooks (hereafter LP, reprinted in *Critiques and essays in criticism*, ed. Robert Wooster Stallman, New York: Ronald Press, 1949; originally published in *Kenyon Review*, Spring, 1943); "Pure and impure poetry" by Robert Penn Warren (hereafter PIP, reprinted in Stallman, from *The well wrought urn*, New York: Reynal and Hitchcock, 1947); "Irony as a principle of structure" by Cleanth Brooks (hereafter IPS, reprinted in *Contexts for criticism*, ed. Donald Keesey, Mountain View, California: Mayfield, 1987); discussions of "The Birthmark" and "A rose for Emily" from *Understanding fiction*, reprinted in *Literary theory in praxis*, ed. Shirley Staton, Philadelphia: University of Pennsylvania Press, 1987 (hereafter SS); and from *Modern rhetoric*, New York: Harcourt, Brace, Jovanovich, 1979 (hereafter MR).

On the other hand, this examination of American seeds of deconstruction does not intend to condone all that has transpired in its name. Contrary to the more extreme relativists of meaning, I reject the notions that there is nothing outside the text (Derrida), that everything is language (Gadamer), that textual meaning is not constrained (Holland), that there are no invariant conditions of meaning (Foucault), that objectivity is dead (Rorty), that all is convention (Fish) and other relativist points sometimes mistaken for the point of deconstruction. In my view, nominalists, pseudo-deconstructors and radical relativists alike confuse the variability of language's uses and forms with its more invariant references and conditions.

the constructed nature of meaning, the irreducibility of artistic form, the fusion of form and content, the heresy of paraphrase, etc. (2) While it is true that they demonstrated something of the constructed character of meaning, their incomplete theorization of this model led to a false contrast between the autonomy of art and the putative stability of normal language. Thus they conceived of the autonomy of the artistic text as a specific characteristic of the literary object, conferring upon it a kind of transcendence of normal discourse. (3) By this supposed aesthetic transcendence, Brooks and Warren imply a misleading detachment of art and criticism – the pedestal effect – thereby fostering illusions of critical transcendence.

Significantly, both New Criticism and deconstruction are practices subversive of normal discourse. The difference between deconstruction and New Critical close reading turns out to be only this: that whereas New Criticism inconsistently invoked a transcendence of normal discourse into aesthetic objectivity, deconstructors show that the constructed character of meaning is ubiquitous and indeterminate, a position that seems to be considerably stronger than the supposed distinction between art and normal discourse. Moreover, without a stronger basis on which to ground aesthetic transcendence than the one New Critics propose, the authority of transcendence becomes an issue of power disguised as an issue of truth.

1. Toward a critical method

Though the New Critics penned numerous influential theoretical essays, it was their practice of close reading that more often transformed the thinking of many American critics.[3] The intention of certain New Critics to democratize critical practice reflects their own faith that their revolution was a methodological one rather than a primarily theoretical one. Still, as members of a young profession, the New Critics were concerned to have a proper object of analysis. This led to their influential reification of "the text itself" as a formal literary object, a conception that derived from the interpretive holism of Aristotle and Coleridge, and the rhetorical legacy of figural analysis.

W. K. Wimsatt's essays on the intentional and affective fallacies are perhaps the clearest expression of the New Critical tendency to view the text as an autonomous linguistic object rather than as dependent

---

3. Furthermore, many of the central theoretical props of New Criticism were prefigured in Aristotle (concrete universals) and Coleridge (organicism).

on either (1) the author's or the reader's subjectivity, or (2) the author's or reader's historical contexts. While subjective and historical factors were not thought by New Critics to be utterly irrelevant, they were thought incapable of accounting for the *literariness* of literature, a feature which, since it could violate any personal intent or social convention, required a specifically literary analysis.

The concept of autonomy found in Brooks and Warren's more theoretical discussions is a powerful and complex extension of this commonplace intuition that great literature makes its own rules, legislates the world (Shelley) and rewrites meaning on its own terms (T. S. Eliot). The power of the artist to create is also his hermeneutic power to question and reinscribe the significance of his history and context. The challenge for the critic, then, is to explain this power as a part of his defense of his own rights and responsibilities. Brooks and Warren approach this problem through the literary characteristics of paradox, irony and complexity, characteristics which are symptomatic of literature's resistance to and power over the received categories of its larger context.

According to Brooks, "there is a sense in which paradox is the language appropriate and inevitable to poetry. It is the scientist whose truth requires a language purged of every trace of paradox; apparently the truth which the poet utters can be approached only in terms of paradox" (LP, 66). Our thoughts normally flatten out meanings into oversimplified categories, though life's complexities and subtleties live on beneath our surface understanding. Just as our cities bury nature under the artifacts of human abstractions, our modern commonsense understanding buries life under abstractions until its subtleties disappear. Wordsworth, according to Brooks, considers this mortifying reduction of life in his "Composed upon Westminster Bridge," where he dramatizes the paradox that it is "only when the poet sees the city under the semblance of death that he can see it as actually alive – quick with the only life which he can accept, the organic life of 'nature'" (LP, 68).

Whereas the normalization of linguistic and social habit mortifies the imagination, paradox breaks the momentum of normalization. Insofar as he believed of poetry that "ordinary things should be presented to the mind in an unusual aspect," so "Wordsworth ... was consciously attempting to show his audience that the common was really uncommon, the prosaic was really poetic" (LP, 69). The poet must reawaken that living quality in the form of "the paradoxes

[that] spring from the very nature of [his] language: it is a language in which the connotations play as great a part as the denotations" (LP, 69).

Typifying the modern world in general, the sciences give a false sense of the intelligibility of life. Unhappily, the tendency of normal language toward artificial simplification is exacerbated by the reductive naturalism of the sciences in contrast with the complex naturalism of the poet. Hence, the apparent necessity of poetic paradox: "The nature [of things] is single, one, unified. But the name is double, and today with our multiplication of sciences, it is multiple. If the poet is to be true to his poetry, he must call it neither two nor one: the paradox is his only solution" (LP, 77). This is nothing less than the human condition, "the paradox of the imagination itself" (LP, 78), the ultimate ground of poetic language. Against the positivist simplifications of modern thought, the poet must restore the complexity of life by forcing the paradoxes still latent in our language.

Elsewhere, Brooks focuses on the ironic structure of literary language, which he approaches through the figuration of fictional metaphor. As art is life by another name, so the complexity of life is reinscribed in the irony of figural representation: "One can sum up modern poetic technique by calling it the rediscovery of metaphor and the full commitment to metaphor" (IPS, 82). Nor is this rhetorical character of literature a matter of embellishment – it is the rhetorical equivalent of Aristotle's conception of poetry as the typical example, the concrete universal: "The poet can legitimately step out into the universal only first going through the narrow door of the particular." Since "poems never contain abstract statements" (IPS, 84), any theme can only be inferentially embodied in the concreteness of the language. "The commitment to metaphor thus implies, with respect to general theme, a principle of indirection" (IPS, 82). All understanding, being linguistic, is also figurally interpretive.

The ironical character of literary language disallows any reductive expectations about meaning, which New Critics take to be as complex as the work as a formal whole. At best, meaning is a compromise between the abstraction of theme and the richness of the concrete context: "any 'statement' made in the poem bears the pressure of the context and has its meaning modified by the context" (IPS, 84); "we have come to see the importance of *context* ... What indeed would be statement wholly devoid of an ironic potential – a statement that did not show any qualification of the context?" (IPS, 83). The unity which must mark the achievement of a complex work of art is achieved out of, not in spite of, this complexity.

Holism for New Critics means multiplying elements in tension. Regarding the heterology of meanings in a rather complex poem by Randall Jarrell, Brooks notes: "None of these meanings cancels out the others. All are relevant, and each meaning contributes to the total meaning. Indeed, there is not a facet of significance which does not receive illumination from the figure" (IPS, 89). The vitality of complexity comes from "the pattern of thrust and counterthrust" (IPS, 87). Yet, despite the tensions of these conflicting elements, the great work *controls* its unity: the great poem is "a poetry which does not leave out what is apparently hostile to its dominant tone, and which, because it is able to fuse the irrelevant and discordant, has come to terms with itself and is invulnerable to irony ... Invulnerability to irony is the stability of a context in which the internal pressures balance and mutually support each other" (IPS, 87). The conflicting pressures of context, that is, are not only acknowledged by poems, but harnessed by the very complexity they constitute.

Of course, it is one thing to say that ironies and tensions are balanced in a formal structure. But once the issues of irony, complexity, and indirection are raised, questions inevitably follow about the assurance with which the poem can control its parts, not to mention questions about the control the critic may or may not have over meaning.

Concerning the poem's self-control, Robert Penn Warren's essay on pure and impure poetry considers true and false poetic integrity. Poetic integrity requires a fundamental break from the prosaic, normalized thought mentioned by Brooks, a break that seeks and finds transcendence of that normality: "poetry wants to be pure. And it always succeeds in this ambition. In so far as we have poetry at all, it is always pure poetry; that is, it is not non-poetry " (PIP, 85).

For Brooks, furthermore, this impulse is not superimposed on nature, or in violation of it, but rather fulfils nature's own tendency: "Nature [in its universalized moment] strains out of nature, it wants to be called by another name, it wants to spiritualize itself by calling itself another name" (PIP, 87). Hence the aesthetic urge for transcendence. Warren takes as an example the archetype of the garden achieved by Shakespeare in the Verona of Romeo and Juliet: "we know that this garden, in which nature for a moment conspires again with the lover, ... is justly admired for its purity of effect, for giving us the very essence of young, untarnished love" (PIP, 87). But unlike Platonic transcendence, Warren's purity does not require complete transcendence, which would be a denial of its context, but more an immanence of the pure ideal in concrete details:

It is time to ask ourselves if the celebrated poetry of this scene, which as poetry is pure, exists despite the impurities of the total composition, if the effect would be more purely poetic were the nurse and Mercutio absent and the lady a more sympathetic critic of pure poems. I do not think so ... Perhaps the lovers can only be accepted in their context. The poet seems to say: "I know the worst that can be said on this subject, and I am giving fair warning. Read at your own risk." So the poetry arises from a recalcitrant and contradictory context; and finally involves that context.   (PIP, 88)

Warren is confident that Shakespeare will prevail not in spite of, but because of, the full complexity of the context he has rendered. And so the purity of true poetic integrity does not deny the richness of its contextuality, the rich concreteness within which its themes find themselves.

False poetic purity, on the other hand, pretends to be able to deny the richness of nature, humanity, and language. It believes that "poetry is an essence that is to be located at some particular place in a poem, or in some particular element" (PIP, 98). This fallacy can take several forms. The imagist fallacy, for instance, appeared to suggest that poetry could be made pure by the reduction of the poem from theme to pure imagery. But as Warren notes, this is an inherently contradictory ideal: "To object to theory in poetry would be like objecting to words there; for words, too, are symbols without the sensuous character of the things they stand for; and yet it is only by the net of new connections which words throw over things, in recalling them, that poetry arises at all" (PIP, 101).

The universal, that is, does not weaken poetic power with abstraction, but is rather the ground or possibility of the human resonance that comes from textual memory, the interlacing of experiences through time. Thus, of a single image in Dante's *Divine Comedy*, Warren can conclude that its power is as thematic as sensual: "It is this long conflict [between divine and human justice], which appears in many forms, this ironic tension, which finally gives body to the simple eloquence of the line in question; the statement is meaningful, not for what it says, but for what has gone before. It is earned. It has been earned by the entire poem" (PIP, 103). The organic quality of complex images and poems requires a thematic dimension to organize that concrete complexity, a dimension that at once utilizes thematic abstraction while grounding it in the sensual aspect of experience.

False poetic integrity, then, is false because it "would purge out all complexities and all ironies and all self-criticism" (PIP, 104). That is, false poetic integrity hopes to reduce literary complexity to one of its aspects, whether by thematic reduction – a false abstraction from concrete richness – or by imagistic reduction – a repression of thematic complexity and abstraction. False poetic integrity buys purity at the expense of the true literariness of complexity and irony.

It is the rich linguistic character of literature that gives it its special power, its characteristically paradoxical achievement of transcendence in immanence. For literary power does not free itself from the actual language that is its flesh; yet it achieves a scope more universal than its local particulars. And so it is that poetic meaning lifts the reader out of his limitations toward larger visions that are new, yet still familiar: "What we do ask is that the poem dramatize the situation so accurately, so honestly, with such fidelity to the total situation that it is no longer a question of our beliefs, but of our participation in the poetic experience" (IPS, 89).

With such forays into literary theory, the New Critics refreshed a number of classical and romantic notions of art, while also laying claim to the specific territory of the literary object. Yet if this is their defense of the autonomy of the text, the integrity of the literary work turns out to be more rhetorical than secure. For while the New Critics have made a plausible case for certain characteristics of literary language, two problems remain for the critic: on the one hand, the properties of literariness make meaning intrinsically difficult to come by; on the other hand, since those characteristics are inherent in life and language, the distinction between literature and the rest of language is problematic. Thus the very irony which the New Critics have valorized threatens the proprietary claims of literary control and critical authority.

What sort of thing, finally, is meaning if it is an irreducibly formal whole, and an ironic one at that? Even if we say with the New Critics that form is content, and that structure is meaning, we are still confronted with the problem of describing that uniquely novel form or structure in either the categories of the critic or of normal discourse. How different is the critic's problem of formulation from that of the poet? With what does the critic mediate the special language of the poet if not the false language of normal or abstract discourse? And how reliable a guide for the reader is this aesthetic unity into which the conflicting tensions are resolved if it cannot be abstracted from the poem without paraphrase? Just how irreducible *is* the literary text, and are not all attempts at critique merely failed approximations to the ineffable depths of its complexity? But then how do we know when we are right if what makes poetry special removes it from critical appropriation?

The problem of a critical appropriation of poetic integrity can take the form of the following trilemma: either (a) critical language duplicates the work of poetic language, or (b) critics succeed in paraphrasing literary meaning in non-literary language, or (c) criticism serves poetry by showing how non-literary language fails to capture poetic meaning, giving rise to the ironies, paradoxes, etc. The "heresy of paraphrase" rules out the second option, and the expository aim of criticism rules out the first. The third option makes a virtue of necessity: since poetic language must appear to normal thought as irony and paradox, these are the wages of criticism's inability to appropriate literary integrity in non-poetic terms.

Today's critic might well anticipate the consequences of this dilemma: on the one hand, by making literary language special, the New Critics appear to give the critic a specific task to address; but on the other hand, by identifying that language by virtue of its irony and complexity, they appear to question the credibility of their critical resources as non-poets. Furthermore, the generality of the distinction between literary and normal language points toward fundamental questions about their theory of language in general. Insofar as the New Critics trace the difficulties of poetic language to the receding complexities of life, the comfortable simplicity of normal language must be something of an illusion – as "Westminster Bridge" suggests – constituting a false consciousness that things are more intelligible than they really are. But if that were the case, then one must raise questions about the status of discourse in general and criticism in particular. To approach this problem as a general problem of language, we turn to Brooks and Warren's theory of rhetoric.

2. The domestication of truth

In Brooks and Warren's *Modern rhetoric*, we find little to help us understand how the analytic function of criticism can avoid the problem of appropriating the mysterious ironies of life in non-literary terms. Rather than offering some account of how the truth of life inherently resists the resources of language, the rhetoric of their manual is quite traditional for its faith in the unity of truth and the fundamental hierarchy of rational and irrational discourses. Whereas the whole thrust of the New Critical concept of literariness appears to challenge the accessibility of truth to the commonsense rhetoric of reason, Brooks and Warren's rhetorical theory appears to assume that truth's rhetorical accessibility as a matter of course.

Brooks and Warren define rhetoric as "the art of using language effectively" (*MR*, 5), though that pragmatic definition requires the traditional distinction between rational (argued for) and irrational (persuasive) effects. "Persuasion represents power," they note, "the 'engineering of consent'" (*MR*, 108), whereas the "end of argument, strictly conceived, is truth — truth as determined by the operation of reason" (*MR*, 109). Argument serves understanding; persuasion the will of the persuader. And while there are many ways by which persuasion may achieve its desired assent — such as slanting, suggestion, identification, etc. — the "characteristic end of argument is achieved *only one way*, by the operation of reason" (*MR*, 109).

Apparently quite complacent with commonsense rhetoric, Brooks and Warren confirm the traditional hegemony of reason over persuasion in a variety of standard ways.

First, persuasion contrasts with what might be called inquiry. In inquiry true conclusions are sought, whereas in persuasion the conclusion is already decided and the reasons are sought. What is often called "rationalization" is "the use of reason not to seek truth but to justify desires, attitudes, beliefs, or actions already determined on emotional grounds" (*MR*, 117). Because rationalization can masquerade as inquiry, Brooks and Warren conclude that it leads to "either or both of two kinds of deception: to deceive the self or to deceive others" into the impression that open inquiry is being practiced.[4] By way of example, Brooks and Warren note that motives of powerful groups (e.g. Nazis, Yankees, slave-owners, and "democratic" imperialists) often engage in practices whose self-interests are glossed with

---

4. Brooks and Warren note that although the rationalizer pretends otherwise, rationalization characteristically *follows* action, decision, attitude, or belief (*MR*, 117).

high-sounding rationalizations.[5] The crux of rationalization, finally, is the motive: "Even a maniac may be faultlessly logical in argument, but we have to inspect his premises and his obsessions. And, too, the context of his argument" (*MR*, 117).

Even in its normal operation, persuasion appears less savory than argument. It begins with "selling yourself" to gain the confidence of the persuadee. Then one must usurp the will of the persuadee in however clandestine a manner: "in the process [the persuader] actually seizes the will of the persuadee. No, he does not seize the will of the persuadee; he lulls it, bemuses it, beguiles it, and he does so by appealing to the desires of the persuadee" (*MR*, 112).

Regrettably, this practice has become one of the great industries of our culture. Brooks and Warren note the irony that our early optimism about modern literacy "did not foresee what in fact has happened in our Western capitalist democracies – the development of a vast mass communication industry, concerned in the main neither with the true nor the false, but with the unreal, the more or less totally irrelevant" (*MR*, 123). The irony, of course, lies in the fact that such practices undermine the rational bases of individual choice: "When the persuadee is persuaded without reference to the grounds of assent, what Jacques Ellul ... calls the 'elimination of individualizing factors' has occurred. That is, the person has ceased to be a person and has become a thing" (*MR*, 124). Such mass persuasion is, in other words, an anti-democratic institution within our so-called democratic culture.

Against these less creditable uses of rhetoric, Brooks and Warren champion the virtues of argument or reasoning. Unlike rationalization, real *doubt* underlies argument, "the process by which the mind moves from certain data (evidence) to a conclusion" according to the rules of

5. "Not only the life history of an individual may reveal such rationalizations, but also the history of a nation. When the Nazis went to war, they went with Hitler's rationalization that Germany was being encircled and that they were acting in self-defense. When the Civil War in America is referred to as a crusade to free the slaves (which is very different from saying that slavery was a *necessary condition* of the war), some historians, remembering Lincoln's statement that the war was to save the Union, are likely to detect here the sweet smell of rationalization. When we consider that slaveholders comforted themselves with the reflection that slavery brought the benighted African into contact with the Christian religion, the same odor begins to rise. Europeans, and some Americans, remembering that the participation of the United States in World War I made us a rich and powerful country, look with suspicion on the slogan created to justify that war – 'To Make the World Safe for Democracy'" (*MR*, 117).

valid reasoning. (*MR*, 157) According to the rules of validity, proponents "claim that one thing (the conclusion) merits belief because certain other things (data, premises, evidence) merit belief" (*MR*, 131). The substance of argument, on this view, is the linking together of the steps of argument according to valid inferences, the violation of which constitute the standard forms of fallacy: e.g. "post hoc, ergo propter hoc"; equivocation; begging the question (assuming the conclusion); ignoring the question; non sequitur; ad hominem; ad populum (*MR*, 161).

Having set up this standard distinction between rational and irrational discourse, however, Brooks and Warren touch upon precisely that point which becomes central for the question of critical authority and the possibility of deconstruction: the question of closure. Given that there are certain inferential rules for moving from one point to another, that still leaves open the question of the first premises and therefore of the validity of all subsequent inferences. Regarding first premises, Brooks and Warren note that "the appeal to reason is the broadest and deepest assumption made in argument" (*MR*, 133), which means that in order for rational discourse not to involve an infinite regress of legitimate steps, one must assume that it forms a closed system with self-evident first premises.[6] And yet Brooks and Warren admit that argument can be "about what constitutes such a standard" (*MR*, 135–6). On their model, then, rational discourse is only so when assumptions are shared, including one's model of the rules of reason. But this assumption, which even they question, is just what deconstruction destabilizes.

So despite the foundationist overtones of Brooks and Warren's references to rationality, their use of it is merely normalizing, reducing thought to a coherence that is only conventional. In fact, here New Criticism and deconstruction coincide to question the possibility of unequivocally rational critical grounds. According to Brooks and Warren's notions of literariness, the relation between truth and commonsense assumptions is *fundamentally* problematic. The evidence of literary meaning, that is, consists largely of witnessing how the normal uses of language fail in the literary context, and how the resulting effect of the literary work is to deny the translatability or reduction of its meaning in terms other than its own.

---

6. "When conflict is involved in argument, the conflict cannot be resolved except by an agreement to accept the dictates of reason" (*MR*, 109).

If the real truth is absent from non-literary language, how can we assume the truth of our commonsense assumptions? Since it is the mark of great literature to challenge assumptions, literary analysis must work negatively, i.e. away from the standard sort of rhetorical closure available to uncritical minds. In light of this shared view of the absence of the grounds of truth, the most notable difference between New Critical and deconstructive skepticism is that the New Critics trust aesthetic sensibility to domesticate this mystery, whereas today's critics bother to point out that any gesture of domestication is both theoretically underdetermined and ideologically invested.

Of course, it would hardly be surprising if literary critics of earlier generations assumed the adequacy of aesthetic sensibility to constitute their authority. The problem is that New Critics seem to offer an objectivism of form and a democracy of literary pedagogy. So their occasional aestheticism raises questions about the coherence of their agenda. For instance, if the assumption of rational closure is a prerequisite for rational rhetoric (*MR*), and if literary destabilization of normal discourse is the final point of literary critique, then Brooks and Warren's rhetorical ideal of rational coherence is complicit with the deadening simplifications of normal language against which Words-worth wrote. From the point of view of the literariness of life, rational discourse is an illusion that truth can be won by properly sequencing the bits and pieces of truth. This contradicts their own organicist model for which the totality of truth becomes more ironic and paradoxical as it becomes more total.

It would appear that Brooks and Warren are invested in two models of discourse – the literary and the rational – whose compatibility is deeply conflicting. The literary model is based on a fundamentally ironic view of language and truth, whereas the rational one merely assumes the traditional univocity of truth. We have, in short, a literary rhetoric of mystery and a modern rhetoric of the obvious.

How damaging is this tension among agendas and models? A close reading of their own work shows just how problematic their rhetoric of reason turns out to be, thanks to their untenable separation of ironic and rational language.

C. Crypto-ideological hermeneutics

As noted above, Brooks and Warren define literariness as a figurative, ironic, and complex use of language that reflects the resistance of life's depths to normal language. On the other hand, Brooks and Warren's theory of rhetoric appears to define rational discourse as evident reason in contrast to the clandestine devices of persuasion. Thus one finds across the rubrics of their work a tension between a literary theory that privileges the elusive and the subversive, and a rhetoric that privileges the obvious and the rational. That Brooks and Warren have not succeeded in expunging either their own rhetoric or their criticism of this tension appears in a closer look at their arguments. For close reading reveals neither the "invulnerability to irony" of literary integrity, nor the manifest reason of exposition that they profess. Language, it seems, is neither as reliably unreliable nor as reliably reliable as they claim. Furthermore, this conflicted view of the nature of truth is not ideologically arbitrary; in their hands it tends to insulate the complex ironies of power from the feeble platitudes of morality.

1. The irrationality of the master — part 1: the rhetoric of the obvious

Brooks and Warren are confident of the capacity of their rhetoric to transcend the irrational. Indeed, so powerful do they suppose the insulating effect of rational discourse that they risk the maelstrom of campus politics in the demonstration of reason's evidence. When they compare student essays on campus issues of the sixties, the controversial material is offered as provocation to thought rather than as material for persuasion to a certain political agenda. Trusting their objectivity as purveyors of civilized discourse (rather than as ideologues), the controversial content of their examples of rhetorical manners is supposed to be neutralized by the issue of good form.

Early on in *Modern rhetoric*, Brooks and Warren tell of the importance of developing a thesis, a "true subject." Our positive example is "a student named Jim" who, when he wrote on "university unrest in the 1960s" found a true subject in the proposition: "At the center the university troubles of the 1960s were antidemocratic." By a "true" subject, of course, Brooks and Warren do not mean that Jim's thesis is true, but that it is a truly controvertible topic. We are first treated to Jim's running notes:

When a student now at X University hears tales of what happened here ten years ago, it sounds like folklore or the discovery of America. But the surprising thing is how little talk actually goes on. We tend to assume that student protest had something to do with ending the war in Asia, but there is very little self-congratulation among students today – and I might add, little excitement about changing the world overnight. Some of us may privately think that changes tend to come slowly and without revolutionary excitement. And we may wonder what became of the heroes of yesteryear.

Some people may think that more students today are selfish, but not a few of us try to think things through.

Brooks and Warren say nothing about the fact that so far Jim has done nothing but strike an attitude and indulge impressions. Happily, though, Jim soon gets down to the work of outlining, at which he is a true champion:

OUTLINE OF "DEMOCRACY AND STUDENT MOVEMENTS OF
THE 1960s"

Proposition: Paradoxically, the student agitation of the 1960s generally claiming to uphold democratic values, attacked those values.
[Introduction and discussion of occasion already prepared]

 I. We should begin by defining democracy, or rather by describing certain aspects of democracy that are especially relevant to our university system.
   A. Democracy aims at the greatest degree of individual freedom. (In government, universal suffrage symbolizes and implements this freedom.)
   B. But the freedom of the individual is limited by one factor: it must not limit the freedom of other individuals.
   C. Although a bulwark of democracy, the university cannot exercise democracy in the same way as society.
      1. Standards for complex instruction cannot be set by popular vote.
      2. The university must maintain "elite" values in order to preserve civilization and solve difficult social problems
 II. In what ways did the student movement of the 1960s violate democracy?
   A. It was not antidemocratic in its ends – antiracism, promoting the attack on poverty, protesting the Asian war – but in its means.
   B. It attacked democracy by direct, violent means – bombings, personal violence, procommunism, holding the law in contempt.
   C. It attacked by indirect means:
      1. It deprived university students of their rights to pursue their chosen occupations by strikes and forced participation in violent acts, by occupation of facilities, and by harassment of faculty.
      2. It threatened special libraries and art collections as symbols of elitism, thereby denying the value of "culture" and depriving others of their rights to use these facilities.
      3. It attempted to dictate curriculum on the basis of "relevance," allowing only subjects of immediate "social" or "revolutionary"

value to society – urban problems, racism, economic ills, etc. "Cultural" and "theoretical" subjects were regarded as irrelevant.
4. By making universities "scapegoats" for social ills, it attacked the idea of rational investigation of problems as a means to democratic solutions.
5. In crudely applying the theory of the "general good," it attacked the rights of the minority.
D. It denied the use of democratic means for social change or protest.
1. It had contempt for the electoral process.
2. It had contempt for the right of peaceful assembly and for legal protest.
III. The ways in which the abuses of the 1960s violated the democratic values of the university can be summed up under several related ideas:
A. The university is not primarily and directly a political organization. If the aim of the university were to disseminate propaganda rather than truth, freedom in research and teaching would be destroyed.
B. The function of the university is to investigate all subjects and issues of human concern.
C. The most important function of the university in a democracy is to create an informed and rational electorate, capable of exercising freedom intelligently.

Though form is supposed to be the issue here, I will note one point, if only because it is so central: that Jim's argument contradicts itself on the main issue of whether or not ends can justify the means. On the one hand he assumes that the sixties protests fall afoul of that principle, while on the other hand he admits that universities also violate democratic procedure as a matter of course (point I, C, 2: universities are elitist defenses of democracy). This double standard is only one of many of Jim's problems to be overlooked by Brooks and Warren, which I will also overlook in the interest of the issue of outlining.

A blind man can see that Jim can outline. Unfortunately, not everyone can outline so crisply, and some don't even try. Witness the sad case of "a sophomore whom we shall call Sally" who "fails to do the kind of preparatory work shown above" (the pseudonym is the only mercy Sally will be shown):

THE GRADING SYSTEM SHOULD BE DISCARDED
I have been in college for two years now, and more and more I feel that the grading system should be abolished. There would, of course, have to be some sort of Pass-Fail arrangement; otherwise "freeloaders" would take over, but the present discriminations do more harm than good. You are almost tempted

to say that the "free-loaders" would do less damage than the "grade-hogs" do now.

The grade-hogs are, as the term implies, not interested in the subject but in impressing people, or even making Phi Beta Kappa. Of course, some are interested in getting better jobs later, but vanity seems to be the main motive. Whatever the motive, the general influence of the system is bad in that it emphasizes the grade and not the subject. The "grade-hog" would as soon make an A in child care as in mathematics. They just want to add up another A.

Furthermore, since all they want is grades, they often don't care how they get them – even cheating. Since they often succeed at this, and are known to succeed, their general influence is bad and a general cynicism and sometimes imitation by other students results. The subject ceases to be important; that's the chief consequence.

The grade system encourages easy subjects, and in doing so draws many students from subjects that would be useful. A chemistry major could use a lot of math, but because math is hard, he goes for Western Civilization, which isn't much help to a chemist.

Furthermore, the grade system doesn't adequately evaluate a student's seriousness and motivation. It tends to be mechanical and doesn't give the student much opportunity for showing creativity. Long-range problems might be a better way than examinations. Of course, there are sometimes term papers, but they themselves are often treated in much the same way as examinations, and not as an index of creativity.

One of the worst features, too, of the present system is that it encourages students to postpone work and cram for quizzes and examinations. They have not concentrated on getting a long-range control of the subject. It is a hand-to-mouth process.

Sally's real name may be protected by a pseudonym, but her discourse is not going to get off so easily: "Clearly the student has here been simply jumping from one notion to another, with no dominant idea, no true subject, except a distaste for examinations. And certainly, she has not distinguished between defects that may be inherent in the system and those that are purely the responsibility of the student." Presumably, these flaws are supposed to speak for themselves, because they receive no analysis. Of course, Jim's outline is impressive. But what is remarkable about Brooks and Warren's reception of Jim's and Sally's work is the stunning irrelevance or inaccuracy of most of their remarks, which cannot finally keep form and content apart.

On the point of preparation, the impressionism of Jim's running notes had little material contribution to make to the outline, although it advertised his distaste for dissidents. On the other hand, we are not shown Sally's running notes or her outline, in which case we do not know what preparation is involved there. More importantly, however, while overlooking Jim's central double-standard about ends justifying means, Brooks and Warren have simply ignored the coherent outline that is implicit in Sally's argument. Rather than distinguish the relevant ˙ from the irrelevant features of the educational system as her argument requires, they dismiss her argument without analysis in their haste to discredit her.

On the point of her argument, in fact, Brooks and Warren's objections to Sally's essay are remarkably incorrect:

(1) "no true subject": the effects of the grading system;
(2) "no dominant idea": the grading system is counterproductive;
(3) "jumping from one idea to another": (by paragraphs)
    a. grades are not worth the trouble
    b. grades are driven by ambition
    c. ambition fosters self-interest
    d. ambition dissuades from valuable challenges
    e. ambition discourages creativity
    f. grades promote short-term over long-term benefits;
(4) "a distaste for examinations": Sally recommends larger projects, whereas Jim inconsistently demands democracy;
(5) does not acknowledge "the responsibilities of the student": as if the student should be indifferent to the ways in which the system favors the ambitious, the dishonest, the selfish, etc.; while Jim does not acknowledge the responsibilities of the university to the politics of the present.

The point, of course, is not that Sally is an exemplary writer. Rather, the point is the strong misreading by Brooks and Warren regarding the real weaknesses of Sally's prose. They have accused her of not having an argument, which is false. If Sally lacks the right stuff, Brooks and Warren are not entirely forthcoming about what the right stuff is. On the point of rhetorical virtue, Brooks and Warren would be more precise to say that she lacks the right form. Just what that means, however, is not as easy to say as they suggest.

Sally's main problem is not that she lacks an outline, which is implicit in her paragraphing. In fact, the body of Sally's essay has its own logic: it moves from the problem of grade-motivation to the effects of that problem, first for the more ambitious students, and then for the less ambitious students. Once logic and style are distinguished, Jim's military-style outline, subordinated down to two levels of subheadings, appears to be merely more vast than Sally's argument, not essentially more coherent. Brooks and Warren simply do not see Sally's outline at all. True, she lacks better grammar, better diction, and bulk. But that is not supposed to be the issue that Brooks and Warren are addressing at this point, which is logical ordering.

Not surprisingly, Brooks and Warren's analytic inaccuracies are coincident with their literary theory in a crucial sense: both their theory and their practice suggest that form *is* content. Jim's outline has that Cartesian clear-and-distinct appearance that makes for easy grading. Sally's prose is not always sure, and never polished. Ergo, Jim's thinking is strong and Sally's is not. But this leads to something very different from the transcendence of subjective preference. Rather, it invites the exercise of some preferences over others. Likewise, their analysis of Sally's form is not finally scientific or objective, but aesthetic and ideological.[7]

Why would Brooks and Warren so violate their own canons of rational discipline and trust peremptory dismissal? Indeed, what is this comparison of students about? Is it possible that the binary order/disorder as represented by the binary Jim/Sally has deeper resonances than are acknowledged? If we perform a literary analysis on Brooks and Warren's example, we arrive at the following pattern:

Good	*Bad*
Jim	Sally
clear outline	implicit outline
good grammar	weak grammar
distaste for dissidents	distaste for grades
affirms authority	questions the system
Yale before 1967	academia after 1970

Of course, one could go on. The point, however, is not the unstated coherence of their repressed contents, but its connection to the form-as-content school of critique, and its significance for the fate of content. It is true that in good writing form does absorb everything, but as Brooks and Warren have demonstrated, that does not yield the formal transcendence of political content, but rather the impossibility

---

7. True, analysis could have strengthened the case against Sally had they offered it, just as their negligent analysis of her implicit outline constitutes a case against Brooks and Warren. Yet it would seem on the basis of Brooks and Warren's example that notwithstanding its subjective character, their distaste for Sally's form-content becomes a stand-in for the rigorous analysis of her thought.

of such transcendence. When form becomes content, we do not have freedom of content so much as a tyranny of form. The rational becomes the aesthetic. All is permitted – if it is done with good form. The irony, however, is that this view is posed as if literary value is thereby made objective, as if content were liberated from mere style into rationality itself.

Belief in this formal transcendence of political content puts the myth of liberal impartiality in the service of a very familiar network of values. On the surface, it is the liberal education model of articulate diversity. Finally, however, it reduces to Kant's conclusion to his essay, "What is enlightenment?": "reason as much as you like, but obey." The up-dated version reads: "Take whatever position you want, but take it with good form, if your background allows for it." But as Brooks and Warren show with merciless rigor, the distinction between form and content tends to disappear in the real world of real professors, and not just theoretically. Despite Sally's implicit logic, her imperfect style renders her, for Brooks and Warren, a body without a head.

Is it just possible that Sally's reception is hampered by Brooks and Warren's distaste for people with a distaste for the establishment? According to their own theory of rhetoric, their prejudices would emerge in the slanting of their argument and in their fallacious departures from the "only one" way of argument, the way of reason. We have already noted their oversight of the structure of Sally's argument and their lack of analysis in her peremptory dismissal. Returning to the literary model of analysis, we might further consider the binary structure of the examples, in which the order/disorder theme is structured in classically patriarchal ways. Brooks and Warren define slanting as "the method by which, without violating the facts in any narrow sense, the persuader suggests such interpretations as are desired by the persuader." While slanting "can be seen in its crudest form in single words or phrases used for connotative values," it could also be seen as suggesting guilt by a pattern of associations.[8]

---

8. Of course, since the New Critics have told us that intentions are irrelevant to literary meaning, we should bracket the intentions of Brooks and Warren on this matter: Brooks and Warren have noted that rationalization can work to deceive oneself as well as others. We will suspend judgment, therefore, on the question of whether, as masters of rhetoric, Brooks and Warren are aware of their own persuasive departures from the only one way of reasoning in the agon of Jim and Sally and the future of the American university.

Here the autonomy of literary form overwhelms the pseudo-objective theory of rhetoric: since the persuasiveness of language cannot be domesticated by reason, connotation must overrun the resources of argument. Persuasion, in other words, cannot be avoided, but can only be harnessed to one's own agenda. The choice between rational and irrational rhetoric is false, however useful for damaging the credibility of those without good form. Still, since Brooks and Warren are on the side of good form, their mastery of rhetoric must finally be accountable to all the devices, persuasive and argumentative, which articulate their conception of good form.

As a tactic of persuasion, the liberal marriage of freedom-of-content and the discipline-of-form serves an important function: to appropriate a liberal face for their own less-than-liberal prejudices. This tactic Brooks and Warren refer to as the need to create as broad as possible a base of identification:

In persuasion, [vs argument], the persuader earnestly seeks to *eliminate conflict from the germ situation* ... The persuader's characteristic assertion is that any difference between his point of view and that of the persuadee is the result of only slight misunderstanding that can readily be cleared up by a little friendly discussion, for they are two persons of essentially identical interests ... In other words, what the persuader seeks is the broadest possible common ground with the persuadee, something far beyond the ground necessary for argument.

The persuader, in other words, pretends to speak for everyone's interests, representing the commonweal which only barbarians would spurn. In their American context, Brooks and Warren stand for that society where the only check on diversity is a minimal decorum, a prerequisite that, since it allows for true diversity, is in everyone's interests, or as Jim's outline puts it, a minimal elitism that allows a maximum of democracy.

What is troubling, however, is the presumed objectivity of this version of democracy as witnessed by their "liberal" treatment of Sally. In fact, they do not fault her lack of stylistic decorum, but fault her lack of an argument. Not only do their prejudices show; they are also guilty of the very irrationalist sins they decry. Though Jim's polished self-contradiction gets plenty of exposure and no criticism, Sally's challenge to the academic norm goes virtually unanalyzed, being dismissed with what – by their own standards – is a litany of fallacies:

(1) post hoc, ergo propter hoc: her essay is unorganized because Sally has no outline

(2) equivocation: "jumping from one idea to another" vs following a logical sequence of points

(3) begging the question: *how* are the weaknesses of the system distinguishable from what is "purely the responsibility of the student"?

(4) ignoring the question: *do* grades reward ambition, promote self-interest, short-term gains, stifle creativity, etc.?

(5) ad hominem: Sally is discredited by her distaste for examinations

(6) non sequitur: Sally has no outline, therefore her essay is unorganized[9]

To grasp the significance of Brooks and Warren's adjudication of the problem of Sally, we might consider how different their example would look if the golden outline had been a part of Sally's case against the grading system. Then the case for liberal education and for the impartiality of reason would have been exemplified by Brooks and Warren's avoidance of a conflict of interest between good form and content they happen to agree with. As it is, however, what we see is something else: an ideal of liberality and objectivity that resists challenges to itself to the point of misrepresenting those challenges. If Brooks and Warren are the exemplars of liberal education they claim to be, the ideal of good form does not liberate content, but rather dissolves it. The emancipation of ideas becomes the colonization of behavior. As the demand for proper form becomes omnipotent, liberalism masks a rigorous elitism of proper discourse.

There is, in this pattern, a genuine impersonality, although not the kind of "end of ideology" neutrality that is supposed by some liberals and some who want to pass for liberals. It is clear, for instance, that abandoning the form and content distinction allows for the most ruthless, if indirect, form of censorship since freedom of content no longer has any meaning. To say that one can say anything with impunity as long as one says it well demands that one be far enough inside the system to have competence in its rules. The tyranny of form, no less than the tyranny of content, demands obedience to establishment logic. Under that rule, only a product of the system can be a legitimate critic of it.

9. Of course, it is difficult to be sure which fallacy is being indulged, since no analysis or reasoning is presented.

Of course, this does not imply that liberalism has no integrity. Rather, it implies that a liberal educational establishment must be judged, not by its surface appearance, but by its enabling conditions. As Brooks and Warren demonstrate, the liberal ideal of proper form is more compatible with reactionary elitism than with radical democracy because it presupposes the conditions of elitism within its operation, even if it offers opportunity for empowerment *in principle*.

The significance of the Brooks and Warren argument for rational rhetoric, finally, is twofold. On the one hand, one sees that the aesthetic nature of form makes the distinction between form and content less rational than liberal assumptions often suggest. Pretending to a univocal rationality, Brooks and Warren's own rhetoric defies their priority of reason over persuasion, truth over style, and objectivity over ideology. Likewise, their critical performance demonstrates that "persuasion represents power" and that "engineering consent" is best done in the name of reason.

2. The irrationality of the master – part 2: the rhetoric of the literary

Whereas Brooks and Warren's distinction between rational and irrational rhetoric can serve to promote a false impression of objectivity, of liberal tolerance of divergent content, and of the representation of a common interest, their notion that literature becomes "invulnerable to irony" through its autonomous mastery of irony, metaphor, and complexity can also serve to naturalize their particular prejudices by projecting them onto the text itself.

a. Putting on a good face: "The Birthmark"

In "The Birthmark" Hawthorne tells a tale of a scientist who becomes preoccupied with a birthmark on the otherwise flawless face of his wife. Convinced of his own powers to perfect nature, he convinces her, over her shame and reluctance, to trust him to remove the birthmark in a great experiment. His momentary victory turns into defeat when her cosmetic perfection results in her death.

For an intelligent high school reader, the meaning of this story is obviously what Hawthorne tells us it is: a man is corrupted by his fantasies of intellectual and moral autonomy at the expense of a

trusting and loving wife. But this obvious moral represents a problem
for Brooks and Warren. For if the tale were no more than an exemplum
of fallen human pride in its modern Faustian form, then it would risk
running afoul of the demand that literature complicate a theme rather
than merely represent it. An irony as obvious as the one Hawthorne
offers – i.e. a moral of the story – would challenge Brooks and
Warren's notion that great art must have intellectual and moral
autonomy, rather than reducing to moral slogans. Furthermore, the
fact that Hawthorne *gives* us the moral challenges the New Critics to
show their transcendence of the intentional fallacy: they must be able
to go beyond Hawthorne's intended moral to the greater complexity
of real art. Thus their reading of this tale becomes an exercise in
proving that Hawthorne is an ironist on their model, not his.

The principle of artistic complexity must have its way. True, Brooks
and Warren admit, "This story amounts to a sort of parable ... [and]
the story ... has a 'deeply impressive moral' [Hawthorne's phrase]"
(SS, 32). But the subtlety of the art is redeemed from the obviousness
of the theme, so Brooks and Warren argue, by the literary richness
which yields both concrete and thematic complications: "the cliché of
fallen pride will hardly be 'deeply impressive' in isolation." The
thematic complications lie in Aylmer's characterization, specifically
the "problem of motivation ... [For] had Aylmer not been a scientist,
a daring experimenter, the birthmark on his wife's cheek would hardly
have come to obsess him." Thematic simplicity is countered by the
irony of Aylmer being a respectable man, even idealistic and heroic.
The complexity of Aylmer's character is supposed to go against a
simple moral condemnation: "We are not, of course, to conceive of
Aylmer as a monster, a man who would experiment on his own wife
for his own greater glory." Aylmer's respectable intentions save him
and Hawthorne's literariness at once.

Their deference to the Great Man saturates Brooks and Warren's
defense of Aylmer's rhetoric, which they refuse to see as an example
of their much despised rationalization, but rather as evidence of good
intentions. Indeed, instead of seeing through Aylmer's rhetoric to
Hawthorne's damning clues, Brooks and Warren simply add yet more
lofty rationalizations to Aylmer's: "The triumph of which Aylmer
speaks will not be for vulgar display and self-advertisement [as if
Georgiana is not treated as Aylmer's prize]. It will be a triumph which
his wife will share [as object] and a triumph to be won for her sake
[Aylmer speaking for her interests]." The hypocrisy of Aylmer's

rhetoric is only exceeded by the blindness of Brooks and Warren to it. What could be more a vulgar display than such a minute feature of his wife's already stunning physical appearance? It is not a triumph for her because it only attests to Aylmer's lack of appreciation and the supposed superiority of his skill over her imperfection.

Aylmer's transparently imperial pride is glossed by Brooks and Warren as being "the kind of pride … which enters into and colors many of man's nobler purposes. What the story emphasizes is not Aylmer's self-conceit but rather his possession of the questing spirit which will not resign itself to the limitations and imperfections of nature." Somehow Aylmer's deceitful overestimation of his powers does not qualify as self-conceit. Moreover, it seems to be irrelevant that, as is so often the case with imperial pride, its quests for perfection are made at someone else's expense, against their wishes, and promoted with deceptions about the identity of the perpetrators, as when Aylmer deceives Georgiana about his previous record of experimental failures.

Since Brooks and Warren claim to know what Hawthorne intends, it is worth seeking Hawthorne's opinion on the point of pride and self-conceit. Aylmer's "confidence" in his right to risk his wife, the confidence which Brooks and Warren refer to in his defense, is the kind of intellectual pride that Hawthorne portrays as the unpardonable sin in "Ethan Brand" or as courting the devil in "Young Goodman Brown," or which Melville portrays at length in *The confidence man: his masquerade*. The fact that for ironists such as Hawthorne and Melville such confidence is never a legitimate defense appears to be lost in the ironies of Brooks and Warren's more sophisticated world of critical elites and their manifest destinies.

Is Aylmer not a monster? And is Hawthorne incapable of seeing him so? In his notebooks, Hawthorne says he intends: "To allegorize life with a masquerade, to represent mankind generally as masquers"; there he sees that "a man seeks for something excellent, and seeks it in the wrong way, and in a wrong spirit, and finds something horrible … and brings to light his accumulated sins."[10] As "Ethan Brand" shows, Hawthorne is not afraid to call intellectual pride the unpardonable sin. The proximity of Aylmer's name to "ail-more" suggests that by

---

10. Coincidentally, these quotations are from *American literature: the makers and the making*, edited by Lewis, Brooks, and Warren (shorter edition, New York: St. Martin's; p. 346).

mitigating the sin Brooks and Warren are reading Aylmer's good form against the greater irony of the tale. Brooks and Warren's denial of Hawthorne's dramatic yet straightforward moral serves their own notion of literature at the expense of Hawthorne's.

To confute Hawthorne's obvious moral of a man corrupted by his fantasies of autonomy, Brooks and Warren must make tragic what is merely grotesque. This requires a systematic misreading of the moral significance of each character. Thus, they charge that "Hawthorne is sympathetic to [Aylmer], and obviously sees in his ruinous experiment a certain nobility." Of course; but how deep, and to what point? They conclude, "it would be misreading the story to infer that Hawthorne dismisses [Aylmer] as merely a foolish man." Instead, there "are many qualifications to be made ... matters of emphasis and matters of application to be taken into account. One cannot range the characters into two absolute categories and the moral itself is not a rule to be applied absolutely and without qualification." But what qualifies as a rule in this case? Brooks and Warren treat moral generalizations as rules, but exempt their notion that great literature is complex from being a critical rule. This inconsistency, however, allows them to pick and choose generalizations as they wish. And so their prejudices are naturalized, seen as objectively in the text itself and as what Hawthorne probably means, even when Hawthorne's own critical remarks suggest otherwise.

Putting aside the many appeals to authorial intention throughout their argument ["Hawthorn does not mean ... " etc.], we might question this irony further. What sort of irony does this discovery of Aylmer's complexity yield? Brooks and Warren hope to destabilize the moral by the fact that Aylmer usually makes a respectable appearance. Thus Brooks and Warren invoke the comparison between Aylmer and his hunchbacked assistant: "Aminadab ... provides a sort of measuring stick for the folly and nobility of the husband and wife. He is, as Aylmer calls him, a 'man of clay.' He lacks imagination for the noble enterprise of daring to surpass nature." Evidently we *can* range characters into two types. Handicapped people – like the destitute in their alleys, the Sallys in their kitchens, and dark-skinned people in their Third World *barrios* – do not dream in a sufficiently lofty form. They wish only to survive with a modicum of happiness.

The irony here, however, is on Brooks and Warren. The way Brooks and Warren read the tale is in fact more parabolic, more allegorical than what Hawthorne gives us. Thus they take the superficialities of good form and hunched backs entirely at face value rather than ironically. They take form as content. Their reading does not complicate the "impressive moral" by complicating Aylmer for us; it flattens the moral into mechanical symbolization by the mere appearances of the characters. The irony is not merely that Aylmer is respectable and kills his wife, but that virtue becomes a pretext for vice. So the reading of Brooks and Warren is ironic in exactly the wrong way: by emphasing the credibility of Aylmer's surface, they repeat his error rather than foregrounding it. The critic becomes an accessory to the crime rather than the agent of its discovery.

In contrast to Brooks and Warren's reading, the subtlety of the tale is the psychology of persuasion – the illusion of good form – by which Aylmer is able to rationalize his thoughts, thereby seducing his wife into risking herself. Hawthorne strews the beginning of the tale with clues that there is nothing scientific, nothing rational, nothing idealistic, and nothing selfless about Aylmer's obsession with his wife's minute imperfection. We see that his interest is not scientific because he is anything but detached about it. It is not rational because it is obsessive. It is not idealistic or selfless because only he cares about it. But what Hawthorne offers as irony, Brooks and Warren take seriously, refusing to critique the rationalization of her sacrifice. The complexity Hawthorne offers is Aylmer's bad faith ruse, which Brooks and Warren credit for its good form.

These New Critical aficionados of irony overlook the fact that Aylmer's failure to find adequacy in his "peerless" wife is a failure of imagination *far more grotesque* than Aminadab's hunched back and his commonplace respect for Georgiana's beauty. Thus their reading of the secondary characters duplicates the ironic barbarity of Aylmer's rationalizations. Brooks and Warren blithely flattened Georgiana and Aminadab into props for the Great Man, helping to perfume the sinister depth of Aylmer's sweaty unrest by dismissing Aminadab as having "a rather obvious symbolic reference" but no moral credibility. The irony that Aminadab is right and Aylmer wrong is lost on Brooks and Warren's aestheticism, and so is the point that the most idealistic rhetoric belongs to the real monster of the piece while more superficially flawed or mundane characters are the more moral. That point is too subversive of the hierarchy of civilization, whose peaks must remain shrouded in the Olympian mists of literary sophistication and visionary sacrifices directed by the powerful at the expense of the weak. Rather than unpacking the irony of the secondary characters,

Brooks and Warren remain focused on the Great Man in the center, exonerating the dehumanization of the weak by Aylmer's flawed rationalizations.

Here the notion of invulnerability to irony is most questionable, and most pernicious. In the name of discovering the deeper irony of the tale, Brooks and Warren pretend to save the story from unironic simplicity. But the issue is not that the story lacks irony until they have found it: the problem for Brooks and Warren is that the tale's irony goes against their worldview – it cuts against their preoccupation with the autonomy of sophistication, the triumph of good form over content. The irony of Aylmer's respectability does not make him better than Aminadab despite his crime; it makes him worse despite his lofty sounding intentions.

What has gone so wrong with Brooks and Warren's analysis? At first we might suspect that the principle of literary autonomy – in its no-abstract-statements version – acts as something of a straitjacket for Brooks and Warren. Like Aylmer's preoccupation with Georgiana's birthmark, they cannot live with the possibility that Hawthorne takes the moral of the story seriously. Thus they must seek complexities against the grain. But that explanation does not explain why they seek irony in unconvincing places, ignoring the more dramatically compelling ironies for ironies that weaken the impact. Mere complexity fails to explain their contortions, which have a deeper pattern, and which violate their own principle of irony by substituting a weaker irony for a stronger one. In this resistance to Hawthorne's moral, we find the rigidity of an agenda which is both aesthetic and ideological.

In Brooks and Warren's closing argument against the "impressive moral," rationality suffers mightily in a last rationalization of the Great Man. They begin by setting up a straw man, a false dilemma between passive quietism and killing one's wife in order to make her perfect:

What is the author's attitude toward the moral itself? Is man to give up all his attempts to conquer nature? Would Hawthorne have men settle down into a supine and passive acceptance of what nature gives? A careful reading of the story will suggest that Hawthorne does not take his own moral in these terms ... Most important of all, it should be apparent that Hawthorne is *not interested in having us apply a rule* – he is not interested merely in trying to win our assent to a particular generalization, or in trying to make us adopt a certain course of action ... His total intention, like that of any writer of fiction, is wider than this.

Who thinks that life reduces to a choice between fatalism and risking other people's welfare? Not Hawthorne. This framing of the tale has nothing to do with Hawthorne's attack on the supposed autonomy of intellectual pride except that it shows that Brooks and Warren cannot accept this challenge to literary autonomy.

Be it known: great stories don't have morals. And yet this becomes just another moral, albeit one they do not acknowledge as such. Once again, power disguises itself as something else: as aesthetic transcendence of morality. The moral is that there is no moral; the rule is that there are no rules. In a grand, final irony of literary analysis, the rejection of rules has become the unchallengeable rule, the autonomy of literature has become the autonomy of the work-critic-Great Man against moral liability, and Hawthorne's unpardonable sin has become the essence of literary virtue.

b. Pseudo-liberation: "A rose for Emily"

Other excesses of Brooks and Warren's fear of morality can be found in their commentary on Faulkner's much anthologized "A rose for Emily." Here again, irony is turned against simple moral points at all costs. As we remember, this story tells of the life of a Southern woman of a fading aristocratic lineage who is sheltered by her patriarchal father from her most significant relationship because the man, Homer Baron, is a common laborer. Eventually Homer disappears and the woman's remaining life is perceived as the increasingly eccentric existence of an aging spinster. In the grotesque dénouement that follows her death, the townspeople discover Homer's much attenuated remains in her attic beside which lay a strand of steel grey hair.

One does not have to work too hard to find complexity in this remarkable example of Southern gothic writing. For Brooks and Warren, however, the risk is that Emily will be seen *merely* as grotesque. To do her and the complexity of the story justice, therefore, Brooks and Warren set out to redeem her heroic qualities.

We are reminded, for instance, that it is "Miss Emily's complete detachment which gives her actions their special meaning for the community." No whining Sally, Emily "is the conscious aristocrat ... consciously 'better' than other people ... above and outside their canons of behavior." Brooks and Warren are not naive, of course, noting that she "can, at the same time, be worse than other people; and she *is* worse, horribly so. She is worse than other people, but at the same time, as the narrator implies, she remains somehow admirable." Echoes of Aylmer's demonic yet somehow redeemed possession are unmistakeable. Is this just the unfathomable irony of life again? In fact, Brooks and Warren risk a thematization of this irony:

Perhaps the horrible and the admirable aspects of Miss Emily's final deed arise from the same basic fact of her character: she insists on meeting the world on her own terms ... This independence of spirit and pride can, and does in her case, twist the individual into a sort of monster, but, at the same time, this refusal to accept the herd values carries with it a dignity and courage.

(SS, 56)

Forget Nietzsche and his Overman: America has the Brooks and Warren reading of Faulkner. Forget that Emily slept with the corpse of her lover whom she poisoned with arsenic that she bought with an unflinching poker face at the local drug store: Emily has backbone. Somebody has to get the better of modern American mediocrity.

Brooks and Warren seem to believe that they can redeem Emily with a combination of traditional heroism and moral complexity:

It has been suggested by many critics that tragedy implies a hero who is completely himself, who insists on meeting the world on his own terms, who wants something so intensely, or lives so intensely, that he cannot accept any compromise ... it can be pointed out that, just as the horror of her deed lies outside the ordinary life of the community, so the magnificence of her independence lies outside their ordinary virtues.

Nor is Brooks and Warren's point so unusual. Milton wrote a once popular poem about that theme, in which the "hero" was known to have said "Better to reign in hell than serve in heaven." Of course, that too, was a morally complex work, but its poignantly dramatic form does not, finally, efface the moral.

Why is this woman "somehow admirable"? For Brooks and Warren Emily is, unlike Sally, her own man. Her kind of civil disobedience, unlike Sally's, is redeemed by its commitment to excellence and definitive action, not to wishy-washy complaints that are not clearly outlined. But what Brooks and Warren overlook (perhaps as displaced remnants of the culture whose decadence Emily embodies) is that Emily is not her own woman. As Judith Fetterly has shown with a far closer reading than Brooks and Warren have offered, Emily is not a paradigm of the strong woman or man. She is not a free will at all, but a victim of her society and her father's constraints on her freedom. The grotesqueness of her necrophilia does not indicate a transcendence of her society's values, but is symptomatic of her profound victimage, an ambivalence so perverse that it destroys what is closest to her. Emily's is nihilism with a vengeance; or perhaps we should say nihilism *as* vengeance. What is grotesque is just her failure of transcendence, an irony obscured by Brooks and Warren's own desire for critical transcendence of morality. For again, Brooks and Warren buy into the "redemption" of the demonic as literary complexity and pseudo-aristocratic independence.

The preposterousness of Brooks and Warren's analyses goes to the heart of the theoretical shallowness of New Criticism. First, the notion that great literature is defiantly complex depends on a categorical distinction between irony and simplicity that is subverted by the tension between Brooks and Warren's literature and rhetoric. It puts them in the position of saying that "more is better" in the matter of complexity, a claim which, given the need to retain an organic unity, becomes incomprehensible. Second, even if we assume that great works are complex, one does not know which works are great until one sees how much they really do resist simple morals. One cannot assume that a work is *going to be* complex in one way or another; one must show it to be so. One does not know in advance what is and is not problematic in a work. The point of irony is that nothing may be as it seems, though that argument in any case must be based on analysis, not *a priori* theses about the complexity of life.

By being theoretically inconsistent – poised between an aestheticism of radical irony and a rhetoric of rationality – Brooks and Warren invite a projection of prejudice in the guise of objectivity. Thus irony is suspended for Brooks and Warren when the Great Man's ideals resound in their ears, or when their nostalgia for aristocratic transcendence is threatened by the encroachments of a more simple reality. Having insufficiently theorized the reach of hermeneutic irony, their attempts at closure unwittingly reflect their own limited horizons of theoretical understanding. Although all generalizations are problematized by life's complexity, they believe that people are redeemed by their good form and dreams of superiority. In a world where substantive grounds of meaning have passed into the complexities of form, they would have us believe, good form is the most we can make of a diminished thing.

D. The ironies of literary professionalism

Since deconstruction began questioning the canons of interpretation and the interests they serve, detractors have said much about the anarchy that deconstruction implies, and the professional irresponsibility it fosters. But this hysteria misses the point of deconstruction for both theory and practice. Deconstruction did not invent bad criticism, the problem of meaning, or the sophistication of moral issues. Rather, deconstruction merely shows that these problems can be neither wished away nor domesticated to an aesthetic world of aristocratic privilege, and that pretending to do so is merely a version of what Brooks and Warren have called "rationalization."

Furthermore, it is an illusion to believe that the problems foisted off on deconstruction have been imported from the decadent Old World. As shown above, the transition from irony to power is just as much at home in New Criticism, however obscured by assumptions of aesthetic transcendence. If post-structural formulations seem more remotely theoretical by contrast with New Critical theory, that is because post-structuralist theory shows how those destabilizing possibilities are intrinsic to language, instead of being features of an aesthetic view of literature. It is that shift from an aesthetic to a linguistic ground that invites the unmasking of the aesthetic ideology itself. A more rigorous hermeneutics is thus able to show that the conjunction of Brooks and Warren's aesthetic autonomy and rationalist rhetoric is both an inconsistent oversimplification of each and a product of a belief in a certain kind of indefinable privilege.

To hope to go back to the unproblematic days of "responsible criticism" is a travesty of critical history, which has quite naturally led to the questioning of meaning and power. Such nostalgia is to betray the demand for rigor put forward by the critics of the fifties, and to prefer a comfortable modicum of discipline to the more demanding need to earn rather than presume the autonomy of aesthetic sophistication. It is to prefer wrapping oneself in transcendental ideals without acknowledging the priestly character of one's power. Critics of the politicizing thrust of deconstruction are blaming the messenger for a message they do not want to hear. Yet, in their very resistance to the message, they prove the point of deconstructive criticism: that the separations of rational discourse from the discourse of power, and of literary from non-literary discourse, are constituted separations, separations that mask a system of power as a system of truth.

As witnessed by the current interest and controversy over cultural criticism, the supposed pluralism of American criticism is less secure than previously thought. The problem is in part the naivety of the liberal legacy, the willingness to take pluralism and rationality at face value. But the image is often as shallow as Aylmer's good intentions. True, American criticism has flourished as a strange hybrid of cultural elitists, liberals, and an occasional academic radical. But whether this *pluralism of representations* constitutes proof of a deeper pluralism is as much determined by what it leaves out as by what it includes.

Except in the abstractions of semiotics, representation is not one function, but a complex of functions. Irony is only possible because in the complexity of real language one can say one thing and do another. Social representation is no simpler than language. The trappings of liberalism can dress up a homogenizing system or a hierarchy of power as easily as a rigorous democracy (sometimes more easily). Society is not understood by the form of its symbols but by their operation. Against the evidence of the representatives, the marginal voices of society remain marginal for precisely those reasons legitimated by Brooks and Warren: their marginality is the condition of Greatness made possible by a system that normalizes good form. The point is not that equality is always good, but whether power is always visible. The pluralism of the liberal representations fosters the impression that reason and justice, not power, is the rule of democratic culture. Good form then appears to be natural rather than institutional.

Like the rationalizations of Brooks and Warren, this naturalization of good form always valorizes one kind of complexity while obscuring another, a point that has ideological consequences for the academy. As Brooks and Warren unwittingly show, the hierarchy of good form may foster a sympathy between liberals and elitists, traditionalists and pluralists, to whose hierarchy of good forms radical critics pose a threat. In this alliance, the Western canon defines good form as a spectrum that reaches from aristocratic elitism to representative democracy of a certain abstract, universalized sort. In this coalition, aristocratic sympathies such as Brooks and Warren's can take refuge behind the putative universality of modern liberalism, while modern liberalism can point to its traditionalist elements and the occasional Marxist as proof of its tolerance of diversity. Thus in the interest of not questioning its real depth, the modern Western form of academic liberalism can ignore its elitist tolerances in the name of its pluralist ideal. Liberals become pluralists in the same way that to understand Aylmer is to forgive him.

This complicity of elitist and liberal sympathies is obvious in the concern that today's radical academics are threatening pluralism with a code of political correctness. Like the naivety of those who are shocked to hear that everything is political, the fear that radicals have an agenda overlooks the fact that societies always have laws, and that universities always have codes of good form. To say the least, that is the point of elitism, and it is also the only way liberalism could have advanced its agenda. Likewise, attacks on political correctness by conservatives are hypocritical by virtue of their own professed moralism, and such attacks by liberals falsely suggest that traditional liberalism has no constraints, being pluralistic in some more rarified sense. That academic radicals are acting under the aegis of political correctness, ironically, is merely to take the moralism of traditionalists and the pluralism of liberals more seriously than is normally the case. The political correctness problem does not change the basic terms of academic debate so much as it changes its center of gravity. By putting the politics of the university in a new light it does not politicize what was formerly not political, but rather exposes the politics of what was supposed to be natural, objective, and universal.

Because American critics were raised on the democratic methods of close reading, the criticism of Brooks and Warren could appear less disturbing than it might, no matter how anti-populist. Still, the fact that so many American critics fear the nihilism of deconstruction but not the amoralism of Brooks and Warren shows the lack of theoretical rigor of the American critical legacy, a lack which post-structuralist theory attempts to address. Notwithstanding the *Time* magazine versions of Derrida and Foucault, post-structuralist theory extends the manifestos of Crane, Frye and others to investigate the theoretical grounds of literary authority. The need for this rigor is now obvious in the pioneering work of Brooks and Warren, a corpus acutely ambivalent about the modern, liberal culture in which it finds itself. The price of their undertheorized work is their embodiment of classically American contradictions about equality and the hierarchies of power. Furthermore, they show how America's curious blend of traditionalism and liberalism can resist with torturous persistence the sight of its own limits, thus sustaining the myth of American universality while veiling the consequences of its power.

As Aylmer, Brooks, and Warren show, excessive rationalization did not begin with deconstruction. If nothing else, post-structural thought shows in what direction candor lies, and shows in greater depth where close reading leads. By noting the fictive character of critical strategies, deconstruction encourages greater care in our assumptions about the privileges of the great, the partiality of the norm, and the obscurity of the margins.

6

Foucault's microphysical politics: Big Brother is missing

> I mistrust all systematizers and I avoid them.
> The will to a system is a lack of integrity.   Nietzsche

A. The politics of theory

The problem of Foucault's politics begins with a paradox. On the one hand, Foucault refers to his "hyper- and pessimistic activism" (*FR*, 343), and professes his interest in "the problem of the regime, the politics of the scientific statement" (*FR*, 54), and in the "new 'economy' of power" (*FR*, 61).[1] On the other hand, he shuns "a pre-established political outlook" or "the realization of some definite political project" (*FR*, 375). This apparent ambivalence toward politics grows out of a deeper theoretical ambiguity that traverses much of Foucault's work, identified by Kellner and Best as a litany of unresolved inner tensions:

[Foucault's] work oscillates between totalizing and detotalizing impulses, discursive and bio-politics, destroying the subject and resurrecting it, assailing forms of domination but eschewing normative language and metadiscourse. He sometimes attacks the Enlightenment and modern theory *in toto* while at other times aligning himself with their progressive heritage. His later positions seek a cultivation of the subject in an individualistic mode that stands in tension with the emphasis on political struggle by oppressed groups.[2]

The apparent ambiguity of Foucault's combination of skeptical and emancipatory interests fosters two views of his politics depending on what philosophical and political commitments one brings to his texts.

---

1. References from a number of commentators are drawn from David C. Hoy's *Foucault: a critical reader*, Oxford: Basil Blackwell, 1986.
2. Steven Best and Douglas Kellner, *Postmodern theory: critical investigations*, Basingstoke, Hampshire: Macmillan, 1991; p. 73.

1. The two Foucaults

On one reading, Foucault's histories are taken as local narratives, limited to "always partial and local inquiry" (*FR*, 47), and to *epistémè*-relative perspectives on "a complex system of distinct and multiple elements, unable to be mastered by the powers of synthesis" (*FR*, 94), while his meta-critical remarks are understood as contextually situated claims about past and present practices. This view emphasizes Foucault's belief in "knowledge as perspective" (*FR*, 80), his repudiation of "the metahistorical deployment of ideal significations and indefinite teleologies," as well as "the search for origins" (*FR*, 77) or for "immobile forms that precede the external world of accident and succession" (*FR*, 78). This Foucault spurns the abstract generalizations and causal reductions of idealist histories in favor of "the hazardous play of dominations" (*FR*, 83) with its contradictory origins of knowledge. This Foucault is epistemically local and globally skeptical, seeking only the "contemporary limits of the necessary" (*FR*, 43) and an *effective history* "without constants" (*FR*, 87), eschewing "the universal structures of all knowledge" (*FR*, 46), preferring the concrete analyses of the specific intellectual to the grand ideas of the general intellectual. Presuming only to present a retrospective, genealogical reading of the present, Foucault's histories include a richness of discursive structures, but, given the shifting structures of truth and the dangers of totalizing theory, he seeks only "how effects of truth are produced within discourse which in themselves are neither true nor false" (*FR*, 60), and so does not presume to prescribe for the future. The future, for the skeptical Foucault, privileges no philosophical or political agenda. This Foucault is a *philosophical skeptic*.

According to another reading – the emancipatory Foucault – his work implies an ideal of freedom which he calls upon, hints at, and courts, even if he never formulates it. In light of this other Foucault's interest in "ascertaining the possibility of constituting a new politics of truth" (*FR*, 74), he thinks "that as an enterprise for linking the progress of truth and the history of liberty in a bond of direct relation, [the Enlightenment] formulated a philosophical question that remains for us to consider" (*FR*, 43). Thus he inquires: "How can the growth of capabilities be disconnected from the intensification of power relations?" (*FR*, 48); thus he believes that "a liberation of the act of questioning [from totalizing theories] seemed ... to have played a positive [political] role" (*FR*, 386); thus he urges: "We must open our eyes ... to what enables people there, on the spot, to resist the Gulag, what makes it intolerable for them, and what can give the people of the anti-Gulag the courage to stand up and die in order to be able to utter a word or a poem" (*PK*, 136); thus he claims that "there is indeed always something in the social body, in classes, groups and individuals themselves which in some sense escapes relations of power, something which is by no means a more or less docile or reactive primal matter, but rather a centrifugal movement, an inverse energy, a discharge" (*PK*, 138); thus he claims: "The point, in brief, is to transform the critique conducted in the form of necessary limitation into a practical critique that takes the form of a possible transgression" (*FR*, 45); and thus he seeks "to give new impetus, as far and wide as possible, to the undefined work of freedom" (*FR*, 46). For this Foucault, there is an emancipatory aim of the decentralization of power suggestive of a kind of *political anarchism*.[3]

As a number of critics have noted, these two strains are not merely complementary. For his critics, the ethical commitments of the emancipatory Foucault require more substantive foundations, more theoretical coherence than the skeptical Foucault appears to allow, without which his ideal of freedom appears to be arbitrary, if not vacuous. Moreover, the emancipatory Foucault, especially in his later incarnation, is prone to appeal to epistemic generality and invariance when he needs it, as when he advocates a "substantive" form of resistance or when he enumerates the possible analytics of power. By virtue of the coherence of the technologies of the self, of the progress in subjectification implied by the improved disciplinary techniques of the modern period, and by certain invariant discursive structures in the ontologies of truth, power, and value, Foucault more than faintly hints at the elements of a pragmatic epistemology and ethics that presuppose more substance than the skeptical Foucault's historical relativism would seem able or concerned to warrant. Hence, a tension between the emphatic foundational austerity of the skeptic and the presuppositions of the critic of domination.

Given the fact that Foucault's work was admittedly in the process of its own development, how does one reconcile or at least explain

---

3. In response to an observation by Cheney Ryan, my usage of the term "anarchism" does not reflect the nineteenth century usage. Rather, mine refers to the etymological meaning, no privileged principle, in light of Foucault's hostility toward totalities, generalities, and collectivities.

these tensions? Given the anarchism of the skeptical Foucault, the Nietzschean enemy of rational systems, how much coherence can be expected? His defenders appeal to this skepticism and to his revisions to shield him from expectations of programmatic commitment and excessive systematicity. But such defenses often overlook his own inner continuity from archeology to genealogy and ethics, and may pose a false dilemma between advocating a general political program and undercutting the very possibility of non-arbitrary critical grounds. This objection can be put genealogically: by what warrant do his more radical defenders provide only a selective account, appealing to the Nietzschean Foucault while ignoring the neo-Kantian Foucault that survives his oscillations between theory and history? A more thorough genealogy of Foucault may reveal unreconciled debts to Kant, Hegel, Marx, and Nietzsche. By the standard of the "effective historical" explanation that genealogy presupposes, these tensions disturb the authority which Foucault claims for his "ontology of the present."

Foucault's conflicted emancipatory interest invites comparison with the work of the Frankfurt School.[4] On the one hand, the emancipatory Foucault shares their interest in the critique of domination and in the problem of practice. On the other hand, Foucault's skeptical and aesthetic-individualist debts to Nietzsche function to remystify the linkage between theory and practice that the Frankfurt School hoped to clarify by the project of critical theory as the critique of domination. Finally, though Foucault adds some quite useful historical material to their legacy, his theoretical conundrums appear to problematize the project of emancipatory theory at its root, reducing his pessimistic activism to a curious sort of utopian despair.

2. The critique of ideology

The unmasking intent of critical theory challenges the emancipatory interest of Foucault's work, and reveals his mixed blessing for critical theory. Central to the legacy of the Frankfurt School is its critique of bourgeois ideology, unmasking capitalism's promotion of a submissive attitude toward inequality and exploitation. Foucault too is sensitive

4. This comparison does not assume a homogeneity among the Frankfurt School theorists, but only a characteristic community on enough points – including the validity of an ideal theorization of society – to allow for comparison with Foucault's more anarchistic formulations. See Chapter 8 for further comparisons.

to this issue of masking and unmasking. Of idealist histories, he claims that "this demagoguery [of unconflicted, continuous history], of course, must be masked. It must hide its singular malice under the cloak of universals" (*FR*, 91). Of sovereignty, Foucault points to the fact that "the essential function of the discourse and techniques of right has been to efface the domination intrinsic to power" (*PK*, 95), so that the theory of sovereignty served to "conceal [the] actual procedures" of the system of right (*PK*, 105). Likewise, he intends his own *Discipline and punish* to be "a genealogy of the present scientifico-legal complex from which the power to punish derives its bases, justifications, and rules; from which it extends its effects and by which it masks its exorbitant singularity" (*FR*, 170).

The theoretical issue of emancipatory validity and effectiveness, however, turns on the *grounds* of such critical strategies of unmasking. If all knowledge claims are historically relative, interested, conflicted, and temporary – as Hegelians, Marxists, and Foucault all agree – then where does one stand to critique a historical epoch and design a new social strategy? Why isn't unmasking merely redescription? What confers truth upon a given social agenda or a utopian preference for progress?

The Frankfurt School remained somewhat flexible (if not inconsistent) and guardedly optimistic about finding grounds for critique. While often eschewing the confidence of Habermas' transcendental pragmatics and orthodox Marxist workerism, the Frankfurt School theorists were disposed to follow Hegel in theorizing a historical rationality of society taken as a whole, an ideal human potential that indicates the emancipatory significance of history's conflicting elements. In Horkheimer's words, "through the cognition of the conditional [nature] of every view ... limited knowledge is ... taken up as limited, one-sided and isolated into the total system of truth."[5] For Adorno, this totality is not grounded subjectively, but in "a constellation of interactions" (Held, 217). Marcuse, furthermore, stressed the *potentiality* of this ideal whole, suggesting that it is by comparison with society's unrealized potentialities that the contradictions of society are judged: "Something is true if it is what it can be, fulfilling all its objective possibilities" (Held, 232). This hypothetically ideal inner unity of the social whole allows for an *immanent critique* of

---

5. David Held, *Introduction to critical theory: Horkheimer to Habermas*, Berkeley: University of California Press, 1980; pp. 176–7; hereafter referred to as "Held".

society's reactionary elements by revealing them as factionally interested obstacles to progress. The evolving, ideal integrity of the social whole, therefore, is the Frankfurt School's answer to the historical relativity they themselves supposed to condition all knowledge and values.

Foucault, by contrast, calls the authority of the social totality into doubt, which is his reason for distancing himself from general intellectuals and the programmatic terms of traditional political practice: "I believe precisely that the forms of totalization offered by politics are always, in fact, very limited. I am attempting, to the contrary, apart from any *totalization* – which would be at once *abstract* and *limiting* – to *open up* problems that are as *concrete* and *general* as possible" (*FR*, 375). In a methodological vein, Foucault refers to "the inhibiting effect of global, *totalitarian theories*" (*PK*, 80), only to conclude that "the attempt to think in terms of a totality has in fact proved a hindrance to research" (*PK*, 81). Since Foucault takes totalizing theory to be intrinsically reductive, he understands the epistemic and emancipatory value of theory to lie in hermeneutic foregrounding and in discovering the questionability of claims to political legitimacy. Thus, "my attitude ... is more on the order of 'problematization' – ... thoughts that seem to me to pose problems for politics" (*FR*, 384). Previous political theories sought to discover privileged principles of order; for Foucault, however, the point is to exchange them for local practices.

This coincidence of epistemological and political localism has led a number of his more enthusiastic defenders to believe that his aggressive localism is consistent with his work as a whole, including its archeological and genealogical components. I believe this is an error, however, for the issue is not whether Foucault's epistemology and politics both profess localism, but whether they can effectively sustain their claims on only local grounds. In neither the foundationist nor the political sense, finally, is the case for localism made as definitively as is sometimes suggested by Foucault and his defenders. And with good reason: a deep defense of localism would require a totalizing theory, landing Foucault in the performative contradiction of generalizing against generalities.

So Foucault never resolves, or even fully addresses, the theoretical contraction to local activity; he merely *advocates* it. But this troubles his discursive authority in two ways. First, regarding the grounds of knowledge Foucault repeatedly appeals to (e.g. his ontology of the present, his archeology of discursive conditions). Second, Foucault simply assumes that resistance to domination can only be, or is most effective when, carried out individually. His anti-holism is epistemically already contradicted and undertheorized.

Foucault's anti-theoretical condition is not an unusual one. A genealogical reading shows that Foucault, like many postmodernists, takes theoretical *generality* to imply theoretical *reduction*. This error puts him in the position of denying the scope of his own theorizing.[6] Based as it is on his post-Kantian confusion of generality with reduction, this anti-holism misunderstands and prematurely dismisses the theoretical preconditions of both a critique of domination and an emancipatory praxis.

True, Foucault is able in spite of this epistemological inconsistency to supplement in specific and illuminating ways the Frankfurt School's interest in the mechanisms of hegemony, as Barry Smart has argued (Hoy, 1986), while also avoiding their sometimes premature reification of the ideologized subject. For this reason, Foucault must be counted among those critics of domination and theoretical reduction who have advanced our understanding of the colonization of the lifeworld. On the other hand, Foucault's selective interest in political theory neglects, if not mystifies, the accountability of the agents of state and class, a level of analysis Foucault obscures between his attention to the ultimate discursive (hypersystemic) conditions of power and his final Nietzschean individualism.[7]

B. Politics: problematizing or mystifying?

In some respects the Frankfurt School foreshadowed some of Foucault's most characteristic insights as in Adorno's phrase, "enlightenment is totalitarian." Indeed, Foucault refines his predecessors' insights genealogically – through the ironic failures and perversions of liberal and communist ideals of emancipation in the practices of disciplinary culture. Still, the radical nature of Foucault's skepticism

---

6. Alternatively, only a revisionary theory of foundations could sustain the kinds of claims to which the emancipatory Foucault commits himself, especially in the final works. The neo-Kantian Foucault moves in that direction, but is jeopardized by the Nietzschean skeptic.
7. At points Foucault appears to admit the continued relevance of class and state. But his localism seems to have made a deeper impression on some of his followers than the more moderate observations.

generates contradictions that inhibit the progressive character of these insights. These theoretical inhibitions take both subjective and objective forms.

Subjectively considered, Foucault's work raises the problem of how the subject could know of its entrapment within its discursive conditions. The ubiquity of these discursive conditions appears to suggest that any putative escape from the system of power only leads to newer, perhaps subtler constraints. History leads "from domination to domination." In this case emancipation would be illusory, a mere effect of consciousness, for if we are necessarily victims of the current epistemic blindness, then Foucault's individualistic choices between techniques of the self are less emancipatory than solipsistic.

This questioning of any claims to depth and progress jeopardizes the meaningfulness of his own interest in "thinking differently." Specifically, it raises the issue of how his late studies in techniques of the self are not always already *too* late, always discovering insignificant differences: if history is the fall of civilization into progressively more subtle means of domination, how important can the Greeks be to us? Discovery of past techniques of self-invention may be, if not must be, irrelevant to current techniques of domination. Foucault admits that we cannot assume the superiority of Greek ethics – since "everything is dangerous" – but he characteristically refrains from providing a criterion of dangerousness.

Logically considered, furthermore, Foucault's discursive conditions of power are *formally* deeper than his individualistic aesthetic freedom – in the Kantian sense of providing pragmatic conditions for the "constitution of knowledges, discourses, domains of objects, etc." Just because these conditions are supposed to be prior to consciousness – i.e. because they are constitutive rather than voluntary or repressive – our deliberate self-fashioning is necessarily within their socially defined parameters. Given the deepening subtlety of the technology of control, the hypersystemic nature of these power/knowledge structures is the more likely to be unchanged by the individualistic, intentional nature of his ethics of the self. With this mismatching between the levels of the discursive power and the techniques of self-invention, this late theoretical turn to individualism begs the political questions Foucault raised earlier by failing to specify what sorts of change are not "empty dreams" of "our impatience for liberty."

Unfortunately for emancipation, Foucault's archeology threatens a "historically *a priori*" argument against his advocacy of resistance and self-creation.[8] For despite his turn from archeological theorizing to genealogical history, Foucault's critique of domination and his calls for a praxis of resistance merely overleap the residual apriorism of the archeology.

How, then, should the critic assess this contradiction in Foucault's attention to the critique of domination?

1. The problem of the variety of power

I sympathize with critics such as Charles Taylor who argue that Foucault's theory of power is incoherently divided between the variety of his insights and the narrowness of his professed methodology of localism and ascending analysis.[9] They are correct,

8. Foucault's late reconciliation with his Kantian heritage comes too late to address this issue of foundations: while Foucault is content to presuppose his three axes of ethical self-constitution, he has not explicated the kind of overall theory which could legitimate such Kantian presuppositions, nor do they solve or even identify the problems of collective domination ignored by the Nietzschean-skeptical Foucault.

9. Charles Taylor suggests that there is a discrepancy between the premises of Foucault's critique and what he appears to conclude from it. On Taylor's reading, Foucault's theory of power rests on three points:

(1) power without a subject –

This point derives from Foucault's search for the conditions of power, "a form of history which can account for the constitution of knowledges, discourses, domains of objects, etc., without having to make reference to a subject which is either transcendental in relation to the field of events or runs in its empty sameness throughout the course of history" (FR, 59). There is a kind of historicist-pragmatic relativity here, insofar as Foucault insists on "seeing historically how effects of truth are produced within discourses which in themselves are neither true nor false" (FR, 60). Though historical, these conditions are deeply constitutive in the sense that "it doesn't only weigh on us as a force that says no, but that it traverses and produces things, it induces pleasure, forms knowledge, produces discourse. It needs to be considered as a productive network that runs through the whole social body" (FR, 61).

(2) power only ascends –

As Foucault admits, his method intends to invert the standard hierarchically descending causal models of social science: i.e. the political scientific method "since the Middle Ages" of assuming the collective juridical power of sovereignty; and reductive Marxist economism, which presumes to explain everything in terms of the global class-struggle. Instead, Foucault argues, "One must rather conduct an *ascending* analysis of power, starting, that is, from its infinitesimal mechanisms, which each have their own tactics, and then see how these mechanisms of power each have been – and continue to be – invested, utilized,

furthermore, to maintain that Foucault's dismissal of theories of state and class is not made good by what he offers instead, notwithstanding his critique of their reductive versions. Nor are these flaws unconnected: for in the interest of avoiding totalizing theories, Foucault falls into a new apriorism of ascending power, a methodological limit which determines his new priorities of specific intellectuals and local critique. The problem for Foucault is that power does not *only* ascend from micro-events; rather, the point is to see how power both ascends micro-physically and descends globally.[10]

involuted, transformed, displaced, extended, etc., by ever more general mechanisms and by forms of global domination" (*PK*, 99).

(3) contextual causality –

This third point Taylor draws from Foucault's remark that relations of power are at once intentional and nonsubjective, and the claim that "the coherence of [a genealogy] does not derive from the revelation of a project, but from the logic of opposing strategies" (*PK*, 61). Against patterned, idealist historiography, the Nietzschean legacy echoes in Foucault's notion of a history constituted by antagonism, discontinuity, and chance. Foucault joins Nietzsche in repudiating idealist subjectifications of historical unities in favor of the blind accumulation of coincident wills, giving the moment a "character" that is at once beyond all subjects and the product of their wills to power, i.e. a "purposefulness without purpose." Against standard analyses of state and class power, therefore, Foucault can argue: "power is exercised rather than possessed; it is not the 'privilege,' acquired or preserved, of the dominant class, but the overall effect of its strategic positions" (*FR*, 174). Hence, contextual causality.

While Taylor finds each of these theses at least potentially illuminating, he also suggests that Foucault may pretend to explain more than he does, at least undertheorizing the relation between his principles. On closer analysis, Taylor argues, the conjunction of the three reveals the incompatibility of their explanatory powers. The problem is that for any one of these points to explain the undesigned systematicity Foucault posits, it appears necessary to transgress one of the other principles. They cannot, therefore, all be prerequisite principles of a Foucaultian method. Taylor concludes that "purposefulness without purpose requires a certain kind of explanation to be intelligible" (Hoy, 87), i.e. "all patterns have to be made *intelligible* in relation to conscious action" (Hoy, 88), and that "Foucault not only does not meet this requirement; it is difficult to see how he could without abandoning some or other part of his declared position." If these principles of genealogical analysis are not mutually compatible, therefore, we want to know their proper critical relations.

10. Indeed, this duplicity is just what Foucault implies when he seeks to discover "how these [microphysical] mechanisms of power have been ... invested, transformed, displaced, extended etc., by ever more general mechanisms and by forms of global domination" (*PK*, 99). That is, only when one sees how ascending forms of power accompany *descending* forms of power do we understand the objects of politics and political economy.

Foucault's fear of totalizing theory – his holophobia – prescribes "the essentially local character of criticism … an autonomous, non-centralized kind of theoretical production" (*PK*, 81), a postmodern reduction that will obscure the general mechanisms of global domination to which ascending power leads. True, it must be granted that Foucault's privileging of ascending analyses of power is heuristically intended to counterbalance traditional political and political economic analysis, but the price of this new priority is too high for critics of the New World Order. Indeed, this methodological pseudo-revolution systematically effaces the determinacy specific to political economy – the complicity of state mechanisms and class interest – and contradicts Foucault's own heterology of methods.[11]

Foucault's thesis of the heterogeneous character of power relations rightly advocates a "variety of tools" for analyzing the various fields of power relations. Such tools include Foucault's ascending ladder of power and praxis – from the microcosmic to the multinational; or his three axes that constitute experience – the historical ontologies of truth, power, and ethics.[12] Seeking terms by which to unpack Foucault's own discourse, I appeal to this variety and propose a different ladder of pragmatic conditions that ranges through practices of increasing generality of agency, a possibility which Foucault undertheorizes. At the top are the most conscious and specific rules of practice; at the bottom are the most general and the most formally presupposed:

(1) techniques of self-discipline: self-invention (e.g. techniques to cultivate pleasure, will power, conscience, etc.)

---

11. It must be allowed, of course, that Foucault's histories do significantly *complement* accounts of the state and class by revealing the reductions of economism and traditional assumptions about sovereignty. The problem is that Foucault's privileging local criticism over global theories suggests the obsolescence of collectivist theories of domination rather than their incompleteness. For a fuller accounting of social determinacy showing the proper relation between his and more traditional critical theories, we need an archeological view of Foucault's analyses and the "whole order of levels of different types of events, differing in amplitude, chronological breadth, and capacity to produce effects" (R, 56).

12. Foucault's archeological critique reacts against the traditional reductions of "serious" epistemic claims to purely formal grounds (e.g. Kant) or to the more standard appeals to the intentions of social actors. Foucault's alternative aim is to discover the mechanics of discursive legitimation, an autonomous level of pragmatic-systemic self-constitution where legitimacy authorizes itself independent of authorial intention and reference to a "real world."

(2) specific public rules: positive law (e.g. poor laws, trade regulation, inheritance taxes, campaign procedures, rules of tenure, etc.)

(3) institutional systems: historical systems of power (e.g. divine right of kings, corporate capitalism, social democracy, academic freedom, etc.)

(4) foundational presuppositions: epochal rationalities (e.g. medieval sacramentalism, seventeenth century mirroring, eighteenth century scientism, evolutionary history, etc.)

(5) purely formal presuppositions: semiotic conditions (e.g. mathematics, formal logic, semiotics, Foucault's three axes "that constitute experience," etc.)

This is one possible axis of levels of events that differ "in amplitude, chronological breadth, and capacity to produce effects." Obviously, the fifth level posits a depth of *a priori* formality that Foucault ignores in his archeology, but which underlies his late ontologies of the present. But whether these are Foucault's own terms is not as important an issue as their significance for Foucault's archeological plotting of "statements," the historical-pragmatic network of discursive conditions of legitimacy. What do these levels tell us about the discursive conditions of power?[13]

2. Some theoretical conflations

When one looks at Foucault's articulation of determinacy and liberty, one finds two privileged termini of Foucaultian articulation, the two extremes of specificity and generality of practices. Archeology delves to the historical-formal conditions of objectification and subjectifi-

---

13. My reference to his late return to individual intentions and neo-Kantian conditions suggests the failure and abandonment of that conception of archeology. But the effects of the archeological ideal linger in his animus against totalizing theories in an intrinsically contradictory fashion. Foucault's interest in genealogy and the human sciences keeps him situated in what Dreyfus and Rabinow call "the middle domain between everyday nondiscursive practices and the formalizable disciplines" (*Michel Foucault: beyond structuralism and hermeneutics*, University of Chicago, 1982, 58), though the failure of his archeological ideal means that his explanations do finally bifurcate to hypersystemic and individualistic grounds. Unfortunately, this leaves a doubly contradictory legacy: his anti-global animus blocks a complete methodology of the middle range of social determinacy (i.e. political economy), and his anti-depth animus blocks a genuine confrontation with the foundational problems of formality and objectivity, whose authority he is forced to assume when needed. Thus, Foucault is forced to presuppose theoretical baggage he hoped to have surpassed, as a genealogical analysis of his claims shows.

cation, the discursive conditions of the *epistémè* where systematicity is preconscious and constitutive. At the other extreme, the final Foucault explores the differing techniques of self-invention that may allow us to think differently. Generally viewed, it appears that Foucault's archeological constitution of determinacy and liberty *polarizes* between collective pragmatic conditions of sense and value, and individual choices about self-creation.

Against localism, this means that his theory is general in at least two senses. First, his focus covers the range of abstraction and generality between formal categories and individual choices, between deep epistemological claims and aesthetic choices about self-invention. Second, Foucault's analysis to conditions adheres to the necessity (at least within the *epistémè*) that the more general rules constitute the more specific practices. This is the presumption, anyway, of his claim that his ontology of the present articulates the three axes "that constitute experience." The late Foucault, in other words, seeks to make his peace with Kant and Nietzsche at the same time.

Given his hostility to totalizing theories, however, we must ask: why privilege these extreme levels of determinacy and agency, this curious mixture of the very general and the very specific, the epistemically foundational and the individual? How does such a privilege reflect Foucault's preference for the specific intellectual rather than the general one? How does *this* totalizing theory except itself from its own delegitimating skepticism?

Typical of universalizing theories, theories of state and class structure have fostered the colonization of power and difference. Within the fields of traditional political theory and modern political-economic theory, sovereignty and class structure functioned as privileged concepts, thereby inviting explanatory reductions that obscured the variety of power relations. In both cases, in fact, theoretical privilege has been complicit with the real dynamics of power which they concealed by exclusion and rationalization, legitimating the centralization of power in the name of universalized ideals of freedom. Given Foucault's stated hostility to such uses of the liberal juridical and Marxist economistic models of power, it follows that his attention would turn from the middle level of determinacy both upwards and downwards, i.e. from the levels that constitute state and class structures to the other forms of power relations.

But despite these sound motives for his suspicions of general theories and his advocacy of local criticism, Foucault has failed to reconcile his own general theorizing with his critique of totalizing theories and his rubric of localism. Thus Foucault's notion of totality remains undertheorized.

First, though Foucault's discourse constitutes a view of power as heterological and historically constituted, that only means that his is not a *reductive* view: it is still global in its implications. That is, Foucault's theories of the discursive conditions of power say as much about the logical conditions of power as they do about history. It is finally this theoretical depth that guarantees their startlingly wide application and subtle comprehensiveness. Allowing that they are situated in the historical *epistémè* does not refute their formal generality. Denying their seriousness – i.e. bracketing their claims to epistemic depth – does not vitiate the possibility that they might be general in a pragmatic way. Foucault's own virtues require a way to distinguish reductive forms of generality and totality from his own.

Foucault's archeology, in other words, shows the need to distinguish the uses and the abuses of totality, for his own work embodies an emancipatory form of theoretical generality. Here Foucault falls prey to one of his own generalities: "My point is not that everything is bad, but that everything is dangerous" (*FR*, 343). That being true, it follows that overall theories and totalities are not necessarily bad, but – just like everything else – dangerous. That totalizing theories may be, if not necessary evils, necessary dangers is implied by the generality of Foucault's residual archeological apparatus. Thus Foucault's revolutionary localism lands him in the contradiction of not being able to theorize his own authority except by being a general intellectual.

The result of Foucault's conflicted prohibition against overall theories is a characteristic postmodern failure to make two kinds of distinctions between theories: between the general and the reductive analysis, and between analytic and prescriptive generality. On the first point, Foucault's theory of the heterogeneous relations of power is a *general* theory intended to block reductions to general principles, though it too becomes *reductive* when he privileges local criticism over global criticism. On the second point, Foucault's theory claims an *analytic* generality in the sense of specifying conditions of possible critique and possible actions; but it is not *prescriptive* in the political sense of asserting a general plan of action. Failing to make these distinctions, Foucault's localism confuses the import of his own project in an anti-foundational contradiction.

For Foucault's analytic purposes (an analysis to conditions of systemic relations of power) the reality of the collective, the totality, or the framework has the critical significance of constituting or identifying "the more general mechanisms ... of global domination" that emerge from the ascent of power, and as such are part of the critique of domination. Foucault appeals to this constitutive and epistemic generality when he theorizes "the regimes of truth," the new "economy" of power, or the "historical framework" which would allow him "to see how these problems [of conditions of possibility, modalities, and constitution] could be resolved" (*FR*, 58). This constitutive and epistemic range and depth allows him to claim that "the individual which power has constituted is at the same time its vehicle" (*PK*, 98); or that "power is exercised rather than possessed; it is not the 'privilege,' acquired or preserved, of the dominant class, but the overall effect of its strategic positions" (*FR*, 174). Foucault could not theorize this "overall effect" if his were not an overall theory. But given his indiscriminate animus against generalized totalities, Foucault does not distinguish between theoretical generality and reduction.

Paradoxically, a heterological foundationism such as Foucault's wants to be general precisely in order to repudiate his target theories. That is, his theory critiques reductive theories of sovereignty and class so powerfully only because it is so general that they cannot escape its implications. But there is a productive and an unproductive way to unpack this paradox. The wrong way attempts to deny the generality of *all* theoretical conditions, whether reductive or not. Foucault's interests are served by a non-reductive notion of generality. This latter tactic requires not the repudiation of generality – a self-contradictory concept – but the complementarity of general and local. This latter stance allows an immanent critique of reductive foundationism.

Furthermore, Foucault's fear of totalizing theories conflates *analytic* generality of conditions with the *prescriptive* generality of repression and discipline. If, as Foucault has said, there is no power without resistance, then analytic generality does not entail domination insofar as it precedes the resistance of the subject. Likewise, it is the point of archeology and genealogy to discover general conditions of the practices of power to make them available to critique. Foucault's diatribe against totalizing theories, then, must be confined to prescriptive rather than analytic versions. In fact, it is to such analytic generality that Foucault must appeal when he intends to make techniques of self-invention available for thinking differently across epistemic boundaries. Such generality is, by necessity, a condition of such trans-historical availability.

3. The price of undertheorization

These confusions have two consequences detrimental to the critique of domination: confusion about the roles of totalizing theory and the general intellectual, and confusion about the causal status of the state and class structure in the institutions of power.

First, Foucault's failure to make the distinction between critical and prescriptive generality vitiates his *methodological* objection to totalizing theories of the state and class, insofar as analytic theories need only *identify* the existence of collective power without either legitimating its representatives or prescribing collective actions. Totalizing theories, that is, may provide a purely diagnostic function. Foucault admits this when he concedes: "It is not that these global theories have not provided nor continue to provide in a fairly consistent fashion useful tools for local research: Marxism and psychoanalysis are proofs of this" (*PK*, 80–1). But rather than specify the limits of local criticism or the better uses of totalizing theories, Foucault only insists that their use be "put in abeyance, or at least curtailed, divided, overthrown, caricatured, theatricalized, or what you will." Foucault, that is, cannot take generality *seriously*.

The second problem concerns the new priority (inverted hierarchy) of local criticism and the specific intellectual. Foucault seeks the discursive conditions of "general mechanisms of global domination," but assumes that they can be discovered by ascending analysis, i.e. an analysis of how the cumulative effects of the microphysics of power rise to more general levels of substantial power. But to assume the sufficiency of this method is merely the inductivist error of the empiricist, the error of assuming that causality is merely the accumulation of monadic or local events. If, besides mere aggregates, there are real wholes in social determinacy – whether linguistic, economic, or juristic – cumulative or ascending analysis won't discover them, since as real wholes they are not reducible to the sum of their parts. As we will examine in greater detail below, this error is the site of Foucault's methodological displacement of political economy and the critique of domination.

For the critique of domination in general, this methodological blindspot results in Foucault's much discussed undertheorization of *agency* in power. Numerous critics have been understandably disconcerted by Foucault's apparent dissolution of social agency into self-constituting systems of power, where all acting members are equally vehicles of the system: e.g. "power is exercised rather than possessed; it is not the 'privilege,' acquired or preserved, of the dominant class" (*FR*, 174). Given the scale of levels of discursive determinacy, this is at best a hyperbolic partial truth whose partiality lies in Foucault's polarized attention between his archeology's mechanisms and his late ethics' individualist determinations. What gets lost in between is obvious: though in one sense we are all victims of the system, some are more victimized than others, some have more choices than others, and the winners aren't reluctant to systematically enhance their advantages. If Foucault's hyper-systematicity explains the discursive possibility of systemic advantages, it does not account for the possibility of systematic exploitation of positional advantages within these systems, a possibility which depends on the character of the system as a whole, and the relative positions within it.[14]

On the issue of totalizing theories, in sum, Foucault's promotion of individualist ethics and discursive foundationism rests on an untheorized methodological privilege, since his objection to totalizing theories turns out (1) to be contradicted by his own generalizing practices, and (2) to be a misleading reduction of analytic theories to reductive explanations and prescriptive political programs.

But given Foucault's powerful historical depictions of the rise of modern systems of control, are not these objections mere theoretical hair-splitting? No. Unhappily for critical theory, Foucault's theoretical confusion (of generality-reduction and analysis-prescription) and methodological reduction (of analysis to ascending forms of power) obscure the most *active* of all resistances to his own individualist

---

14. Nor are Foucault's methodological prescriptions merely passive regarding this omission: his animus against totalizing theory and his preference for local criticism repress the only terms in which it could be understood. By his campaign against totalizing theories, Foucault mystifies the level at which class interest is determined by the totality of market conditions, where global and local strategies intersect, where legal rationality and class irrationality coincide, where purposeless purposes are achieved, i.e. the level of political economy. Foucault's local criticism thus systematically obscures class advantage within institutionalized domination both as a collective cause of social structure, and as a possible target of political action. This, of course, is why his version of political economy appears to some of his readers to suggest the inevitability of domination and political paralysis.

emancipation. For by privileging blind systemic control and individual choice, Foucault mystifies the institutionalization of interested domination. By focusing on discursive conditions and individualist techniques of determinacy Foucault may bring significant aesthetic choices to individual consciousness; but by obscuring the collective origins of resistance to liberty (i.e. state and class resistances), Foucault occults the *resistance to resistance* that critical theory needs to discover.

C. The ghost in the Foucaultian machines

The tension between Foucault's anti-holism and his desire for resistance can be further specified in terms of the problem of collective action and social formation, a problem which requires conceptualizing fields of power and the relations between its members. Clearly, Foucault suspects theories of collective action insofar as they suggest that the interests of all can be reasonably determined in advance: "The problem is, precisely, to decide if it is actually suitable to place oneself within a 'we' in order to assert the principles one recognizes and the values one accepts; or if it is not, rather, necessary to make the future formation of a 'we' possible, by elaborating the question. Because it seems to me that the 'we' must not be previous to the question" (*FR*, 385). Fine; let us formulate no "we" without taking contexts and personal histories into account. The question still remains, however, about what allows us to decide on the suitability of the "we." Does Foucault's localism make it easier or harder to decide on the suitability of a "we" even with such considerations in mind?

Insofar as all collectivizing theories are taboo, Foucault's position makes it harder: because every "we" is a collective theory of action, a theory of overall effects in the context of a whole. Thus, to decide on the suitability of a "we," we need at least two stages of totalizing theory.

We need first an *analytic* theory of the collective insofar as determination of even individual interests depends on the total shape of the field of power. One cannot strategize atomistically merely by considering one's dyadic relation to other individuals as individuals: for then one could not anticipate their coalitions. When one adds the dyads, one finds that their characters change in light of the whole. The battle one fights as an army is different from the battle one fights in a brawl; the deal one cuts as a union member is different from the deal one cuts alone. The wholeness of the whole, that is, is more than the sum of its parts; the whole has its own reality. Likewise, strategy depends on knowledge of the whole configuration of all members of the field.

Only in light of an analytic theory of the whole context can the suitability of a collective theory of action be considered, since it depends on the possible coincidence of individual interests as determined by the total field of relations. The prescription of collective interests is an inference from the whole back to the individual's interests to which it is dynamically related. For example, it may be that today the most ecologically irresponsible mutual investment funds yield the best short-term returns just because they are an undeveloped market. But perhaps if everyone invested in long-term, ecologically sustainable investments, short-term, unsustainable advantages would decline, making short- *and* long-term interests coincide. Such considerations, however, depend on theories of collective action that theorize totalities of possible actions (e.g. assuming a finite field of investment parameters), not merely as accumulations of independent, local intentions. Such considerations, that is, must be strategic. Without an allowance for a theory of global constraints, Foucault's individualism falls prey to the shallowness of previous individualisms.

There is, however, another defense of Foucault's anti-holism that the Foucaultian could bring forward. Foucault, he might argue, does not discredit all theoretical wholes, but merely wholes whose influence *descends* through the relations of power in totalitarian fashion, whether as sovereign state or vanguard party. Foucault himself, he counters, offers the more emancipatory route to knowledge of systems of power: through analysis of power's ascending influence from specific microphysical sites of action. Indeed, this appears to be Foucault's view at points. I suggest, however, that it does not cohere as a political strategy just because it rests on the erroneous inductivist-methodological assumption that ascending analysis is sufficient to discover the fields of power and domination. Here Foucault comes head to head with Marx: for Marxist economist reduction is one of Foucault's primary targets, whereas Marxist political economy depends on a theory of the operative power of the total field of commodity relations. Thus the Marx-Foucault issue goes to the heart of Foucault's attempted revolution in the study of institutional power.

1. Standing Marx on his head

Liberal legalism and Marxist economism, for Foucault, turn out to be offspring of the same error: totalizing theory. According to Foucault, the contract is the crux of modern theories of state and market power, and the link between juridical and economistic reductions of the relations of power to homogeneous fields.

Foucault notes that in legalism "power is taken to be a right, which one is able to possess like a commodity, and which one can in consequence transfer or alienate, either wholly or partially, through a legal act" (*PK*, 88). In this contractarian view, social power is "that concrete power which every individual holds [by virtue of] a legal transaction involving a contractual type of exchange," a view that fosters analogies "between power and commodities, power and wealth" (*PK*, 88). Both capitalistic and legalistic liberalisms, that is, make power a totality of contractual events, but do so by falsely assuming the adequacy of the contractual model of power, as if the conscious will of the contractor were an adequate representation of the diverse relations of power.

In Marxism, on the other hand:

> there is ... an economic functionality of power ... present to the extent that power is conceived primarily in terms of the role it plays in the maintenance simultaneously of the relations of production and of a class domination which the development and specific forms of the forces of production have rendered possible. (*PK*, 88)

Marxism, that is, subordinates individual contracting to a total economic pattern or structure of power which constitutes the primary social factor. Thus legalism and economism each practice a kind of totalizing theory: legalism theorizes the system of right that formally legitimates the individual contract, while Marxist economism theorizes the economic structure that explains the total configuration of social power. The former yields an ideally reductive juridical totality, the latter a holistically reductive economic totality.

Economism, in this view, includes all reductively totalitarian "models of functional subordination or formal isomorphism that will characterise the interconnection between politics and the economy" (*PK*, 89). Against the reduction of power to economic interests, however, Foucault wants to ask: "is power always in a subordinate position relative to the economy? ... is power modelled upon the commodity? Is it something that one possesses, acquires, cedes through force or contract, that one alienates or recovers, that circulates, that voids this or that region?" (*PK*, 89). Foucault's hypersystemic and heterological theory of power – as something so varied and so prior that it constitutes even the possibility of agency and intention – suggests otherwise. Furthermore, against a homogeneous field of power relations, Foucault wants to posit the heterology of power, requiring "varying tools in its analysis – even ... when we allow that it effectively remains ... profoundly enmeshed in and with economic relations and participates with them in a common circuit" (*PK*, 89).

For Foucault, Marxism remains too close to Hegel when it assumes there is a materialist rationality to history. Marxist political economy's suggestion of an essential, formalizable relation between political and economic mechanisms of power commits the fallacy of totalizing theory. Instead, Foucault's heterology of power implies that political economy is not a science defined by a generic object, but by chance hybrids of different relations of power, with their differing kinds of forces and strategies. Typically, Foucault's martial image of the political terrain suggests the *irrational* confluence of political and economic relations. As a kind of Nietzschean motif, Foucault reiterates his version of Clausewitz' maxim: politics is war by other means.

The question remains, however, how much of an improvement is Foucault's war metaphor over Hegel's and Marx's dialectical and antagonistic models of power? Can Foucault improve upon the reductive models without losing their explanatory power?

To begin with, Foucault uses the antagonistic image to characterize his genealogical method in contrast to traditional idealist histories:

I have attempted to analyse how, at the initial stages of industrial societies, a particular punitive apparatus was set up together with a system for separating the normal and the abnormal. To follow this up, it will be necessary to construct a history of what happens in the nineteenth century and how the present highly-complex relation of forces – the current outline of the battle – has been arrived at through a succession of offenses and counter-offenses, effects and counter-effects. The coherence of such a history does not derive from the revelation of a project but from a logic of opposing strategies.

(*PK*, 61)

To say that the coherence of this history does not derive from a project but from opposing strategies puts it beyond the designs of the state apparatus, of the law, or of representative men. Genealogy is irreducible to pattern and design because it is the logic of opposing strategies, of assertion and resistance, of excess, and of Nietzschean chance. And yet, to say that genealogy is the logic of opposing strategies does not make it entirely unpredictable, entirely random, entirely other. There are ways of dealing with the rationality of such irrationalities.

Indeed, if the logic of opposing strategies sounds familiar, it is because it is also the logic of classical economics, the science of the struggle over scarce resources as mediated by the market. In a number of fundamental ways, Foucault's microphysics of specific actions parallels the free market model. According to Adam Smith, competition is a socializing force guided by an invisible hand toward an equilibrium of prices, making the free market a kind of internally self-adjusting system. Likewise, Foucault's systems of power "can retreat here, re-organize its forces, invest itself elsewhere ... " (*PK*, 56), constituting a curious "intentional yet nonsubjective" agency of self-promotion. Furthermore, Adam Smith's system produces its collective effects by the accumulation of independent, self-interested economic men, each with their own motives, histories, and capabilities; likewise, Foucault's systems result from "an *ascending* analysis of power, starting, that is, from its infinitesimal mechanisms, each with its own history, its own trajectory, its own techniques and tactics" (*PK*, 99, altered translation).

What Foucault has described is what capitalists and Marxists alike both find in the market mechanism: a system that adjusts the totality of individual strategies according to the *contextual causality* of supply and demand. In the genealogy of contextual-causal theorists, Adam Smith's invisible hand is the father of Foucault's purposefulness-without-purpose of the economy of power, the ghost in Foucault's Nietzschean economic machinery.[15]

The market model illuminates the core of Foucault's localist logic.

---

15. Why then is Foucault not Adam Smith in disguise? The difference lies in Foucault's historicism. Just as Foucault wants to deny that genealogy discovers a rationality of the Hegelian sort, so he shuns the prescriptivism of free-marketeering. Furthermore, unlike the invisible hand of classical economics, the invisible hand of Foucault's heterological economics does not lead to equilibrium, but rather to domination. So where Smith's invisible hand leads free class competition to converge on the ideal of rational prices, Foucault's invisible hand guides the competition among mechanisms of power toward no ideal but survival, constrained only by chance intersections of relations of power. Where Adam Smith's hand seeks the rationality of equilibrium, Foucault's invisible hand of power seeks the irrationality of domination. Foucault's political economy is a Nietzschean, non-ideal, heterological, non-reductive economism.

Insofar as totalitarian theories and systems suggest that economies can be legitimized or controlled by the *descending* influence of political authority, they misunderstand the nature of economies, the "logic of opposing strategies." Thus, by defending the intrinsically antagonistic economy of power from resolution into *a priori* or top-down prescribed unities, Foucault's political economy rectifies an error of totalitarian economism. When legalistic and economistic authoritarians super-impose political patterns on economic heterologies, they assume that descending power can utterly displace or at least control ascending power. When legalistic and crude economistic histories derive historical meaning and causality from a plan, they too superimpose a pattern over something that is unpatterned and conflictual by nature. By stressing the heterological economy of opposing strategies, Foucault's model shows not that economics should not be reductive, but that it cannot be.[16]

Let us credit Foucault, then, with having identified a certain kind of confusion of politics and economics, of theory and history, a politically conceived confusion that hopes to reduce by prescription the heterology of struggles – the economy of opposing strategies – to a privileged pattern, principle, or term. What does Foucault provide instead? Foucault provides two things: a rebuke of Marxist political economy, and his promotion of the analysis of ascending power relations. But the step to these points is far too great for the evidence Foucault provides. Indeed, Foucault's perspective crucially mis-represents the genealogy of Marxist political economy, and contra-dicts his own heterological model by privileging the analysis of ascending relations of power to the detriment of the analysis of descending relations of power.

2. A case of mistaken identity

Crude Marxism aside, how reductive is Marx's critique of political economy? A closer look absolves Marx's political economy of the

16. Unfortunately, Foucault equivocates on the term "economy," using the narrower sense to refer to reductive theories of economic determinacy, while elsewhere denoting all struggles of opposing strategies, as in his search for "a new economy of power." This latter sense redeems economics from its reductive sense by opening it up to the heterology of power relations.

reduction Foucault takes for Marxism. Moreover, this genealogical simplification by Foucault indicates a general point about theoretical reduction which Foucault's straw man obscures.

Foucault implies that if one grants the heterology of power, reductive political economic analysis is repudiated. True, but only insofar as it is *too* reductive. That leaves open two questions that Foucault does not answer: to what extent are there reductive systems of power? and how much does Marx's work obscure the underlying heterology of political economic relations? Here the record of Marxist commentary is mixed and controversial, thus requiring more genealogical care than Foucault has expended.

True, one must allow that Marxist theory has allowed for or at least suffered a number of theoretical reductions, all of which appear in the guise of Marxist economism. To begin with, the standard distinction between productive base and the more conflicted superstructure of culture and politics will not absolve Marxism from the charge of reduction, because crude Marxism reduces the heterological top to the homological, commodified base. Nor is the theory of the class struggle invulnerable to a reductive dialectical determinacy, such as gave rise to the "inevitability" of the Revolution. Furthermore, Marx appeared willing to accept the reality of class dialectics for prescriptive purposes as well as for descriptive purposes. And so Marxism's resistance to reduction must be found elsewhere: in the meaning of Marx's theory of surplus value for his theory of history. But this point requires some precision.

If one were asked whether Marx believed in the reduction of values to economic values, unfortunately one would have to say yes and no, for it is a fundamentally ambiguous question. Or more accurately, Marx's answer would be: historically, yes – epistemologically, no. Homology of values, for Marxian theory, is not a transcendental reality, but a historical product of the commodity system. Indeed, the heterology of relations is precisely what the commodity system is supposed to displace, invest, colonize, etc. as exchange values equilibrate different use values and relations of power. This accounts for the apparently reductive moments in Marx's rhetoric, as when he claims, "It is not consciousness that determines life, but life that determines consciousness."[17] But to read this too reductively dismisses

17. Karl Marx and Frederick Engels, *The German ideology*, Moscow: Progress Publishers, 1976; p. 42. Or later in the same work: "This sum of productive forces,

too quickly two complicating elements of Marx's theory: the historical determinacy of society, and the heterological character of the superstructual relations. These elements go against the possibility of a completely reductive economism.

This point is implied elsewhere by Marx regarding the distinction between base and superstructural relations for the transformations of society:

> in considering such transformations the distinction should always be made between the material transformation of the economic conditions of production, which can be determined with the precision of natural science, and the legal, political, religious, aesthetic or philosophical – in short, the ideological forms in which men become conscious of the conflict and fight it out.

One can read this as a distinction between the homologizing power of the commodity system and the heterological elements of culture.[18] The extent of economistic homology and ideological false-consciousness are not aprioristically given, but are empirical questions for Marx, which thus require assessing the actual extent of commodification.

Furthermore, not only is economistic reduction for Marx an empirical question rather than an ahistorical methodological axiom, but his attitude toward the homologizing of value by the commodity system shows his principled rejection of economistic homology. Indeed, the false homogeneity of exchange values is a central target of

capital funds and social forms of intercourse, which every individual and every generation finds in existence as something given, is the real basis of what the philosophers have conceived as 'substance' and 'essence of man' ... " (p. 62). Yet in the same work, one finds a more reciprocal formulation of the causality of consciousness and its conditions, as when Marx and Engels write: "circumstances make men just as much as men make circumstances" (ibid., p. 62). Thus it is best concluded that Marx was not entirely consistent on the degree to which he was committed to reducing social causality to material circumstances although he believed he had sound *historical* reasons for stressing the primacy of the conditions of production.

18. Or in the words of Anwar Shaikh: "[The centrality of the commodity system] does not mean that [other legal, political and personal relations within society] lack a history and logic of their own. It only means that within any given mode of production, they are bound to the system by the force field of this central [commodity] relation, and characteristically shaped by its ever present gravitational pull." *Marxian economics*, New York: Norton, 1987; p. 169.

Marx's critique. Far from assuming that all values are economic in the bourgeois sense, Marxists and Tories alike have historically joined in charging the commodity system with producing an artificial homogeneity of power relations, including, for Marx, the commodification of the "incommensurable magnitudes" of land, labor, and the means of production.[19]

Frankfurt School theorists anticipated Foucault's rejection of homologous reductions of value in capitalist, fascist, and totalitarian contexts, but did so in the former case under the aegis of Marx's critique of the commodity system as a systematic illusion of natural values. As their critical theory shows, the fundamental issue of Marxist economics for the critique of domination is not whether crude Marxism has sometimes erred in reducing values to economic values – which it has. The issue is rather what relation between state and class fosters the greatest liberty, or if Foucault prefers, inhibits non-consensuality, and what tools allow for the analysis of the mechanisms of domination. Likewise, this emancipatory issue questions whether Foucault fosters a better analysis of political economy as a dimension of domination.

To this question, one must again answer that Foucault obscures the terrain. Foucault's hybrid of hypersystematicity and anti-collectivist individualism simply veils the inner dynamics of the commodity system as a social force. Likewise, the class structure of domination vanishes into the new *causal homology* of Foucault's hypersystemic view in which everyone is equally a vehicle of the system, in which no one possesses power, in which power "is not the 'privilege,' acquired or preserved, of the dominant class, but the overall effect of its strategic positions" (*PK*, 174).

3. A Foucaultian homology

What is the significance for political economy of making power this constitutive systematicity *rather than* something that can be possessed by agents within the system? If not power, how else should we distinguish those who have more and less influence or choice within the system? Short of such a reconstruction of *intra*systemic domi-

---

19. *Capital* vol. III, Moscow: 1971; p. 823. Cited in Mepham and Ruben, *Issues in Marxist philosophy*, Atlantic Highlands, New Jersey: Humanities Press; p. 46.

nation, how useful can this hypersystemic model of power be for emancipatory and unmasking purposes?

By undertheorizing state and class, Foucault's concept of power is both too general and too specific to articulate domination as a differentiating feature of social roles, effacing the very institutional or collective dynamics to which his ascending analyses lead. The anti-holist Foucault faults traditional history for being a "comprehensive view excluding differences" (*FR*, 91), but Foucault threatens to lose real differences of power between social roles through his homologizing of power throughout the system. This erasure of differences appears when Foucault says, "The purpose of history, guided by genealogy, is not to discover the roots of our identity, but to commit itself to its dissipation" (*FR*, 95). This subverts the Nietzschean unmasking function of genealogy by making its power epistemic in the wrong sense: i.e. by attributing to genealogy a nominalist power to deny the reality of collectivities, rather than the power of *discovering* the effectivity of *all* relations of power. Genealogy should not dissolve identities but track their effects; and it does so by multiplying distinctions in power, not by effacing them.

But even if Marx can escape the charge of a homogenizing economism, surely he must be guilty of historical metanarration, of collectivizing political commitment, of prescriptively totalizing theory. Historically, the question of whether Marx's class structure is a descriptive system or prescriptive system is controversial. At least one prominent commentator, however, has attributed descriptive intentions to Marx. Thus Isaiah Berlin writes: "Marx denounces the existing order by appealing not to ideals but to history: he denounces it not as unjust, or unfortunate, or due to human wickedness or folly, but the effect of laws of social development that at a certain stage of history one class, pursuing its interests with varying degrees of rationality, should dispossess and exploit another."[20] On this reading of Marx, what is of primary significance for economic theory is the reality of collective forces, not the desirability of solidarity. Of course, Marx chose sides on the issue of the class struggle, but his reasoning went from fact to value, not the other way around.

What is at stake here is not an antiquarian point; the issue is the status of the social totality – as an epistemic or moral consideration – in political economic analysis, as well as the demands of political

20. Isaiah Berlin, *Karl Marx: His life and environment*. Oxford, 1963; p. 7.

economy on Foucault's localism. Does Foucault want to say that collective force does not exist as such – as some nominalists do – or does he simply not *trust* collected force? His critique of Marxism is, once again, ambiguously poised between the two. But whatever later Marxists might say, Foucault could not attribute to Marx a preference for parties over facts. Marx wanted science, not moralism. Part of the Hegelian legacy Marx remained committed to was the reality of collectivities as such. Thus, even if Foucault has objections to totalizing theories, he cannot dismiss Marx's theory of collective force out of a distrust of parties.

Neither the charge of reductive homology nor the charge of political prescriptivism can be carried to the heart of Marxist political economy. Likewise, Foucault's conflation of Marxism with reductive economism and class promotion is, ironically, genealogically reductive, reading the problems of later Marxist politics into Marx's critique of capitalism. Foucault's critique of Marxism, therefore, misses an opportunity to do better than counterpunch totalitarian theories. As a result, Foucault's portrait of Marxism loses much of the complexity of the original work of Marx as well as the more supple Marxist thinkers that followed him.

4. The lure of inverted hierarchies

Still, Foucault's defenders might claim that even if Foucault sidesteps the task of presenting a genealogically full critique of Marxism, his model of ascending power provides a counter-model which can be empirically compared to Marxist political economy. According to this defense, the Foucaultian could say that the point is not to deny collectives, since Foucault could get whatever collectives he needs through his ascending analysis of power. Foucault's ascending analytic, on this view, might yield as much collectivity as there really is, while not assuming the *a priori* collectivity that merely refines the mechanisms of domination. Since power ascends, that method must discover "how ... mechanisms of power have been – and continue to be – invested, colonised, utilised, involuted, transformed, displaced, extended etc., by ever more general mechanisms and by forms of global domination" (*PK*, 99). Foucault, in this case, need not begin with the totalizing theoretical apparatus of the German philosophical tradition, but can amass what generalities he needs empirically, and "put [it] to the test of reality" (*FR*, 46). Perhaps the issue is not finally whether collective power exists besides hypersystemic power and individual choice, but rather what is the best method to discover the operation of power, collective or otherwise.

Regarding his method, Foucault reminds us that he intends to invert the over-generalized methods of political science and economism in order to make criticism local, concrete, and reflective of the logic of opposing strategies. But Foucault's inversion of the traditional method of analyzing the descending influence of power from state and class falsely implies that because an exclusively descending analysis is reductive, an exclusively ascending explanation solves the problem. Furthermore, that premise, however heuristically useful for redressing a previous imbalance in political theory, contradicts Foucault's own heterological demand for "varying tools" in the analysis of power. Foucault wants to stand Marx on his head, exchanging ascending explanations for descending explanations. Unfortunately, this inversion of method merely inverts the error of crude Marxists. Foucault's political economy achieves its liberation from the dogma of descent at the threat of a dogma of ascent. Of course, if political economy lived by ascent alone, Foucault would simply be right. But the test of reality suggests otherwise.

To begin with, what is the object of political economy? Political economy, by definition, is the interaction of ascending and descending power. It is the intermediacy of state and class, the collective and the collected, the planned and the spontaneous, the descending and the ascending relations of power. It studies the dynamic of the state-as-consciously-unified-system and the classes-as-products-of-opposing-strategies, the dynamic of state as juridical causality with market as contextual causality. Foucault is, of course, right to resist reducing economics to political fictions or to class determinacy alone. But whatever role the state and class do have in the economy can only be determined by a theory of the whole that attends to descending influence as well as ascending influence.

For the critique of domination, the cost of Foucault's methodological inversion of Marx's class analysis is high: by warranting only ascending analysis, Foucault fosters the dissolution of political reality into the chaos of monadic economics. By privileging the ascending movement of power over the descending, he idealizes political history as a free market where power accumulates by the "chance" result of individual contracting. By privileging local relations of power, however heterogeneous, Foucault neglects the fact that as it accumulates, centralized power automatically descends along whatever paths are available, eclipsing the microphysics of power with the mediacy of whatever wholes can be appropriated by the most powerful.

5. Post-essentialist class theory

What then are the implications of the heterology of power relations for class structures? And if Foucault's localism misses the dynamic that leads to a certain degree of class structure, how should the problem of classes be framed in order to avoid either global or local reductions?

Take Edward Said's paraphrase of Foucault that "in the modern period ... there is an unremitting and unstoppable expansion of power favoring the administrators, managers, and technocrats of what he calls the disciplinary society" (Hoy, 150). A Foucaultian purist could object to Said's appeal to class-structured power rather than into a succession of pragmatic regimes for which "all parties are equally vehicles." But that deep-technologistic objection requires a new analytic dogmatism of ascending power: it implies that power necessarily transcends its structure of field-defined, interpersonal domination. Here Foucault's vacillation between deep pragmatic conditions and micro-events cuts out the dynamics that define the middleman, the power broker.

How dispensable is this figure of the dominating subject? To suggest that the disciplinary system would have succeeded if it had not *enhanced* the effectiveness of domination of some over others is not only un-Nietzschean; it is incomprehensible, and counter to Foucault's own generalizations about the increased technology of domination. For whom does control increase? The only commensurable measure of such generalizations is the dominating subject. Foucault's allegorization of systems-promoting-themselves does not efface the fact that in the panopticon, person A can watch everyone else, but not vice versa. Power is not symmetrical, and hypersystematicity's impersonality obscures such asymmetries.

Indeed, Foucault's oscillation between hypersystems and self-invention does not so much problematize hierarchies as it problematizes the critique of them. On the levels of hypersystems and self-invention they respectively disappear into equal-vehiclehood and self-absorption, while on the level of social intercourse they are given a kinder and gentler aspect by Foucault's demand that we account for them as they emerge democratically, by the ascent of power. Since, contra-Foucault, contextual causality is holistic, the microphysical view makes domination appear to be blind complicity.

Because hypersystemic regimes *live through* the positional domination they enable, descending power and ideology remain at the crux of critical theory. For the critique of domination, the significance of class structure is not vitiated either by deeper discursive conditions of power or by a heterology of mechanisms of power. Quite the contrary, these Foucaultian insights merely revise the notion of class into non-essentialist terms: rather than polarizing into the final struggle of capitalists and labor, the threat to emancipation is just that classes can be multiplied as needed to stabilize the structure of domination. The Revolution was not postponed for lack of a class struggle; it was avoided because capitalists could fraction social structure by co-opting – i.e. by constituting – new classes. Ideology did not end: it was blurred.

Foucault's fear of collectivist action misses the point of the critique of political economy, which is not an iron law-like metanarrative. The issue is whether or not the collective aspect of economic determinacy is a *historical* fact, and why. Here Foucault's confusion of general and reductive theories muddies the issue of economic determinacy. Whether or not a collective theory of action is desirable, an analysis of collective determinacy certainly is.

Foucault is right to reject the reductions of crude economism which suggest that everything reduces to class forces or that the economy can be entirely controlled from above. But by framing the question of power between an anonymous non-subjective system and the strategic choices of arbitrary individuals, Foucault helps mystify the descending influence of the collectivities already at work in the political economic field: those that have already invested, displaced, and colonized the systematic interactions between culture, politics, and economy. For concrete questions about social power have as much to do with concentrations of power by classes as they do with philosophical presuppositions or with individual choices about aesthetic existence. Foucault's reductions to systemic conditions and individual choices eliminates the most powerful players in the game, the agents of the middle level of the hierarchy of formal generality, the brokers between the institutions of state and contextual causality of economic force. We want to see the Big Brothers, but they have disappeared from Foucault's battlefield.

D. Big Brother is missing: destroying critical theory in order to save it

Of the many problems Foucault presents to the reader, the problem he brings to critical theory involves the linkage between freedom, progress, and critical grounds. Here Foucault's histories and his theoretical work must be distinguished. Like a poet who writes inferior commentary on his own work, Foucault's theorizing subverts his own emancipatory interests, turning his anti-foundationist jitters against his best potential effects.[21]

Foucault wants to save critical theory from premature totalization. Unfortunately, all criticism is premature; but we cannot postpone action indefinitely. The problem is not that Foucault chooses to question certain theoretical problems. Rather, the problem is that the skeptical Foucault muddies the very possibility of global theorizing by anti-foundational generalities that even he cannot consistently respect. Foucault's "preference for ethics over politics," for instance, misses the issue of the interested nature of his work and his sympathy for resistance: for the kind of judgment that is involved in politics and ethics is the same – the application of concepts of value to particular contexts.

As noted repeatedly, however, this contradiction follows from Foucault's pattern of contradictions. His bifurcation between para-structuralist discursivity and individualist self-invention effaces the concepts that link individual choice to social consequences. His networks reveal systematic connections, and his techniques of the self show the self-constituting consequences of our practices. We see, that is, how systems displace other systems, and how individuals help or hurt themselves. But the conjunction of these two levels of analysis

---

21. This is not to say, of course, that his theoretical work is not significant or useful. However, its utility is overshadowed by its partiality and by its lack of clarity about its own theoretical commitments. This is less true of his historical work. Furthermore, Foucault's contradictions are important for his reception. Open-minded critics have sometimes attempted to reconcile his contradictions for him, either by glosses of their own or by selective attention, while his staunchest defenders have treated his contradictions as productive methodological innovations, a level to which they do not always rise. Foucault's vacillation between Nietzschean and Kantian emphases shows that his tensions do not always follow from an illumination of power but from unreconciled appropriations, where "unreconciled" means, not that he has too little unity, but that he has *underestimated* the acuteness of the contradiction in his own work.

leaves out the interested character of social roles, the ways in which action and position profit one person at the expense of another. Rather than highlighting more subtle strategies of domination, Foucault's hypersystemic revision of power makes domination a problematic category in the same way totalitarian theories efface individual responsibility by referring to the determinacy of history. Unlike the illuminating effects of his histories, this epistemological commentary is morally confusing, if not paralyzing.

By opposing overall theories, collectivities, the power of the whole, class structures, and descending power – rather than appropriating all of these tools in a more fully heterological methodology – Foucault's methodology unwittingly propagates reductions of its own, with incoherent consequences. We just noted how his hypersystemic analyses converge with certain radical left forms of collectivism by refusing to contextualize agency. Ironically, Foucault's later denial of collectivities for ascending power converges on the right with Edmund Burke's organicist distrust of rationalist critiques of traditional authority; it converges with Darwinian and Social Darwinian legitimations of atomistic survivalism; it converges with Thatcher's revelation that "Society doesn't exist"; it converges with the right libertarian economic claim that individual contracting is the only moral framework for judging the ethics of economic phenomena. These are uneasy bedfellows for Foucault, a fact which represents his failure to theorize fully the implications of his work.

It is not unreasonable to conclude, as Said has, that Foucault winds up on the side of power, apparently theorizing both the inevitability and the futility of resistance. This suggests that Foucault may finally be guilty of the fallacy of imitative form: as the analyst of power and contradiction, Foucault's work suffers an unproductive degree of resignation and inner conflict. Of course, his histories will undoubtedly continue to instruct by their revelation of the immanence of power and knowledge. But as another example of postmodern anti-foundationism, Foucault's philosophy and politics will continue to jeopardize the very interest in liberty he embodies.

7

Habermas' neo-formalism: theory as praxis

A. Modernity's rationalization of the world

The Enlightenment optimists believed that Reason would save the modern world from what Kant referred to as man's self-imposed tutelage. Kant's view reflects the spirit of modern philosophy in two ways: insofar as modern philosophers believed rational reflection to be the *justifying* and *integrating* activity of mankind through both pure reason and practical reason. The careers of modern philosophy and modern society, however, suggest that the project of rationalizing the world has a problematic record on both counts.

Those who are more skeptical of the possibility of rationalizing culture, at least in the ways typified by the Enlightenment legacy, have abandoned or condemned that legacy in the name of a postmodern perspective. On the other hand, those who are more optimistic about the power of reason – i.e. to foster real progress in cultural development, to create liberating social structures, and to provide grounds for the critique of domination – wish to reconstruct, reinterpret, or reform the Enlightenment ideal of a rational society. Among the defenders of modernity Jurgen Habermas may be the best known, although Habermas' defense of modernity includes his own diagnosis of its errors and its ills.

1. Modernity: pro and con

On the issue of reason's progress there is the evidence of modern science. Even if only in the most crudely pragmatic terms, the productive power of science has emancipatory significance. Technology has extended human powers for meeting biological needs as well as for disseminating the power of technique through the globalization of communication. Beyond the manipulation of natural forces, however, there arises a host of philosophical questions that are less easily accounted, and which may require a perspective that is broader than the technological austerity to which modern empiricists often confine themselves. One must, therefore, question technology in the larger view of emancipation and morality.

Philosophical modernity involves the epistemological turn of Descartes, Hume, Kant, and Hegel; a turn which expresses the desire for philosophical self-legitimation, the requirement that modernity "create normativity out of itself," as Habermas has put it. Spawned by a critique of classical philosophy's unself-critical attitude, modern philosophy is not content to know being, but intends to theorize itself as knowledge. Modern philosophy is *reflexive* at once for its own and for society's rationality.

Moreover, the rationalism of modernity also has its *individualistic* thrust, the democratization of control over the lifeworld made possible by integrating critique and popular sovereignty. Thus, the universality of reason not only legitimates democracy as a society of moral equals, but also requires a critical discourse by which its citizens can constitute their individual autonomy while constituting "one out of many." Ideally, the technological and institutional structures of society would foster free inquiry out of which civic progress can emerge on individual and social levels at once.

The question, then, for social critique is the proper interrelation of technology, foundational theory, and emancipatory critique. Whereas the promise of each of these aspects of modernity is perhaps commonplace, the problem is that modernity has failed to harmonize the elements. The emancipatory potential of modernism, it seems, has been deflected by an internal fragmentation of modern discourse, and by pathological developments within the actually existing forms of power.

2. Habermas and the disintegration of reason

Contrary to one feature of Enlightenment rationalism, the technologizing (or Weber's "rationalizing") of the world has not integrated life but rather disrupted reason into a number of spheres. Here social philosopher Jurgen Habermas follows Weber in seeing modernism as the division of society into the autonomous domains of science, morality, and art. Furthermore, Habermas suggests that the fragmentation of society has been invested by new forms of domination. Following Horkheimer and Adorno's observation that "enlightenment is totalitarian," Habermas has been concerned to note how the rise of instrumental reason has intensified the techniques and effects of domination at the expense of modernism's emancipatory potential. These Habermas identifies in several symptomatic developments:

(1) The fragmentation of discourse: the proliferation of local, specialized techniques fractures knowledge into compartments. As Stephen White notes: "Everyday consciousness is robbed of its synthesizing power; it becomes fragmented."[1]

This tendency empties language as a vehicle for communication as subjects disappear into a world of objects: the "communicative infrastructure is threatened by two tendencies which are intertwined and mutually reinforcing: by systematically induced reification and cultural impoverishment" (W, 104). Objectivist discourse appropriates for itself an undertheorized and all-engulfing ideal of control, establishing a technocratic authority that obscures its own limits. Thus knowledge advances at the expense of communication and widespread understanding.

(2) With the dominance of technology in place, philosophical and moral options are foreclosed, obscuring deep-theoretical, aesthetic, and moral aspects of private and public interests. No distinction is made between (a) the moral and political questions of the ends of social action and (b) the logistical questions of technology. Emancipatory critique of the whole is subverted by a paradoxical homogenization and fragmentation of instrumental reasoning.

(3) In the moral void, a technocratic monologism arises in which efficiency legitimates whatever means are suited to the interests of decision makers. The hegemony of instrumental discourse becomes a hegemony of the technocratic elements of society where the sphere of communication is coopted by the interests of technocratic and economic power. As White notes, the "colonization of the lifeworld" occurs "when the systemic media of money and power begin to displace communicative sociation in … cultural transmission, social integration and socialization" (W, 110). As various social domains are appropriated by specialists, active participation by citizens – a prerequisite of a rational society – is displaced by interests "co-ordinated by money or power … [with only] an objectivating attitude and an orientation to success" (W, 110). The public sphere thus

---

1. Stephen K. White, *The recent work of Jurgen Habermas: reason, justice, and modernity*, Cambridge, 1988, p. 117; hereafter referred to as W.

becomes progressively less public and more the reflection of a managerial class.

The eclipse by technology of an integrated reason may begin as an internal development within modern discourse, but is exacerbated by the social interests that are in a position to take advantage of it. And what is worse, the dominance of instrumental reason tends to obscure precisely the sort of moral awareness required to call its legitimacy into question. Thus modern liberal societies tend toward a crisis in their moral coherence or public legitimacy, a crisis that is at once theoretical and political.

The alienation of the public consciousness from the public domain coincides with the rise of the modern state's interventionist strategies for fostering a growth economy and coping with the instability of capitalist markets. As modern states intervene into the economy in order to stabilize it, they transform their function from representatives of juridical equality to defenders of the economic *status quo*. And since this involves protecting the economic structure of inequality, the state becomes invested in creating the illusion of egalitarian sovereignty to maintain its legitimacy. As White observes: "On the one hand, [late capitalism's political] actions must accord with the class interests of capital in continued accumulation and, on the other, with the demand of the population that the political system express universalistic, democratic values" (W, 111). This tension within the state's twofold guardianship of political equality and economic inequality fosters a "legitimation crisis."

The late capitalist state's preservation of inequality in the name of equality is accomplished through the rhetoric of technique by putting into question the means but not ends of political action. Thus contemporary political rhetoric subverts the critical and democratic ideal it was supposed to serve by obscuring the ultimate effects of sovereignty within the discourse of technocratic fragmentation. This fragmentation becomes a functional successor to ideology: whereas ideology formerly rationalized the free market society as the locus of true freedom, technocratic capitalism spontaneously obscures the inequality of state services by its specialized rhetoric of technical efficiency and economic stability.

Of course, the defenders of the modern capitalist state would challenge Habermas' contention that democratic sovereignty is not intact. Given the rise of conservative opinion in the 1980s, defenders of capitalism could suggest that Habermas' suspicions about the compatibility of late capitalism and democracy depend on the highly problematic concept of false consciousness: that is, Habermas must claim (a) that the modern capitalist public is not getting what it really wants or needs, and (b) that Habermas knows better than they do what is good for them. To answer such critiques of his critique, Habermas wants trans-ideological standards by which to judge the rationality of society. He wants transcendental standards of the rational society, not just his own idea of reason. And yet he also wants these standards to be practical: they should demarcate rational and irrational social practices, and prescribe practical goals. Against the domination of technology and its exploiters, Habermas wants to bring together the theory *and* practice of human rationality.

B. The terms of critique

To critique and redress the pathologies of modernism, Habermas seeks a theoretical framework suitable for identifying its irrationalities and for resynthesizing its elements into functional harmony. Echoing influences ranging from Kant, Hegel and Peirce to Marx and Freud, much of the thrust of Habermas' vision is found in this declaration of intent:

to develop the idea of a theory of society with practical intention ... [this project] aims at achieving an explanation of social evolution which is so comprehensive that it embraces the interrelationships of the theory's own origins and applications. The theory specifies conditions under which reflection on the history of our species by members of this species themselves has become objectively possible; and at the same time it names those to whom this theory is addressed, who then with its aid can gain enlightenment about their emancipatory role in the process of history. The theory occupies itself with reflection on the interrelationships of its origin and with anticipation of those of its application, and thus sees itself as a necessary catalytic moment within the social complex of life which it analyzes.

Here are found three of Habermas' primary theoretical interests: (1) a foundational theory with pragmatic implications, (2) a theory with reflexive awareness of its own historical and theoretical origins, and (3) a theory with emancipatory authority.

1. Modes of inquiry

Habermas' first step toward defining the adequate grounds of critique is classically dialectical, targeting first what he rejects: positivist empiricism and hermeneutical traditionalism, the first being too presumptuous and narrow regarding its own theoretical grounds, and the latter being too historically and contextually relative to yield critical transcendence. In order to define critical grounds that avoid the positivist and hermeneutic snares, Habermas makes a distinction between three kinds of inquiry:

There are three categories or processes of inquiry for which a specific connection between logical-methodological rules and knowledge-constitutive interests can be demonstrated. This demonstration is the task of a critical philosophy of science that escapes the snares of positivism. The approach of the empirical-analytic sciences incorporates a *technical* cognitive interest; that of the historical-hermeneutic sciences incorporates a *practical* one; and the approach of critically oriented sciences incorporates the *emancipatory* cognitive interest that, as we saw, was at the root of traditional theories.[2]

The idea of discriminating forms of reason is not new. In fact, despite other differences, Gadamer proposes a similar scheme which he borrows from Aristotle's modes of knowledge: *technē* (craft), *phronēsis* (interpretation, estimation), and *epistēmē* (theory).

Habermas' scheme coincides with Gadamer's on the insufficiency of instrumental reason (*technē*) as a foundation for philosophy, as well as agreeing on the open, historicist, and perspectival character of *phronēsis* and on the logically rigorous character of *epistēmē*. Furthermore, as Gadamer and Habermas agree that technocracy has obscured the currency and specificity of political questions, both thinkers believe that the critique of instrumental reason depends on distinguishing the logics of technique and morality. Hence, both hold that political questions are questions of ends, requiring a purpose-assigning judgment, whereas technology involves questions of means, requiring only instrumental reason.

The issue between Habermas and Gadamer, therefore, lies in determining whether the moral authority of the social order lies primarily in the cognitive practice of *epistēmē* or in that of *phronēsis*. Likewise, for Habermas as a critical theorist, this foundational issue determines whether epistemic or hermeneutic authority is the more properly *emancipatory* form of judgment, constituting the foundation of emancipatory praxis. Indeed, this difference defines Habermas' reconstruction of critical philosophy and his critique of post-

---

2. Jurgen Habermas, *Knowledge and human interests*, Boston: Beacon, 1968; 308.

modernism, while defining his well known differences with Gadamer over the status of modernity.

Against the ambitions of modernism – whether in the form of positivist scientific methods or rationalist faith in reflective consciousness – Gadamer's philosophical hermeneutics is concerned to show the openness and infinite questionability of thought. He therefore highlights the dis-closure of *phronēsis* (i.e. the openness of practical, prudential, moral, aesthetic, and interpretive thought) against the objectivism of *technē* (science, technology, control, mechanics) and the formal rigor of *epistēmē* (epistemology, formal necessity, logical conditions), claiming that the universal scope of hermeneutic reflection can open up the grounds of all knowledge.

Ever the modernist, Habermas believes that reason must solve reason's problems. The hegemony of *instrumental* reason (*technē*) has undercut the democratic ethos: the moral and political functions of public discourse are dissolved into a managerial hegemony of the few. This current irrationality of modernity is a pathological relation between cognitive modes and social spheres, but not a necessary one. It can be further rationalized by the proper integration of social elements and cognitive interests. The question is: what harmonizes the disequilibrated spheres of society?

Habermas seeks critical substance. Typical of the Enlightenment progressive, he associates tradition with the arbitrariness of custom, and emancipation with rational critique. In Habermas' view, Gadamer's conservative claims for the historicity and traditional prejudices of knowledge serve to block rational critique by placing the origins of authority in the past. This backward, historicist view leaves us without a transcending criterion of progress, without a non-arbitrary ground of emancipatory critique to distinguish rational social conditions – the "invariant regularities of social action as such" – from arbitrary social forms – the "ideologically frozen relations of dependence that can in principle be transformed."[3]

In terms of foundational practices, Gadamer and Habermas differ over the relative authority of *phronēsis* and *epistēmē*, of prudence and science, of tradition and reason, of understanding and critique, of hermeneutic questionability and critical theory. Habermas follows the tradition of ideological critique by conferring special critical and emancipatory authority on the epistemic foundations of social

3. Ibid., 310.

rationality. Where Gadamer looks to *phronēsis* or interpretation and questionability for his emancipatory authority, Habermas follows Kant in looking to an ideal reason, referring critique to the "quasi-transcendental" authority of *epistēmē* or reconstructive theory. Not surprisingly, therefore, Habermas dubs the critical or epistemic mode of cognitive interest the "emancipatory" mode.

At once recalling and revising his Kantian roots, Habermas claims to discover in the formal conditions of democracy a mandate/ procedure for more public participation in the management of society. In particular, he finds the rational grounds of social critique in the formal conditions of inquiry and communication where equality and freedom of thought are supposed to coincide. By theorizing a democratically ideal speech situation – where all are allowed to make claims and all are obliged to justify their own – Habermas hopes to mediate scientific, moral, and artistic interests by providing the standard of rationality and the ground by which to critique the irrationalities of domination.

2. Reconstructing the conditions of free inquiry

Habermas is aware of the critiques of Kantian abstraction and wants to avoid liability to them. Hence Habermas honors the post-Kantian critiques of mere formalism, and he intends to include empirical arguments in the justification of social rationality. Moreover, he acknowledges the deconstruction of Cartesian reflective consciousness by the empirical fallibilism and hermeneutic historicity of Hegel, Peirce, Marx, and Freud. Still, he wants to discover beneath the variety of social practices a universally implied social ideal which must finally constitute an ultimate social practice. Habermas believes he can reconstruct a post-apriorist universalism, a "quasi-transcendental" obligation that is at once formal, empirical, and practical.

In his view, reconstructive sciences seek the formal structures that make various practices possible (and therefore discover a formal necessity), though these structures must also be found in real practices, not merely in speculative ideas. Reconstructive sciences discover the formalities of practical competences:

[the] various conditions for the validity of meaningful expressions and performances ... [discovered by] rational reconstructions of the know-how of subjects, who are entrusted to produce valid expressions and who trust

themselves to distinguish intuitively between valid and invalid expressions ... [such reconstructions yield] accounts of the pretheoretical knowledge and intuitive command, let us say, of the rule systems by means of which competent subjects generate and evaluate valid expression.   (W, 129)

This project must be evaluated both by the epistemic criteria of theoretical coherence and by the empirical criteria of communicative practice. Habermas notes that this brings the project within the fallibilist limits of pragmatic theory: "It is important to see that rational reconstructions, like all other types of knowledge, have only a hypothetical status ... They are in need of further corroboration" (W, 130). Furthermore, they must reflect the seasoned intuitions of practical reason: "The normative implications of the model must also stand up to the standards of our most reflective moral judgments" (W, 131). Habermas' social foundational theory thus seeks to mediate the necessity of formal conditions, the fallibilism proper to empirical science, and the concepts of practical reason.

Despite his concessions to empiricism, Habermas' strategy for the critique of domination owes much to the Rousseau-Kant lineage, whose notion of social rationality appealed to the formal grounds of social equality. Habermas believes that such grounds are found in the structures presupposed by the logic of communication. Such a logic is deep-structural insofar as it need not be conscious, though it is logically implied by our actions. Like the rules of grammar, the logic of communication is practiced before it is known, and is effective whether conscious or not.

Indeed, in the specification as well as in the interpretation of the ideal speech situation, echoes of Kant's formality and moral universalism re-emerge. Being anonymous, speech roles must be reciprocal. Being rational, they must be uncoerced. Determined by the ideal of inquiry, these roles require that speakers (1) speak intelligibly, (2) speak the truth, (3) recognize the appropriateness of the context of the speech, and (4) respect the accountability of claims. These conditions contribute to a formal wedding of "autonomy and responsibility" that obligates interlocutors equally in the search for truth, a kind of social-logical framework where duty and freedom of inquiry are two sides of the same implicit social contract. So where speakers are equally free to contribute their perspectives on the ideal of truth, that moral freedom depends on the universality of the rational ideal that inquiry implicitly presupposes. Thus Habermas steps from formal universality to moral universality.

The Kantian element is crucial in Habermas' claim that, though empirically discovered, these deeper logics are universal in a quite strong ideal sense (although Habermas is sometimes vague on the exact degree of strength). "When the pretheoretical knowledge to be reconstructed expresses a universal capability, a general cognitive, linguistic, or interactive competence (or subcompetence), then what begins as an explication of meaning aims at the reconstruction of species competences. In scope and status, these reconstructions can be compared with general theories."[4] Likewise, successful reconstructive theories can claim to have determined "precisely those rules that are operative in the object domain" in question, which Habermas takes to be the domain of social rationality and its emancipatory conditions (*CES*, 16).

Since free inquiry is coextensive with the public domain of the rational polis, Habermas extrapolates from the necessary conditions of a given practice (free inquiry) to the essence of humanity, i.e. to a *species competence*, a degree of universality that is the key to Habermas' strong moral-practical claims. Communication, he believes, can be taken as the paradigm of rational social behavior, allowing a universalistic extrapolation from formal conditions of social under-standing (free inquiry) to practical conditions of democratic agreement (consensus formation), and from a procedure for producing agreement to the structure of legitimation (social rationality in general).

Such a logic is, he believes, a *pragmatic* logic, which can be discovered empirically by reconstructive sciences. Thus reconstructive theory yields a hybrid product that is not quite formal or empirical science alone. Its theorization is empirical, hypothetical, and therefore fallible; yet it specifies formal conditions that necessarily hold in a given object domain.

Here, however, the notion of *domain* is fatally ambiguous for Habermas' reading of his model, insofar as society is made up of numerous overlapping domains. The question then is whether Habermas can legitimately extend his epistemic analysis of the formal conditions of democracy into the universalist moral/political claims he makes, since the public domain, while coextensive with society, is not the only domain that is coextensive with society. In that case, there may be a tension between multiple universalities within the same

---

4. *Communication and the evolution of society*, Boston: Beacon, 1979; p. 14; referred to hereafter as *CES*.

context that impinge on the absoluteness of each. In fact, that is precisely the problem of competing cognitive interests that gave rise to the pathologies of modernism in the first place: i.e. the possibility that the logics of the different social domains or spheres could inhibit each other's operations. Here is where Habermas' faith in reason continues to be strong foundational in the face of his own heterology of principles.

Habermas wants a model that not only *allows* for the mediation of differences; he wants a model that *obligates* a specific, unique procedure for mediating them. This move, however, conflates the logics of *possibility* and *obligation*. Or to put it in his own modal terms, while it is the mode of *epistēmē* (analysis to formal conditions) that determines the necessary preconditions or possibility of democratic consensus formation, it is the mode of *phronēsis* (application of categories in particular contexts) that decides when that practice is called for and hence in what circumstances that model obligates us. It is perhaps Habermas' central error to mistake the *formal* preconditions of a single practice (communication) and a single social sphere (democratic politics) for a universal *practical* obligation, or even for social rationality itself.

Unfortunately, the strategy of universalizing the moral claims of democratic consensus formation confuses a practice-specific formal necessity with practical universality in general, a distinction that is demanded by Habermas' assumption of different cognitive interests. Ironically, Habermas' own premises exclude his right to assume that democratic consensus-formation is the only species competence in question. Hence, even as the communication model seems to bring together freedom and responsibility, individuality and mutuality, form and value, theory and practice, Habermas' three modes of cognitive interest will return to haunt the supposed critical universality of the model.

3. Modes of reason: pragmatic distinctions

A critique of Habermas' argument finally turns on his cognitive interests, since they are the most transcendent level to which he appeals.

As a critical strategy, distinctions between kinds of knowledge or methodology have been controversial. For some thinkers, categorizing disciplinary methods (into natural and human sciences), or cognitive interests (Habermas), or forms of judgment (Aristotle), or faculties of reason (Kant), excessively reifies theoretical abstractions. They wonder: have not Gadamer, Kuhn, Feyerabend and the sociologists of knowledge revealed the interpretive dimension of natural science? And have not psychologists and sociologists revealed the susceptibility of human action to empirical (e.g. statistical, operant conditioning) methods taken from the natural sciences? Are not, then, such modal distinctions between faculties and disciplines discredited from all sides? And does not Richard Bernstein speak for many social theorists when he charges Habermas' categories of cognitive sciences with being "a fiction – and not a very useful methodological one"?[5]

To the question, "Are there modes of knowledge?", the best we can answer is: yes and no. The problem of modes of knowledge depends on what one means by categorically different types of knowledge. The problem is to see how disciplinary elements interpenetrate each other while still distinguishing separate disciplinary practices. If one took Habermas' three modes to mean that interpretation, validation, and control are wholly isolatable forms of judgment, then such distinctions would be specious, since interpretation, validation, and control cannot be entirely separated in practice. This mutual involvement of faculties, this practical *modal intermediacy*, follows from its origin in the phenomenological foundations of semiotics, where the conditions of thought coincide. All epistemic practices involve power, knowledge, and meaning – they all depend on technique, formal distinctions, and practical contexts that situate theory and consequence. Because all forms of knowledge share these general constraints – albeit in different ways – they necessarily involve each other's implications.

But while we may not be able *practically* to separate knowledge into strict categories, we can differentiate cognitive practices whose elements may still overlap. In doing so, we differentiate these practices' forms by their methodological emphases (e.g. quantification, prediction, instrumentation, observability, etc.), by theoretical priorities (e.g. generality, precision, level of abstraction, formal consistency, simplicity, etc.), and by differing pragmatic aims (e.g. interpretation, measurement, control, intervention, etc.). Indeed, differentiating inquiry is precisely the point of scientific methodology.

5. *The Restructuring of social and political theory*, Philadelphia: University of Pennsylvania, 1976; p. 223.

This can be done in abstraction, as semiotics theorizes forms of signification, or in the concrete methodologies of empiricism.

Furthermore, the mutual involvement of disciplinary elements that underlies this diversification of methods is also disguised by the fact that in each science different elements are taken for granted while others are questioned. Philosophy gravitates toward formal generality, empirical science toward objectivity, and hermeneutics toward history and interpretive uniqueness; yet they all must depend on the same phenomenological conditions. According to their different foci, aims, and methods each discipline sets the priorities of its practices, bracketing those of the others when necessary. As Max Horkheimer notes, "identical objects provide for one discipline problems to be resolved only in some distant future, while in another discipline they are accepted as facts." This conventional and pragmatic aspect of method determines what foundational elements get bracketed and obscured, and which are made questionable.

Notwithstanding their distinguishable practical extensions, however, the intermediacy of foundational elements renders the cognitive modes interdependent and equally universal at the foundations of thought. Technology, philosophy, and hermeneutics represent orientations toward different but equally fundamental and universal forms of significance: power, knowledge, and meaning. The "contest of the faculties," like the strong foundationist error, only arises when one mode of inquiry attempts to reduce or govern all epistemic issues with privileged methods, principles, and interests.

Habermas' error is not that he differentiates the modes of knowing, but that his use of them succumbs to the "contest of the faculties" mentality. Habermas wants to ground freedom in critical knowledge, the "emancipatory mode," *rather than* the less determinate contextuality of the historical-hermeneutic mode. In the traditional strong foundational pattern, Habermas wants the clearest and firmest grounds possible for freedom's warrant. But necessity, not freedom, is discovered by formal analysis, and freedom of ends is as much the burden of action as are the formal conditions of the ends we happen to choose.

Indeed, Habermas' universalist reading of the epistemic mode ignores his own distinction that "the historical-hermeneutic sciences [incorporate the] *practical*" interest, which indicates that practical reason cannot be reduced to a formal necessity. This confusion prevents him from seeing that the necessity which attaches to formal conditions – even of free inquiry – is a practice-specific necessity and is not universal in the widest sense. Practical reason ultimately depends on the appropriateness of practical ends in context, not on the formal conditions of any one practice. This pragmatic heterology means, against Habermas' privileging of free inquiry, that there can be no universally rational social practice.

4. From cognitive modes to social spheres

Equally important to Habermas' analysis are the distinctions between social spheres, an important legacy of modern sociology. Indeed, such distinctions virtually gave rise to critical theory when Weber surmised that bureaucratic technique rationalized production at the expense of a meaningful world. For Weber, post-mythological alienation is the price of modern efficiency; technology makes a rational world but an inhuman worldview. Post-Marxist theorists have also been concerned to note the interplay between politics, economics, and culture in the social contradictions of capitalism. Like earlier critical theorists, Habermas seeks a unifying form of reason to adjudicate the influences of the various social domains. Thus, Habermas' theory depends on both a triple distinction of cognitive interests and a triple distinction of social spheres.

What sort of distinctions are these distinctions of spheres? They begin as theory, though they have important practical consequences.

When one advocates the principles of democracy (such as one-person-one-vote and equality before the law), one holds that natural differences must be ignored in order to guarantee freedom of opportunity and prohibit oppression. In considering the citizen one abstracts differences between individuals, thereby considering them only as participants in a social contract (as proposed by Rousseau's theory of the General Will, Kant's theory of the Kingdom of Ends, Habermas' communication model, and Rawls' "original position"). Democratic theory rationalizes this abstraction from natural inequalities of condition and ability by performing a kind of generic or formal analysis of society as a social contract. Since reason is the human essence, so the theory goes, and since reason can only be developed by free participation in the dialogue that is the contract, the form of the system must *precede* its concrete circumstances rather than follow from them. The principle of moral equality is not supposed to be empirically given, but must be foreseen by theory as a moral abstraction whose conditions democratic theory approximates through legal structures. Freedom is not the precondition of a free society, but its ideal rationale, and therefore must be built into the social structure as a regulative ideal.

The abstract formality of democratic logic has a counterpart in the logic of the market. By contrast, markets are not egalitarian moral fictions: equality of voting power is not transferred to the realm of earnings and wealth in capitalist societies for a number of reasons (e.g. for freedom of expression; for differentials in productivity, length of employment, caliber of work, talent for disposal, etc.). Unlike the network of citizenship and the constitution of the state, the marketplace is supposed to be informal and inegalitarian. Yet the market has its own fictive ideal: i.e. how the market would behave if everyone were wholly self-interested, had perfect information about products, had full mobility to change markets and employers, etc. Though seeming less artificial than the democratic ideal, the ideal of the free market is an abstraction as well.

Thus the state and the market are different systems, both of which are accounted for by formal abstraction from the complex object (society) that reduces to neither alone. And here we find the parallel with the foundations of the cognitive modes. Where the modes combine interrelated epistemic elements in different ways to yield the different methodological practices of the sciences, so the spheres of state and economy are distinguishable in the abstract, yet are interrelated in their operations. The point may be to conduct oneself in each sphere according to its proper logic – as much as possible. But the fact that the different spheres are abstractions, and that their operations interrelate, means that the practical problems of applying their logics do not reduce to mechanical deductions from their ideals. In fact, since the spheres themselves can make competing demands, the adjudication of spheres is a *practical* problem beyond the theoretical problem of defining their principles.

The principles of different spheres, in other words, are only adequate in the abstract. And here arises the much debated issue of the border line between the state and the market, between public and private domains. While necessarily a practical problem, the foundational issue remains especially vexed because it often confuses two kinds of problems, the problem of theorizing an ideal model of the state or market versus the problem of deciding where to draw the lines between them in reality. One is a theoretical and formal issue, the other a practical problem of reconciling the demands of each.[6] This distinction between formalization (theory) and application (practice) has crucial consequences for Habermas' universalistic reading of the conditions of free inquiry.

On the one hand, to analyze the formal conditions of democracy or the logic of the free market is to think in abstraction from the complexity of real practical choices. The *application* in context of state and market logics, on the other hand, involves moral and political questions of valuation and purpose that are not predetermined by the models themselves. Analysis to formal conditions (whether political or economic) does not predetermine the real, but only the ideals that must be applied to it. Theorization in the abstract does not substitute for practical application to real circumstances because the application of the ideal is a different form of judgment (theoretical practice, or cognitive interest) from the theorization of the ideal itself. Modes of judgment must be distinguished as practices, even if their elements overlap in practice.

Habermas' distinctions of modes of reason capture some of this complexity of our multi-systemed society, although the posing of those distinctions involves implications Habermas ignores. Ironically, having made the distinction between the different modes of judgment and their extension into different social domains, Habermas' failure to acknowledge consistently the very distinctions he has defended blinds him to the limits of his model of social rationality. His desire to have a litmus test for social rationality leads him to mistake the formal conditions of free inquiry for the universal standard of social legitimacy. Thus he confuses the formal conditions of discourse in a democratic public domain with practical or moral necessity in general; his idealization of the rational polis overlooks the fact that even consensus has a wider practical context.

6. In light of this point some economists have claimed that economics is not an empirical science, but a formal one. Others have claimed, of course, that economics *is* an empirical science, although that may only mean that what begins as a formal science becomes empirical when we decide to apply it or track models empirically. In the latter case, economics may be historical by choosing to be descriptive without being either *a priori* or predictive. These disputes over the status of economic modeling, some of which are merely semantic, do not in any case influence my main point: that the distinction between formal and applied logics is real, and that to cross that boundary has real consequences.

C. The pragmatic limits of epistemic analysis

If there was Enlightenment hubris in Kant's blueprint of the limits of knowledge, others have questioned the power of reflection to discern such timeless boundaries, especially concerning social rationality. By way of historical reflection and economic analysis, Hegel and Marx made the analysis of the social nexus dynamic and progressive. In these two cases, the unconscious elements of past critical reflections were supposed to have been exposed by the light of the emerging end of history. Unfortunately, the nineteenth century failed to mark the end of historical irrationalities, and the search for the essence of social reason continued.

In the wake of philosophy's linguistic turn Habermas hopes to find the dialectic that can appropriate Hegelian and Marxian dynamics while recuperating a neo-Kantian formality. Where Marx found in labor an unconscious ground of reason unavailable to Kant's abstract reflection, Habermas believes that language allows for a mediation of theory and practice, concept and action, all by way of communication's pragmatic; deep structural preconditions. For Habermas, the formal conditions of communication define the pragmatic-social nexus of theoretical, productive, and moral interests, a discovery that hopes to improve upon both Kant's conceptualism and Marx's economism.

1. Conflating modes and spheres

Of course, it is for Habermas' practical universalism that traditionalists and postmodernists alike charge him with the reductive rationalism of the Enlightenment. Furthermore, they can convict him with one of his own arguments: they can appeal to his defense of the *autonomy of practical reason* against positivist reduction.

Habermas' critique of the technocratic state depends on maintaining the autonomy of practical reason – the political accountability of state actions – against the managerial state's persistent appeal to efficiency, as if only the means, but not the ends, of society are in question. But as Habermas wants to defend practical reason against the hegemony of instrumental reason, so we must wonder why the autonomy of practical reason can be reduced to the *formality* of communicative preconditions. It seems that Habermas is trying to have it both ways with the autonomy of modes: on the one hand, he wants politics to be irreducible to instrumental reason (H: practical reason *is not* reducible to instrumental reason); on the other hand, only if his modes of reason were reducible to each other could Habermas pass from the necessary conditions of communication to universalistic moral claims (H: practical reason *is* reducible to formal reason).

The analysis of formal conditions is not, of course, wrong in principle; it constitutes the proper task of epistemology and transcendental pragmatics. Furthermore, the communication model is right to seek the emancipatory significance of the formal conditions of free inquiry – those "formal properties of the modern understanding of the world" required for modernism's and democracy's reflexive self-legitimation. But the mere discovery of the formal conditions of free inquiry leaves unsolved the problem of the practical appropriateness of inquiry itself as a practice. To discover the necessary conditions of free inquiry does not show the *universal* appropriateness of free inquiry, and to believe it does reduces practical reason (the question of the appropriateness of any given practice) to the results of one form of epistemic theory (the formal conditions of communication).

Habermas does not appear to see his project as a reduction of practical reason to epistemic reason. Rather, he articulates it as if he had found the point at which epistemic and practical modes mediate each other. This is in part true, because communication is a practice, because free inquiry is a central practice for democratic societies, and because it has formal conditions. Likewise, the concept of transcendental pragmatics (to which Habermas and Karl-Otto Apel both appeal) combines both transcendental analysis and practical rationality, both formal and applied logics. Likewise, following Kant's extension of practical reason to a universal ideal of the rational and free society (Kant's Kingdom of Ends), Habermas' transcendental pragmatics intends to specify the form of rational legitimacy, the ideal against which irrational social practices can be measured. Just as neurotic speech expresses a reason-distorting resistance to self-understanding, and just as propaganda distorts truth for an ideological agenda, so transcendental pragmatics is supposed to provide an ideal to demarcate "systematic distortions in communication" from free inquiry.

It appears that formal analysis and real practices converge on one particular practical ideal. But here is where the distinction between modes of inquiry must allow that even when they are not divisible, they still require distinction as practices. Even if modes overlap or are convergent in particular practices, that does not mean the modes are identical or reducible to each other. Failure to make that distinction leads Habermas to extrapolate a limited formal necessity into a universal moral necessity.

Not surprisingly, many critics are wary of this project insofar as Habermas' intention to bridge formality and practice, necessity and contingency, analysis and hypothesis, appears to flout many of modern philosophy's most cherished distinctions. Nor are his critics assuaged by his prefixing a "quasi" to his "transcendental." And yet the problem with his ideal is not the hope of discovering the transcendent conditions of a practice, which are just its deep-structural logic; for such preconditions need not transcend the limits of the practice in question. The *necessity* of such conditions only means that they are part of the enabling logic of that practice.

Instead, Habermas' problem lies in the claim to practical *universalism*, to an ultimate social rationality, and in the expectation that the formal conditions of a given practice – in this case free inquiry – can spare us from the problems of practical reason: i.e. hermeneutical indeterminacy and ideological relativism, the problems which arise in applying formal or ideal principles to concrete contexts. For even allowing that the ideal conditions of free inquiry are the paradigm of democratic public discourse, a number of problems arise.

2. The practical limits of quasi-transcendence

Habermas intends for his ideal speech situation to be a universal standard of social rationality. In a democratic age and under normal public circumstances, Habermas' universalizing of free inquiry may at first seem unproblematic. For instance, it is obvious that the procedure of free inquiry is intended to adjudicate misunderstanding and difference through the mutual respect of rational beings, thereby leading to the consensus appropriate to a democratic society. Thus it may appear that free inquiry is the very heart of the democratic social mechanism. But what does it mean to make this formal point morally universal? And what does this moral universality mean for the practical limits of this ideal speech contract? When we look closely at his argument, we discover that the practical limits of free inquiry are obscured by the confusion of formal and moral claims.

On the question of the practical limits of free inquiry, Habermas acknowledges that not all speech acts are motivated by free inquiry and mutual understanding. Strategic communication, for instance, (e.g. lying, deception, manipulation, etc.) happens often enough; but such practices can only be understood as derivative of ideal speech: the liar hides the truth, the manipulator depends on what you assume he is doing instead, etc. For Habermas, these exceptions do not vitiate the force of the ideal of truth: they merely highlight the necessary presupposition of truth against which such deviations work, and thus re-enforce the universality of the ideal of truth by implication. Deviant practices do not vitiate the universality of the free inquiry ideal, because that ideal still functions both as a theoretical possibility and as a moral injunction against which deviant practices are understood as deviant.

Still, despite the cogency of the argument to presuppositions, at least two lines of objection suggest that the ideal speech model of social reason is not adequate to Habermas' claims of universality.

(a) Consider a debate between a fundamentalist Hindu and a fundamentalist Christian over the theocratic laws of their subcultures. If they dialogue sufficiently over differences in beliefs, they may arrive at an intractable difference: the former referring to the absolute authority of the Vedas, the latter referring to the absolute authority of the Bible. Here the free inquiry model fails to improve consensus because of prior commitments not necessarily liable to the force of dialogue. Habermas believes that his model is progressive because it intends to free up dogmatic impasses. But that merely presupposes that we are already committed to his consensus model as a paradigm of rationality rather than to dogmatic first premises. The effectiveness of Habermas' model, that is, depends on us having already abandoned the kinds of first premises that it is not fit to handle. The critique of dogmatism is, practically at least, a circular argument.

Such dogmatic examples, though extreme, suggest that foundational differences cannot merely be assumed to be resolvable by the procedure of free and equal inquiry. This is the problem of the *epistemic sufficiency* of inquiry as a means to consensus.

Even this counter-argument, however, does not challenge the desirability of the free inquiry ideal. More difficult questions regarding practical universality arise over the appropriateness factor in the ideal speech situation. Indeed, the questions of how much consensus is enough and whether free inquiry is always the appropriate practice (even for achieving the necessary consensus) are the central obstacles for Habermas' project. Counter-examples are obvious: one does not assume the need to engage in reciprocal inquiry with animals, infants, and homicidal sociopaths. *When*, in that case, is free inquiry the appropriate social practice? And what is it that tells us when free inquiry is or is not the appropriate procedure?

(b) That free inquiry fails to specify its own epistemic limits as a formal model of action has practical consequences leading to this second line of critique. This line questions the *practical appropriateness* of free inquiry and consensus. What happens when the effectiveness of inquiry appears to fail, or when the failure of one party to meet ideal conditions jeopardizes not only the effectiveness but even the appropriateness of the ideal of consensus? Is there some point at which we are not obligated to achieve consensus, and what determines *that* point?

The practical universalization of the model leads to a curious paradox: its universality would require that nothing is outside the model. When the preconditions are not met, however, the whole problem is that we are outside the model. In that case, to assume that the formal preconditions are practical obligations is to confuse ends and means: for while formal preconditions may be necessary to practice the model, that does not mean that the model is the necessary way to achieve the preconditions. That would be the case only if the preconditions of free inquiry were not *ideal* preconditions, but always already met. Only then would there be no practical circumstance outside the formal legitimacy of the model. But just because achieving the preconditions of free inquiry is a practical problem, the application of the model is an open question.

This problem of achieving the preconditions of inquiry is apparent even if one grants Habermas the notion that free discourse is a universal social ideal. What is one supposed to do when living under a ruthless, coercive tyranny? If one promotes free discussion, one is silenced. Since even minimal preconditions of free discussion are not met, the ideal speech situation does not indicate what constitutes rational social behavior.

Or to take a less drastic example, what about life in a society where there is apparently free discussion, but where the means of socialization are all under the control of a superficially benevolent elite which supports barbaric regimes from afar? Because of the combined appearances of benevolence and free inquiry, discussion can in fact *be* free without threat to the elite: one's protests can be politely tolerated as marginal distortions or as evidence of freedom. According to the ideal speech model, one's resistance is limited to dialoguing, however vainly. And what is worse, in all other matters one remains complicit with the *de facto* subversion of true democracy. In any case, the practical universalization of the preconditions of free inquiry reinscribes them from preconditions to ends-in-themselves, regardless of the consequences of their iron rule.

These examples expose the free inquiry model's silence on its own limits, on what to do when its preconditions are not met. The model's abstraction from the real, that is, ignores the competing practical demands that constitute its own precondition of contextual appropriateness. One need only consider several of the more effective emancipatory actions of recent times: the Civil Rights movement in America, the embargo of the apartheid regime in South Africa, or even Gorbachev's perestroika. None of these are instances of dialogic inquiry; indeed, their means are implicitly condemned by their departure from the discursive ideal. Yet it is not clear that communicative action would have been morally preferable, or especially effective, or that the moral cost of these irrational actions is intolerable.[7] Habermas, therefore, has not established the practical universality of his model.

3. The circle of Kant

On a strong reading of Habermas' universalism, there should be nothing *outside* of the obligation to achieve consensus, though we have found reason to question that reading. Furthermore, when we examine his strategy, we can trace the genealogy of his blindness to the limits of his model. Despite his wariness of Kantian formalism, Habermas' desire for universality leads him into the same thicket in which Kant became embroiled, the thicket where formal necessity and universality appear to become interchangeable in a confusion of analytical and practical modes of reasoning.

Assuming that pure reason is a closed system, Kant failed to see that

---

7. This discussion of the limits of Habermas' argument is but a brief version of the more extended discussions such as McCarthy's in *The critical theory of Jurgen Habermas* and Benhabib's in *Critique, norm, and utopia*. My point is not to survey the extent of others' critiques, but only to draw attention to Habermas' failure to universalize his grounds, a point which the other treatments support at greater length.

analysis to formal conditions does not define the pragmatic boundaries of reason.[8] By misapplying the closure of mathematics to epistemology and practical reason, Kant confused the formal necessity of a system's internal coherence with the practical problem of right action. Kant believed that formal analysis could define *a priori* practical obligation (the task of the categorical imperative). So while Kant's distinctions between pure and practical reason are the prototype of a modal theory of judgment, his theory is even more significant as the prototypical reduction of all judgment to *a priori* principles, including the reduction of practical reason to epistemic reason.

Though Habermas has avoided the stronger epistemic reduction of Kant by following Peirce's fallibility thesis, he follows Kant's confusion of formal and moral necessities. But it does not follow from (a) the fact that the formal conditions for free inquiry hold universally for ideal speech, that (b) free inquiry is always the ultimate moral or practical necessity. The formal necessity of ideal speech conditions is practice-specific, and its universality only applies to all rational beings *within* the context of rational inquiry *once the appropriateness of free inquiry has been determined by practical reason* (the appropriateness precondition for a speech act writ large).

Overlooking the shift from formal to practical modes of rationality, Habermas invokes the Kantian strategy of grounding practical reason in universality: "only those norms are permitted which can find general recognition in their domain of application. The principle serves to exclude, as not admitting of consensus, all norms whose content and range of validity are particular." [9] In other words, the necessity and sufficiency of consensus are assumed, although the whole thrust depends on the qualification "*in their domain of application*," which is where the question of the limits of dialogue lies. In ignoring this practical question for the formal one, Habermas mistakes one element of practical reason – its formal or ideal element – for the whole, and begs the question of application.

---

8. Having assumed that the mind processes all knowledge according to an ultimate set of categories, Kant concluded that reason's self-reflection would discover these ultimate grounds of knowledge, the structure of pure reason, knowledge's ultimate limits. Transcendental analysis and deduction were supposed to reveal these necessary grounds. But Kant underestimated his own metaphor of the mind's construction of reality.

9. Quoted by Thomas McCarthy, *The critical theory of Jurgen Habermas*, Cambridge: MIT, 1978; p. 313.

Habermas overlooks the problem of application because he fails to see that practical reason is ultimately a prudential problem, not a procedural problem. Against the grain of Habermas' universalism, the essence of practical reason is not so much its ideal character, but its *applied* character, i.e. the need to apply abstract ideals to the real world – precisely what Kant and Habermas hope to avoid by appeal to formal necessity. The problem of application, however, demands of practical reason not only the formal conditions of some privileged practice, but the choice between different practices or ends. Indeed, in terms of the distinctions in cognitive interests, it is just its concern with the *particulars* of application which practical or moral reason shares with instrumental reason, as opposed to the formal generalities of epistemic inquiry.

The problem in Kant's and in Habermas' cases is the same: the equivocal character of the term "necessity" that attaches to formal conditions. Transcendental analysis assumes a practice in order to discover its necessary conditions. But while the necessity of those conditions is practice-specific, its formal necessity for that practice is mistaken for practical universality; it is mistaken, that is, for a moral priority over other possible practices. *That* question is a question of real moral contexts, not a question of the presupposed conditions of one practice. But having confused formal necessity with practical universality, Habermas assumes that the obligation of free inquiry must always be in force. This confuses what we must do to communicate with what we must do.[10]

Habermas' confusion of formal and practical universality shows that rather than escaping the formalism of Kant's transcendental subject,

---

10. As with Kant's system of pure reason, Habermas falls into the trap of practical self-closure. The contextual dimension of practical reason – the issue of appropriate practice – entirely drops out of the picture in the name of categorical universality. When Kant extrapolated his notion of categorical duty to institutionalized authority, he discovered that rebellion could not be legitimated since, if universalized, it would mean that no order (anarchy) might be preferable to imperfect degrees of law and order, a conclusion Kant thought to be incoherent. Thus Kant sympathized with the French Revolution but was forced to condemn its rebelliousness. Habermas' ideal speech situation faces a comparable problem. As a version of the ideal contract, it seems sufficiently just. But it assumes that a rational procedure for achieving consensus is not only a good idea, but always the best idea. We are forced back into Kant's maxim: exercise freedom of thought, but obey – in this case the rules of consensus formation.

Habermas has merely socialized it into the duty to achieve rational consensus.[11]

4. When partiality becomes dogmatism

Habermas gives the impression of having discovered the universal form of rationality by assuming the inquiry model, analyzing to its necessary conditions, and then assuming that the model is adequate to establish its own preconditions. This argues in a circle, which is exposed in the case of the parties who are not already committed to consensus. Habermas' only possible response to the debating dogmatists is a dogma of his own: do not stop dialoguing until you have achieved the consensus implicit in the possibility of dialoguing.

As McCarthy notes, "The crucial step in [Habermas'] argument is obviously that from the universality of truth (and rightness) claims to discourse as the proper mode of their redemption" (McCarthy, 323). But the practice in question, far from being rationally sufficient, may not even be practically sufficient to achieve its own preconditions. Moreover, the fact that the problem of practical reason is wider than the scope of free inquiry means that the necessary preconditions of free inquiry do not specify either their own limits or what to do if their conditions are not met. We must conclude that Habermas does not warrant the move from the formal necessity of inquiry's preconditions to the universal obligation to solve all social problems dialogically.

These aporias show that Habermas has not reduced social rationality to the formal conditions of inquiry. The formal necessity of ideal speech conditions for inquiry do not necessarily constitute *the* universal or ultimate social obligation; they are merely presupposed by a given ideal of public discourse whose scope within the various activities of a society remains an open question. Even if one must be able to talk or listen to be human, one need not *always* talk or listen to be a rational human, even in the face of disagreement.[12]

11. McCarthy notes that the domain of rightness may lend more cogency to the consensus model than the domain of truth, since "the connection between consensus and rightness is initially more plausible than consensus and truth" (McCarthy, 314). Or, as noted above, consensus may be just, yet not true.
12. This formal-practical confusion may contribute to Habermas' confusion of truth with conditions of agreement. For even if Kant and Habermas have identified the transcendental conditions of consensus formation, consensus does not guarantee

D. The critical error of universality

Ironically, the case against the universality of communicative reason is a version of Habermas' own critique of systems theory. Habermas rightly argues that the abstract functionalist structures into which systems theory analyzes society cannot capture the contingency of meaning, the hermeneutic dimension of the lifeworld, which does not reduce to systemic formality. Meaning, Habermas argues in that case, is not purely formal, but contextual as well. Yet this is just the problem with Habermas' own formalism: the ideality of critical debate does not capture the practical complexity of social contexts in which its applicability may be contested, a complexity for which there is no ideal procedural solution. Practical reason cannot be formalized.

On the one hand, Habermas is right to correct Kant's formalism with the ideal of democratic will-formation. The public sphere so defined "would morally become strictly universal" in the sense that it would apply to all. Yet Habermas' over-reading of this universality becomes formalistic in spite of himself when he believes that this structure of public discourse is somehow the ground of subjectification rather than merely its public limit. This formalistic excess appears when he claims: "Internalization [of the conditions of ideal speech] would only be complete when ... the readiness to engage in discursive clarification of practical questions ... was *alone* internalized, but in other respects the continuous interpretation of needs was given over to communication processes" (my italics). Habermas' argument does not earn this reductive a notion of the ethical subject.

In view of these limitations, Habermas' analogy between psycho-analytic diagnosis and critical theory turns out to be a misleading product of his formalism. Habermas believes that, like symptoms of psychosis, symptoms of domination would be reflected in systematic disorders in communication. But to make communicative reason the *a*

truth. Even if consensus formation is a *just procedure* of inquiry, that is, it does not warrant facts, but only agreement. As Thomas McCarthy has put it, "'truth' is a normative concept and thus cannot be tied to the de facto achievement of consensus: not just any agreement that comes to pass can serve as a warrant for truth" (Thomas McCarthy, *The critical theory of Jurgen Habermas*, Cambridge: MIT, 1978; p. 304). Thus a committee of scientists may concur that a new theory appears to be the best among a group of candidates, though its predictions may then turn out to be wrong: consensus does not determine the outcome of the experiments. Consensus theories as such are authorized by intersubjective agreement on truth conditions rather than by an objective notion of truth.

priori solution to domination confuses the medium with the message: though it may play an instrumental role in such pathologies, formal incompetence is neither a necessary nor a sufficient condition for either psychosis or domination. Indeed, extremes of creativity are often destined to appear irrational, though it does not mean they fail of competence or fail to communicate. And those who are most likely to propagandize are very likely to be careful about appearing to follow the rules of free inquiry. Communicative competence is not the *sine qua non* of freedom or the rationality of the subject, just as poor grammar is not the psychopath's primary problem. Likewise, for critical theory the issue is not always the form of free inquiry, but of the appropriateness of a practice in a given context.[13]

What does it mean, then, that the claims of communicative reason do not turn out to be practically universal? What would it mean to reject Habermas' reduction of practical reason? It means that domination is not merely the negation of a single practice. It means that society is constituted by contexts of multiple practical claims that are not *a priori* hierarchized. It means that epistemology is not "the emancipatory mode." It means that practical reason does not reduce to a single ideal of social rationality, an ultimate practice (free inquiry) that always governs all other practices. It means that critical theory is grounded by the universality of all three cognitive practices (instrumental, formal, and practical), rather than by the universality of

13. The issue of universality indicates a point on which Habermas loses an insight of the early critical theorists. Whereas Habermas presumed to improve the rigor of Marxist critique by moving the grounds from labor to language, the Frankfurt School theorists shunned formalism of any sort. The earlier theorists avoided privileging a systematic ground precisely because they respected the creativity of the forces of domination as well as those of a free people.

More recently, Foucault speaks well to this point: "... I do not think that there is anything that is functionally – by its very nature – absolutely liberating. Liberty is a *practice*. So there may, in fact, always be a certain number of projects whose aim is to modify some constraints, to loosen, or even to break them, but none of these projects can, simply by its nature, assure that people will have liberty, automatically, that it will be established by the project itself. The liberty of men is never assured by the institutions and laws that are intended to guarantee them. This is why almost all of these laws and institutions are quite capable of being turned around. Not because they are ambiguous, but simply because 'liberty' is what must be exercised ....The guarantee of freedom is freedom" (*FR*, 245).

"If one were to find a place ... where liberty is effectively exercised, one would find that this is not owing to the order of objects, but, once again, owing to the practice of liberty" (*FR*, 246).

any one. Of course, these limitations do not render the free inquiry model useless for critical theory, but they subordinate it to the wider scope of practical reason.

As a social model, Habermas' ideal speech situation has much moral cogency. As a democratic ideal, it provides a standard against which societies can be judged for systematic obstructions of free inquiry. Indeed, it sets a credible standard by which thin theories of democracy (elitist, managerial, indirectly representative, etc.) can be critiqued as manipulative and unrepresentative. Insofar as the notion of public consent is taken to mean freely *informed* consent, the structures of public discourse are subject to the various principles Habermas has identified: reciprocity, symmetry of roles, non-coercion, appropriateness of context, etc. This provision of institutional standards gives Habermas some of the social-critical grounds he needs, although not the universalism he wants. He has found a central paradigm of democratic rationality, but he has not found the only form of social rationality, or one that can always tell us what to do.

The considerable interest in the work of Habermas derives from his linkage between the fate of modern politics and the fate of philosophy itself. Yet our analysis suggests that he has raised questions which he and his critics have not only failed to settle, but failed to frame adequately. For while he has denounced the hegemony of technique over political choices, and the subordination of human welfare to the play of meaning, he has failed to square these antireductive arguments with his reduction of practical reason to the communication model. On the other hand, while his critics have denounced his distinctions between cognitive modes and his reduction of emancipatory practice to free inquiry, they have failed to provide the kinds of theoretical frameworks that can account for the critique of domination, including the permanent theoretical possibilities to which Habermas, Gadamer, negative theorists, and Foucault's self-invention all appeal according to their own critical agendas. Using his own cognitive modes, this immanent critique of Habermas suggests that even his failure confirms the indispensability of those critical conditions appealed to by him and his critics.

Framing the problem of foundations, then, appears to be at the heart of the problem of emancipatory critique. Postmodernists fear foundational reductions, and they are right to do so. Modernists fear the disappearance of the real into the fabrications of meaning, and they are right to do so. The rightness of both, therefore, demands a notion of philosophical foundations that is neither reductive nor arbitrary. Or put in terms of the modes of cognitive interest, foundational and practical thought do not compete for emancipatory priority, but rather constitute different moments in the critique of domination. In that case, moving beyond modernist reductions and postmodern arbitrariness demands acknowledging both the generality of foundations (e.g. the pragmatic conditions discovered by epistemological analysis) and the practical indeterminacy of appropriate action (i.e. the indeterminacy of practical and hermeneutic contextuality).

The generality of this point attests to the continued force of philosophy as a general and theoretical practice in its own right. But regarding the kind of practices that are central to social critique, philosophy's generality yields to the contingencies of specific social contexts. Philosophy, that is, remains a player in the arena of social critique, but less as a final judge than as a critic of initial terms. As the critics of technocracy correctly believe, philosophy remains an ally in the articulation of generic possibilities, even by warranting a plurality of possible utopias. But practical reason, not epistemic reason, is the final judge of social action. Thus Habermas' fondness for formal necessities must give way to the plurality of social spheres and the indeterminacy of practical reason, whose autonomy he should defend against formal reduction as vigorously as he defends it against technological reduction.

8

Critical theory and postmodern localism: rebels without a cause:

Today, with theory paralyzed and disparaged by the all-governing bustle, its mere existence, however impotent, bears witness against the bustle. This is why theory is legitimate and why it is hated; without it, there would be no changing the practice that constantly calls for change. Those who chide theory anachronistically obey the *topos* of dismissing, as obsolete, what remains painful as thwarted.   Theodor W. Adorno

A. The problem of critical theory

Kant epitomized the revolutionary rationalism of the Enlightenment when he said, "Our age is the age of criticism, to which everything must be subjected."[1] The age's critical spirit led to revolutions in several domains: a technological revolution in the name of control over nature, social revolutions in the name of democracy, economic revolutions in the name of industrial and socialist economies, and cultural revolutions in the name of free inquiry, self-expression, and rational thought. The impact of these developments is difficult even to estimate; the modern world is a transformed world whose legacy cannot, in many ways, be undone.

Yet a number of challenges to modernism have placed its legacy in an ambiguous light. On the one hand, traditionalists such as Gadamer highlight the contingent and historical grounds of even rationalist thought, pointing to its roots in the prejudices of our ancestors. According to Gadamer, all thought is at once motivated and bound by historically conditioned ideas and commitments. Such grounds allow for change *within* tradition, but allow the subject no revolutionary or "rational" break *from* a traditional past into an objective, unprejudiced state of knowing:

the thing which hermeneutics teaches us is to see through the dogmatism of asserting an opposition and separation between the ongoing, natural

---

1. Footnote to the first preface to the *Critique of pure reason*.

"tradition" and the reflective appropriation of it. For behind this assertion stands a dogmatic objectivism that distorts the very concept of hermeneutical reflection itself. In this objectivism the understander is seen ... not in relationship to the hermeneutical situation and the constant operativeness of history in his own consciousness, but in such a way as to imply that his own understanding does not enter into the event.   (*PH*, 28)

The reflective consciousness idolized by the Enlightenment is in fact always structured by a historical background – however silently immanent its influence. As rationalism's ideal of critical objectivity seeks an impossible escape from historical conditions, modernist rationalism was fundamentally misconceived as a transcendence of the arbitrary and local prejudices of traditional cultures.

From a different angle of critique, postmodernists agree with traditionalists on the limits of modern rationalism and the reflective consciousness, denying the full self-presence of the subject. They too conclude that modernism's promise has been disillusioned by history, although they are more skeptical than Gadamer about the validity of traditionalism. Post-structuralism suspects traditionalism and modernism for the same reason: i.e. for authorizing privilege, whether on historical or rational grounds. In the postmodern view modern rationalism merely substitutes a pseudo-rigorous analytic authority for traditionalism's more haphazard, arbitrary, and local legitimation of privilege. By contrast to both, postmodernism considers any privileged form of cultural authority – whether institutional or theoretical – to be questionable in principle.

Modernism's faith in reason involved a belief in real progress. For postmodernists, however, the ambiguities of modern progress – with its commodified, normalized, and abstracted productions – profoundly discredit the "global theories" of truth and legitimacy that led to such expectations. Postmodernists believe that the world and its history cannot be assessed as a whole, or "totalized" as modernism's universal ideal of progress implies is possible. Thus Foucault refers to the "inhibiting effect of global, totalitarian theories" (*PK*, 80), while Shoshana Felman notes that "human knowledge is by definition that which is untotalizable, that which rules out any possibility of totalizing what it knows or of eradicating its own ignorance" (BI, 18). For Stanley Fish, hermeneutic theory errs in its attempt to govern practice "from a position above or outside it" and to reduce meaning to "universal rules" rather than "concrete practices" (*AT*, 110).

Furthermore, modernism's rationalization of the world is not only a fantasy of knowledge; it is a fantasy of power as well, the Baconian equation of knowledge with objective, universal power. Through strategies that theorize the essence of rationality, the common good, or reflective truth, totalizing theories elevated themselves into a position to legislate knowledge, truth, and justice for all people in all contexts. Given the submission of progress to the calculation of maximum productivity, the designation of rational needs, the rationalization of the workplace and school, the commodification of the quality of life, and the enforcibility of freedom, postmodernists have come to see theory as an intrinsically colonizing force, the Chief Academic Officer in the empire of discourses.

As a counter-memory (in Foucault's phrase) to traditional and modern theory, postmodernism critiques modernism's strategies of authorization such as the essentializing of the human subject, the universalization of needs, the moral neutrality of scientific discourse, and the interpretive transparency of consciousness. The works of such seminal figures as Bakhtin, Derrida, Foucault, Lyotard, Deleuze, and Lacan have challenged the epistemological assumptions of rationalist politics − especially the assumption of the representability of subjects with their complex contents and contexts − as well as modernist theories of political legitimacy.

The combined failure of modernist foundationism (either in its rationalist or empiricist forms) and its imperial consequences has led to the hermeneutics of suspicion, to anti-theory, to anti-epistemology, to anti-foundationism, to anti-metanarrativity, to strong conventionism, and all such projects for decentralizing knowledge, meaning, and authority. And yet, while fulsome in their criticisms of modernist theory and politics, postmodernists have been less forthright about their own theoretical commitments and the political implications of their own discourse. At some cost to their coherence and accountability, numerous postmodernists have generalized their critiques against logocentrism's foundationist generalities, seemingly unaware or indifferent to their own implicit commitments to theory, epistemic reduction, and their appeals to unspecified notions of freedom.

Indeed, postmodernists generalize not only about the limits of epistemology, but about their political implications as well. Having concluded that philosophy has no ultimate foundations, Rorty suggests that philosophy can do nothing more enlightening than facilitate understandings between the varieties of provincialism. Similarly, since conventional commitments are all we have, Fish suggests that any claims to transcendent professional integrity are meaningless: professional behavior is the behavior of professionals. Since theories of class and the state are bankrupt, according to Foucault, there appears to be no collective interest that a political party could legitimately claim to represent. It would seem that social critique, in such views, is bound by nothing more than the arbitrary stipulations that accidental beliefs confer. This prison house of moral localism is the legacy of postmodern social theory.

Even more fully than Rorty and Fish, however, Foucault's work embodies the political contradictions of postmodernism. Foucault shuns political theories because he is skeptical of the "rationality of dominations," the centralized systems of power that are legitimated in the name of freedom. Yet, his refusal to rationalize a new political ideal admits of two notable exceptions: the notion of the specific intellectual and the ideal of ascending power. These exceptions show the theoretical tension in his profession of localism.

As a "pessimistic activist," Foucault shuns the "general intellectual" in preference for the "specific intellectual," the technological savant who would be able to facilitate resistance to established authority by knowing where the most effective points of intervention would be, who "by following lines of fragility in the present" can manage "to grasp why and how that-which-is might no longer be that-which-is."[2] Instead of the general intellectual's "descending" theories of sovereignty and class power, Foucault believes that insofar as resistance rises from below, we need ascending theories of power: "One must rather conduct an *ascending* analysis of power, starting, that is, from its infinitesimal mechanisms, which each have their own tactics, and then see how these mechanisms of power each have been – and continue to be – invested, utilized, involuted, transformed, displaced, extended, etc., by ever more general mechanisms and by forms of global domination" (Kritzman 36). By virtue of these changes, Foucault hopes to exploit theory for its emancipatory potential, and avoid its appropriation by the rationality of dominations.

Foucault's recommendations are stimulating, and his own work shows how to put some of those recommendations into fruitful practice. Yet is not clear that emancipation and resistance can be fully effective with only those tools Foucault has recommended. For

2. Michel Foucault: *Politics, philosophy, culture: interviews and other writings, 1977–1984,* ed. Lawrence D. Kritzman, New York: Routledge, 1988; p. 36; hereafter referred to as "Kritzman."

instance, it is not clear that one can have *only* specific intellectuals (1) without at least one general intellectual to mediate the specific ones – as Rorty's hermeneutic mid-wife could do under the advisement of a larger plan, or (2) without specific intellectuals being both general *and* specific in order to mediate themselves. How, for instance, could the specific intellectual identify the lines of greatest fragility in centralized power without a general perspective in which to compare strategies? Nor do we know what Foucault means by "substantive" resistance without a pragmatic notion of depth or generality of interests to motivate collective action. These objections are not necessarily fatal – for Foucault might just *happen* to gain massive numbers of converts who spontaneously and effectively decide to resist centralized power without a global plan – although without a general theory such a hope is simply utopian. These problems point to the political liabilities of postmodernism's hostility to theory, liabilities that are compounded by the hint of a general theory disguised as a spirit of localism.

To the contrary of the ultra-marginal model of critique, the critique of domination of the Frankfurt School theorists, which shares the emancipatory aims of postmodern critics of modernism, demands a more ambitious role for theory. Capitalist and socialist industrialism also left these earlier critical theorists skeptical about centralized power, although they allowed that theory was as much the victim as the culprit in the cunning of power. It is true that the first generation of critical theorists did not have the benefit of the postmodernist critiques of language, and that their proximity to the language of Hegel and Marx leaves many of their formulations ambiguous at best, and too liable to reduction at worst. It is also true that they did not perfect the tools that their theoretical ideal required, and that they sometimes despaired of finding a redemptive form of reason outside art. Still, some of the most useful insights of postmodernist thought are glimpsed in such seminal essays as Horkheimer's "Notes on science and the crisis" (hereafter, NSC), "Traditional and critical theory" (TCT), and Marcuse's "Philosophy and critical theory" (PCT). Moreover, some of the contradictions of postmodern anti-foundationist generalizing are avoided by their view of theory while inviting a reconstructed notion of foundations.[3]

3. Marcuse's essay appears in his *Negations*, Boston: Beacon, 1968; Horkheimer's essays appear in his *Critical theory: selected essays*, New York: Continuum, 1986. My defense of the philosophical implications of these essays does not imply

Given the responsiveness of the Frankfurt School theorists both to philosophy and to the critical interests of social theory, I suggest that a dialogue between the Frankfurt School and postmodernist theory is a useful exercise for current political and social inquiry. Indeed, this essay can be understood as a speculation on Foucault's own remark, "if I had been aware of [the Frankfurt School when I was a student], I would not have said a number of stupid things that I did say and I would have avoided many of the detours which I made while trying to pursue my own humble path" (Kritzman, 26). In this spirit, the following discussion of the Frankfurt School critical theorists will be less a history or overview of their thought, or even a close reading of some of their more influential critiques of culture, than an attempt to advance some of the more promising (if insufficiently refined) ideas that can be found in their essays on the foundations of critical theory.[4]

B. Re-membering Frankfurt theory: the three grounds of social theory

The legacy of Frankfurt School theory is not a static emancipatory paradigm, but rather an open-ended project of critical theorizing, a dynamic ideal that follows from their reflections on the conditions of social critique. On the one hand, their theory improves upon its

approval of other, better known theses, many of which are not necessarily entailed or representative of these essays. It must be noted here that the relation between these quite foundationist essays and the narrower analyses by the Frankfurt School theorists is complex and problematic.

In particular, I acknowledge difficulties in the work of Frankfurt School theorists regarding such issues as realism vs nominalism, the nature of the subject, and the relation between pleasure and happiness. Many of the Frankfurt School analyses that followed these early essays remained too committed to a philosophy of the subject to avoid compromising a theory of praxis (see Seyla Benhabib's *Critique, norm and utopia*, New York: Columbia University Press, 1986). Furthermore, with its strong commitment to the historical constitution of subject and object, the method of immanent critique (which connects the Frankfurt School to the legacy of Hegel and Marx) was not averse to being cast in the guise of nominalism (Adorno), which strategy threatens the recuperation of objective critical grounds that the essays examined here reveal to be possible.

4. Several fine summaries and commentaries on the Frankfurt School legacy provide the historical and genealogical work to which this essay owes much. These include: Martin Jay's *The dialectical imagination: a history of the Frankfurt School and the Institute of Social Research, 1923–1950*, Boston: Little, Brown, 1973; David Held's *Introduction to critical theory: Horkheimer to Habermas*, Berkeley: University of California Press, 1980; and Douglas Kellner's *Critical theory, Marxism, and modernity*, Baltimore: Johns Hopkins Press, 1989.

predecessors and competitors by avoiding the formalist reductions of rationalist epistemology, the objectivist reductions of positivism, and the historicist relativism of hermeneutics. On the other hand, critical theory identifies the formal, objective, and historical factors that are the theoretical conditions of critique. This balanced ideal of critical complexity avoids the Scylla and Charybdis of reductive and anarchic conceptions of critical foundations.

By reconstructing critical authority, the Frankfurt School theorists hoped to escape the reductive excesses of Enlightenment progressivism while salvaging its emancipatory ideal. Thus they conceived of their project as mediating the legacies of Hegel and Marx, hoping to avoid the rationalist excesses of the former and the positivist excesses of the latter, while also acknowledging historical determinacy. From their reconstructions of their predecessors, the critical theorists distil out an inchoate epistemology where formality accounts for the systematic legacy of philosophy, objectivity captures the empirical substance of modern science, and historicity reflects the evolutionary and contextual particulars that must be accounted for in a theory of social change. By mediating epistemic abstraction, empirical determinacy, and contextual uniqueness, the Frankfurt School theorists hope to reconcile the virtues of traditional theory and postmodern particularity in the interest of emancipatory social praxis.

1. Science as objectivity

It is not surprising that critical theory should take objectivity seriously, being inheritors of the legacy of historical materialism. True, Frankfurt School theorists tended to relax the mechanistic quality of the Marxian dialectic. And Adorno professed to nominalism rather than to realism as a foundationist perspective. Yet Horkheimer acknowledges science's technological ground when he notes: "In the Marxist theory of society, science is regarded as one of man's productive powers." Even though science becomes caught up in "social values," which in turn "[take] shape in methods of production," yet science "constitutes a means of production" (NSC, 3). This productive ground of science is a social-structural substance as well as an epistemic transcendence of human constructions into the exteriority of natural forces: "There will always be something that is extrinsic to man's intellectual and material activity, namely nature as the totality of as yet unmastered elements with which society must deal" (TCT, 210). For critical theory, the grounding force of nature comes from the fact that it is *not* totalized by theory, that it remains transcendent and immanent in scientific theory at the same time.

While objectivity appears as a transcending constraint in critical theory, it does not reduce to a static abstraction. For, while approximating the "laws" of nature, theory also reflects the objectivity of historical and social context, including the pragmatic interests of scientists and their society: "What scientists in various fields regard as the essence of theory thus corresponds, in fact, to the immediate tasks they set for themselves" (TCT, 194). This combination of particular circumstances and general interests shapes the criteria of truth: "That new views in fact win out is due to concrete historical circumstances, even if the scientist himself may be determined to change his views only by immanent motives" (TCT, 195). This point anticipates Foucault's fusion of discourse and power as a network of relations at once technological and linguistic, at once objectively grounded and untotalizable in the direction either of nature or of language.

On the point of objectivity, science can help keep philosophy in line. To subdue philosophy's transcendental urges, Marcuse situates the internal logic of rationalist philosophy within the externality of objective science. Whereas rationalist philosophy theorizes truth as abstractly as possible, that transcendence is finally challenged by the need of those abstractions to confront nature-as-empirical-science and history-as-social-science, a confrontation that limits formalism with reality: "The untruth inherent in all transcendental treatment of the problem thus comes into philosophy 'from outside'; hence it can be overcome only outside philosophy" (PCT, 150). Philosophy, to make the untruth of its abstract concepts true, needs the externality of objective science and the concrete application that only practice can bring to abstract reason. Thus the systematic abstraction of philosophy and the objective concreteness of science constitute complementary balances in the notion of truth.

But just because objectivity is only one of three kinds of constraints upon critical theory, it is possible that its influence can be exaggerated, an exorbitancy which is the theoretical vice of positivism and the social vice of the hegemony of instrumental reason.

In classical and modern rationalisms, the hegemony of instrumental reason was checked by the primacy of logical necessity: the contingency of nature deferred to the abstract certainties of metaphysical and rationalist philosophies. The "abstract freedom of the thinking subject" (PCT, 150), the Enlightenment's autonomous rational subject, was the culmination of philosophy's traditional thrust toward abstract universality and self-certainty. In the age of empiricism, however, the progressive character of technological power displaced the ambiguous and much-disputed abstractions of reason. Suggesting that the contingencies of nature are rationally domesticated by technological objectivity, empiricism reduces knowledge to power, reason to instrumental reason.

For positivists, technological objectivity is no longer understood as an independent constraint on thought, but rather as reason itself in the form of the empirical method. Positivism becomes the modern version of philosophical transcendence, whose mythic aura of power privileges an evolving technological practice under the aegis of efficiency and success. "'Production,'" Horkheimer notes, "means 'the creative sovereignty of thought.'" Despite this apotheosis of reason-as-power, however, the open-endedness of science means that there is in fact no theoretical closure: "Since everything about the object is reduced to conceptual determinations, the end-result of such theoretical work is that nothing is to be regarded as material and stable" (TCT, 198). With an inflated sense of autonomy, instrumental reason appropriates the rational world altogether, a self-constituting fiction whose technical success becomes the sign of its self-sufficiency: "The determinative, ordering, unifying function is the sole foundation for all else, and towards it all human effort is directed. Production is production of unity, and production is itself the product" (TCT, 198).

Anticipating similar claims by Heidegger, Gadamer, and Habermas, the Frankfurt School theorists insisted that science overextended its role as one constraint in the process of knowledge. The objectivist pretensions of instrumental reason have substituted for the dogmatic errors of traditional metaphysics a modern dogma of reason-as-technique. The critical legacy of science is therefore ambiguous: though it is a necessary partner in the critique of domination, its propensity for totalizing reduction makes it a willing agent of domination.

2. Science as pure theory

To counterbalance the excesses of scientism, critical theory intends to preserve the virtues of traditional theory, "one side of which is formal logic" (TCT, 216). Formality, then, stands as one kind of limit to epistemic authority, and a counterweight to the constraints of nature and history. For truth cannot reduce to either the facts of nature or the accidents of social history. According to Horkheimer, truth must find its ideal content in theory as both the product and judge of history:

It is not for social interests to decide what is or is not true; the criteria for truth have developed, rather, in connection with progress at the theoretical level. Science itself admittedly changes in the course of history, but this fact can never stand as an argument for other criteria of truth than those which are appropriate to the state of knowledge at a given level of development.

(NSC, 3)

Knowledge is fundamentally a theoretical affair, and thus depends on the formal preconditions of the various human practices as well as on science's developing control over natural forces. As the ancients taught and as Kant reaffirmed in his notion of the critical tribunal of reason, "primary propositions of traditional theory define universal concepts under which all facts in the field in question are to be subsumed" (TCT, 224). Analytic theory, therefore, cannot be written off as mere fiction, but must be accounted in terms of its own authority as theory and as truth: "When critical theory comes to terms with philosophy, it is interested in the truth content of philosophical concepts and problems. It presupposes that they really contain truth" (PCT, 148).[5]

This does not mean, of course, that abstract theorizing must be accepted at face value. Adorno's *Against epistemology* emphasizes critical theory's suspicions of rationalism's foundationist pretensions. For whatever formal conditions a practice may require, whatever truth conditions a language might allow, social knowledge involves an empirical and historical judgment based on the historical specificity of the context of action. But rejecting rationalism only means that theory cannot reduce truth to pure abstraction and complete theoretical autonomy. Critical theory's suspicions about epistemology do not warrant a dismissal of formal conditions in principle, but only rationalism's *reductive* uses of formal conditions. The point, finally, is to reconstruct epistemology from its abstractly universalist interpretation to the hermeneutically opening and pragmatically differentiating

5. Compare the Frankfurt School's concern with the problem of truth with an admission of Foucault's in a 1977 interview: "The problem of the truth of what I say is very difficult for me, and it's also the central problem. It's essentially the question which up to now I have never answered." (*Remarks on Marx*, 32)

effects of practical reasoning. This requires reconciling traditional theory with pragmatic epistemology.

When Horkheimer examines "traditional theory," he finds the standard deductive systemic ideal that descends from Aristotle to Husserl. Following Descartes, philosophy posits that "the order in the world is captured by a deductive chain of thought" (TCT, 189). Or as Husserl formulates it, theory is "an enclosed system of propositions for a science as a whole" (TCT, 188).[6] Here especially postmodernism suspects the totalizing ambitions of theory as a reactionary defense of hierarchy against difference and substantive change. For as Horkheimer notes: "The basic requirement which any theoretical system must satisfy is that all the parts should intermesh thoroughly and without friction. Harmony, which includes lack of contradictions, and the absence of superfluous, purely dogmatic elements which have no influence on the observable phenomena, are necessary conditions" (TCT, 190). The question for critical theory, then, concerns the cogency of traditional hierarchical conceptions of theoretical grounds, especially in light of philosophy's failure to achieve its idealized closure over pure reason, and empiricism's failure to come up with something better than verificationist or instrumentalist forms of reduction.

The path beyond the hierarchical reductions of pure theory and the blind power of instrumentalism is found in the logic of theoretical progress. As Hegel's foundationist sublations imply, and as Peirce theorized in his abductive theory of theory-invention, the key to the openness of theory – especially in its foundationist moments – lies in the hypothetical and dynamic character of its totalization. Though theory may be "the sum-total of propositions about a subject," Poincaré notes that "a theory always remains a hypothesis." Furthermore, its hypothetical character is directed by its context, its placement in what Lakatos calls a *research programme*. Such methodological frameworks, Poincaré observes, "must direct generalization, so as to increase ... the output of science" (TCT, 188).

The problem with traditional theory, then, is not that it failed to discover aspects of the formal conditions of thought, but rather that it

6. Also, "a systematically linked set of propositions, taking the form of a systematically linked deduction"; Horkheimer adds: "a certain totality of propositions ... , emerging in one other manner from theoretical work, in the systematic order of which propositions a certain totality of objects acquires definition" (TCT, 188).

failed to appreciate the practical context of theory itself, either in the hypothetical practice of theorizing, or in the differentiation of formality into an indefinite variety of practices rather than a single scientific practice. Certainty and universality – the epitome of the hierarchical ideal – mischaracterize the foundations of knowledge, whereas the discrimination of practical contexts turns out to be the final interest of epistemic authority.

This pragmatic turn highlights the questionability of foundational moments in philosophy and science, the historical substance that situates practice. If the formality of pure theory and the objectivity of science are thus inevitable constraints on knowledge, the constraint of historical context on practical reason must be accounted as well.

3. Science as historical practice

Freedom was the goal of reason for Kant and Hegel, but the passage from theory to practice faltered. Once epistemology seeks the freedom beyond foundational knowledge, philosophy defers its totalizing authority to the interests of history: i.e. after Hegel and Marx, "philosophy became superfluous as an independent scientific discipline dealing with the structure of reality" (PCT, 134).

To critique domination, critical theory builds on Marx's critique of Hegel. Marcuse revises Hegel's end-of-history-thesis, displacing (a) philosophy's abstract theorization of freedom with (b) the practical intent of critical theory: "With the concept of reason as freedom, philosophy seems to reach its limit. What remains outstanding to the realization of reason is not a philosophical task" (PCT, 137). Whereas Hegelian theory tended to collapse the freedom of reason into the necessity of the moment, critical theory recognizes that the "subsequent construction of the new society cannot be the object of theory, for it is to occur as the free creation of liberated individuals" (PCT, 135).

As an on-going, historically bound project, critical theory provides no permanent blueprint for the new society, no privileged paradigm, but critically identifies or "negates" the counter-emancipatory tendencies of the present. This rejection of predeterminacy allows "a state of affairs in which man's actions no longer flow from a mechanism but from his own decision. The judgment passed on the necessity inherent in the previous course of events implies here a struggle to change it from a blind to a meaningful necessity" (TCT, 229). Where history spontaneously was, there conscious reason must be.

Respect for history prevents a collapse into an objectivistic naturalism. Thus historical materialism maintains that, "[on] the one hand, neither the direction and methods of theory nor its object, reality itself, are independent of man, and, on the other hand, science is a factor in the historical process" (NSC, 4). So while pure theory gravitates toward "the ultimate and most general grounds of Being" (PCT, 135), and while science grounds reason in the blind determinacy of matter, Marcuse warns that "[l]imiting reason to 'pure' theoretical and practical achievement implies an avowal of bad facticity" (PCT, 140). Instead, history-in-reason must be acknowledged in human and social rationality.

Horkheimer argues that critical theory's "opposition to the traditional concept of theory springs in general from a difference not so much of objects as of subjects" (TCT, 209). As post-Newtonian physics has also insisted, the subject that thinks must be factored into the empirical validity of science. Here again critical theory anticipates the postmodernist conception of knowledge as a pragmatic-discursive strategy embedded in social practice, whether in the form of Foucault's power-knowledge linkage or Rorty's denial of essential or morally neutral categorizations: "The classificatory thinking of each individual is one of those social reactions by which men try to adapt to reality in a way that best meets their needs" (TCT, 199).

Yet postmodernism errs in conceiving itself in too revolutionary a fashion. The historical contextualization of pure theory and objectivity can only surpass these older notions by continually *seeing through* their limitations, if not in a linear progression, at least in a wider consideration. By reconstructing formality and objectivity, not as absolute determinations, but as constraints on history's own substance, philosophy surpasses Naturalism as the point of knowledge. And so the beginning of the end of philosophical history starts with Kant's formulation of the goal of reason as freedom, Hegel's mediation of freedom by history, Peirce's mediation of all thought as a sign process, and Marx's insistence that abstractions without practice cannot emancipate society.

While the practical emphasis of critical theory distinguishes it from traditional philosophy, Marcuse concludes that philosophy's history is itself a record of the limitation of reason by an objective history however ideologically encoded: "in its historical forms philosophy also contains insights into human and objective conditions whose truth points beyond previous society and thus cannot be completely reduced to it" (PCT, 148). The constraints of traditional philosophy include social and theoretical facts as well as theoretical limitations (whether as pure theory or in the confusions of formalist and positivist reductions). Objectivity does not dismiss the importance of historical context: it guarantees it.

The problem is to sort out the mix of theory and practice, freedom and determinacy, conscious and unconscious elements. Following Marx, critical theorists identify in the economy (i.e. society's organization for self-reproduction) a recalcitrant hybrid of reason and unreason. In this view, philosophy is only one element within the social structure, appearing "within the economic concepts of materialist theory." Given this balance of factors in social theory, if the social context of philosophy is ignored, the abstractions of philosophy only "threaten [critical] theory as a whole" (PCT, 134–5). Here critical theory joins the postmodern anarchist against crude Marxism and liberal universalism. For against such reductions to socio-economic facts and universalized citizens, historical concretion appears to the anarchist as the domain of the indeterminate, the unique, and the spontaneous. In line with Foucault's ideal of "thinking differently," the critical theorist, "[if] he pursues the idea of man, ... must think in opposition to facticity" (PCT, 150).

C. The openness of practical reason: critical theory as practice

Postmodern objections to totalizing theories are of two kinds: theoretical and practical. Theoretically, postmodernism suspects such theories of attempting to comprehend more than can be figured into one field of variables. The world is heterogeneous, and theories are homologous, reducing the blurred variety of things to misleading singularities and dominating centers. Defining its terms abstractly, theory defines knowledge as if from somewhere beyond the limitations of context. But postmodernists insist: despite their pretensions, theories remain partial, interested, and place-specific.

On the other hand, totalizing theories are suspected for practical and political reasons as well, i.e. as totalitarian, power-centralizing. By oversimplifying the interests of the many, they allow for the empowering of some people on behalf of all the others. Since truth is a thing of this world (Foucault), and since humans have no essence whose interests can be universalized, totalizing theories are inhibiting, if not misleading. Such postmodern considerations have made critical theory's interest in collective action and freedom problematic in principle.

Is the universal of freedom, however, like other universals? For instance, is it necessary to posit an essential self in order to critique domination? Or isn't it rather that domination is a structure that inhibits a freer self, in which case one critiques a structure of domination by appealing to an undefined, universal freedom rather than a defined, essential self? And is not the revolutionary authority of universal freedom an analytic universality that deconstructors appeal to in the name of the universal scope of hermeneutics and the ubiquitous readiness of language for deconstruction? Is not Foucault's own return to the Enlightenment as a "privileged domain for analysis" in the interests of "our impatience for liberty" a sign of the revolutionary character of the universal of freedom?

It cannot be doubted that many of the greatest travesties of justice have been perpetrated in the names of universal ideals, including freedom. Yet postmodern thought has not succeeded in making sense without such ideals; it has only succeeded in making sense by appealing to them implicitly and by being ready to give them up (a readiness that does not distinguish them from empirical fallibilists). Here Derrida's suggestion that we can only recycle Western metaphysics, not escape it, indicates an important limit to any localism that pretends to escape commitment to generalities. True, if we take postmodern localism as a heuristic counter-practice (as Foucault has suggested), its current emphasis is warranted. That is, if we take Foucault's appeals for specific intellectuals *rather than* general intellectuals, his appeals for local critique *rather than* theories of collective interest, and appeals for theories of ascending power *rather than* descending power as redressing an imbalance of past theorizing, they cannot but be welcomed. On the other hand, if such preferences are intended to discredit universals and global theorizing in principle, then they are untrue to Foucault's own generality of application and to the emancipatory scope of practical reason.

1. Utopia as history

Foucault has directed postmodern critique toward the prospective critique of the present: "That is my own belief...about the work of the intellectual, that it is fruitful in a certain way to describe that-which-is by making it appear as something that might not be, or that might not be as it is. Which is why this designation or description of the real never has a prescriptive value of the kind, 'because that is, that will be'" (Kritzman, 36–7). We are well advised not to assume the inevitability of the future, as Marcuse's and Jameson's emphasis on the utopian potential of the present suggests. The epistemic problem, however, concerns the preconditions for mediating the possibility of the future and the facticity of the present. What is required to know the present tendencies and future openings? And what can we urge on that basis? Does social emancipation have any currency, or only individual self-emancipation as Foucault's later work might suggest?

What substance can critical theory give the notion of prospective freedom? Marcuse says "freedom here means a real potentiality, a social relationship on whose realization human destiny depends" (PCT, 143). Unlike the indulgences of utopian dreaming, "these are exclusively potentialities of the concrete social situation" (PCT, 142). Furthermore, here is where the global perspective is indispensable, for future possibilities must be strategic as well as concrete: "the transformed social existence must be determined by its ultimate goal even at its inception" (PCT, 145).

On this point of the moment of power, crude Marxism and some postmodernists fall prey respectively to fallacies of premature positivity and infinite postponement, both of which can be avoided by reconceiving the utopian moment. Against scientistic denouncements of utopian thought, Marcuse reminds us: "The utopian element was long the only progressive element in philosophy" (PCT, 143). Against rationalist abstractions, which could include Habermas', he also warns: "The abyss between rational and present reality cannot be bridged by conceptual thought." Anticipating recent critiques of philosophy of science, Marcuse concludes: "In order to retain what is not yet present as a goal in the present, phantasy is required" (PCT, 154). And like those pragmatic critiques of science, Marcuse notes that the scientific method does not achieve closure over itself. The ultimate ground of science's hypotheses, its deepest theoretical structure, is itself hypothetical, its future-orientation never fully redeemed: "In the theoretical reconstruction of the social process, the critique of current conditions and the analysis of their tendencies necessarily include future-oriented components" (PCT, 145).

In addition to requiring phantasy, the problem of decisive evidence is compounded for social sciences since, as Popper insists, social theory is itself part of the process of change. Hence, the practical legitimacy of the theory is premised on the need and power to falsify current facts with a better reality, including a new practice. Given this counterfactual position of critical social theory, Marcuse hyperbolically states that critical theory "can invoke no facts in confirmation of the theoretical elements that point toward future freedom" (PCT, 145). Facts may be certain, but they are not certain of the future. Likewise, as successful critical theory becomes part of the new social whole, it too will require critique: "critical theory is, last but not least, critical of itself and of the social forces that make up its own basis" (PCT, 156). Its truths, likewise, must involve a "continuous alteration of the theoretician's existential judgment on society" (TCT, 234).

2. Pragmatic universals

Such concessions to the fictive character of social theory link critical theory with post-structuralism, though Horkheimer is not so sanguine as Foucault about surpassing traditional theory with only local critique. True, Foucault makes concessions to homogeneity, systematicity, and generality in the later essay "What is enlightenment?" – and yet we may wonder if he can achieve the "analytics of power" through his "local tests" and his "ascending" method of accumulating the instances of microphysical events. Horkheimer thinks not.

Referring to earlier theoretical controversies in the methods of the social sciences, Horkheimer refers to those who, like Foucault, sought to work up to generality from the "microphysical" data of local observations. According to these partisans of the local: "The way that sociology must take in the present state of research is (it is argued) the laborious *ascent* from the description of social phenomena to detailed comparisons and only then to the formation of general concepts" (TCT, 192; my italics). This is classic inductivism. On the other side, however, stood Durkheim, who opted "for an abridgment of the inductive process":

[Induction's] role is to put into our hands points of reference to which we can refer other observations than those which have furnished us with these very points of reference. But for this purpose it must be made not from a complete inventory of all the individual characteristics but from a small number of them, carefully chosen ... It will spare the observer many steps because it will guide him ... We must, then, choose the most essential characteristics for our classification.[7]

7. Durkheim, *The rules of sociological method*; quoted in TCT, 192.

Horkheimer understands that Durkheim's insight – which was anticipated by Peirce and reaffirmed by Hanson, Kuhn, Lakatos and others – goes to the heart of theory invention and the discovery of the new: the totalizing moment in foundational theorizing.

The ordering of a whole context of elements is not an accumulative process, but a constructive one. The whole must be actively ordered, not mechanically deduced or passively collected. Its legitimacy is neither deductive necessity nor probabilistic generalization, but the persuasive arranging of less general under more general elements into a coherent context: "Such a subsumption or establishing of a relation between the simple perception or verification of a fact and the conceptual structure of our knowing is called its *theoretical explanation*" (TCT, 193; my emphasis). In its organizing aspect, theory is global; in its totalizing aspect, explanation is hypothetical; in its inventive moment it is imaginative, prospective, and practical: "Constructive thinking, then, plays a more important role than empirical verification in this theory as a whole" (TCT, 221).

What does this mean for the ascending method? The problem is that mere accumulation never discovers a whole, because the whole is a *sui generis* consideration. Furthermore, one cannot really begin without a whole, because it is the whole that directs the process of accumulation. On this view, the ascending method of analysis does not so much free itself of totalized concept as enclose itself within whichever ones it already has. Ascending analysis, that is, does not solve the problem of totalized concepts so much as drop them from its empirical procedure on the false assumption that, having begun without them, legitimate generalities will mechanically follow from local accumulations. This localist hypothesis merely represses or assumes the inevitable generalities that are already there.

True, postmodernists are correct to wonder about the scientific character of practical reason. Epistemologically, it is both aesthetic and totalizing: aesthetic in its dependence on a sense of the "fitness" of all the parts, totalizing in its requirement that all the parts be accounted for, constitutive in its demand that the future follow its lead. On the other hand, it seems that such constitutive generalities are consistent with postmodern critiques of traditional epistemology. The postmodern sense of texts is as much aesthetic as analytic; postmodern deconstructions are parasitic on totalizations such as Derrida's general system, finding their fissures by noting where wholes escape conceptual closure; while postmodernism highlights the practical element of its discourse. Critical theory's totalizing and post-modernism's critique are merely two moments in the same process, two aspects of the hermeneutic circle of theory and application, both of which are anticipated by the self-critical understanding of critical theory.

3. The openness of theory

Since, for critical theory, the unity of theory and practice requires that even theory be understood as a practice, the demonstration of the *practical* dimension of knowledge constitutes the theorist's proper theoretical mediation of thought and being.[8] Theory must not deny its formal and objective constraints; it must find the significance of these grounds in the practical and discursive context of its work. Thus critical theory grows historically with practice: "Since the theory is a unified whole which has its proper meaning only in relation to the contemporary situation, the theory as a whole is caught up in an evolution" (TCT, 238).

Recalling the above discussion of social totalities, critical theory has two aspects to its openness, both of which are implied by Adorno's notion of immanent critique. The first is the social-institutional aspect, the aspect ignored by positivist science: "science has to do with a knowledge of comprehensive relationships; yet, it has no realistic grasp of that comprehensive relationship upon which its own existence and the direction of its work depend, namely, society" (NSC, 8). Insofar as social reality shapes philosophy and science, social context must be a part of theory's reflexive critique.

And yet, to contextualize the institution of philosophy and critical theory in order to leave it open to revision is not enough. Theory must recognize the pragmatically open structure of theory itself. This appears in the totalizing, foundational moment. In the past, science took these moments too much for granted, rendering them under-theorized: "science accepts as a principle that its every step has a critical basis, yet the most important step of all, the setting of tasks, lacks a theoretical grounding and seems to be taken arbitrarily" (NSC,

---

8. Postmodernism typically suspects foundationist claims of requiring privileged binary oppositions. Critical theory also begins by questioning the binary mode of philosophical analysis, especially in its modern Cartesian legacy: "The inability to grasp in thought the unity of theory and practice and the limitation of the concept of necessity to inevitable events are both due, from the viewpoint of theory of knowledge, to the Cartesian dualism of thought and being" (TCT, 231).

8). To truly rationalize science, therefore, is to de-rationalize its acontextual assumptions. We must not only ask what the past data are, but what the past assumptions are, nor only ask where its predictions are leading, but where science itself leads.

Paradoxically, therefore, to *totalize* theory as practical reason is to open it, i.e. to *contextualize* theory in both the formal context of practical reason and the objective and conventional context of the social future. This pragmatism shuns rationalistic and objectivist determinisms: "the kind of theory which is an element in action is not a cog in an already existent mechanism" (TCT, 216). On the other hand, it does not reduce social action to arbitrariness either. It depends on both the objective capacity for economic production and the intersubjective capacity for social reproduction and creativity.

Regarding the conventional substance of social reproduction, critical theory recognizes its need to become a factor in determining the future. Critical prognosis extends a current tendency in which it intentionally participates. Thus despite critical theory's dependence on objective, technological factors, it is finally *moral* [pace Marx] rather than objectivist in its authority: "the state of affairs upon which judgment is passed in [critical theory] and the tendencies inciting men to build a rational society are not brought into existence outside thought by forces extrinsic to it, with thought then, as it were, accidentally recognizing its own reflection in the product of these forces" (TCT, 217). As an instance of practical rather than objectivist authority, critical theory is consciously and counterfactually consti- tutive: "The historical significance of his work is not self-evident; it rather depends on men speaking and acting in such a way as to justify it. It is not a finished and fixed historical creation ... [I]n regard to the essential kind of change at which the critical theory aims, there can be no corresponding concrete perception of it until it actually comes about" (TCT, 220).

Of course, such tentative circumstances put critique on shaky foundations, as Habermas suggests when he objects: "Must [critical theory] not open itself to the historically variable source of experience provided by the socially concrete life-world, prior to all methodo- logical objectivations, in order to legitimize the critical initiative as such?"[9] Unfortunately, the answer is yes. But if the Frankfurt School view is correct about the grounds of practical reason, the openness of practical reason does not vitiate the critical force of pragmatic ideals

9. *Theory and practice.* Quoted in Held, p. 479, fn. 12.

by contextualizing it since they do not believe an *a priori* standard of social rationality is available. Unlike Habermas, the Frankfurt School theorists insist on mediating the universalist ideal of freedom with history rather than a privileged practice, and on mediating relativist localism and individualism with the ideal possibilities of the social whole.

D. Critical theory: foundations and (dis)closure

Since Marx, mediating theoretical totalities and local political practice has been a problem for both theory and practice. The risk has been to gravitate into either collectivist blueprints or local anarchy. Rather than choosing between theories of social wholes and the openness of practice, the Frankfurt School view of foundations affirms both.

Regarding the openness of practical reason, the Frankfurt School theorists take a position between Habermas' universalism and the more skeptical localism of Foucault. While holding out against localism for substantive articulations of collective interests, they do not believe that a formalist paradigm or procedure of social rationality can be found to which all critical issues can be referred.

For Habermas, however, the openness of reason can be rationalized as the formal conditions of free inquiry.[10] Reciprocal, uncoerced, justified dialogue becomes the essential public practice. According to Habermas, this discursive openness is universally presupposed by the very logic of communication. Social rationality is thus universally formalized as a public procedure of consensus formation. But while Habermas' model has obvious appeal as a model of public discourse, it has more limitations as a paradigm of social rationality than Habermas admits. It is silent, for instance, on how its own domain should be limited by the private sphere, by aesthetic-creative demands, or for security purposes. Its reflexiveness, it seems, is circular: when faced with questions about the limits of consensus, it can only enjoin us to keep debating until we agree. The necessity of its formal conditions, it turns out, are necessary only *for itself* as a practice, while the limits of its practical applicability remain open to question. Habermas reduces the openness of practical reason to one central social practice – free critical debate – whose imperfect reflexivity yields an unspecified relation to other practices. Habermas' communicative reason, therefore, while formalizing the openness of *one* kind of practice, fails to universalize social rationality *in general*.

10. See Chapter 7 on Habermas.

Yet, while falling short of his universalism, Habermas' case for the universality of free inquiry and its moral superiority to either self-interest or uncritical traditionalism does, as a refinement of Kantian themes, manage to surpass some of the problems of Kant's more abstract formalism. It is, for instance, a *social* model. Likewise, while postmodernists are understandably nervous about his universalist claims, it is telling to see how loyal they are to the principles he posits as binding. He is right to maintain that postmodern critiques acknowledge the ideal of public justification, even as they deny universalist commitments. Insofar as postmodernists continue to argue with Habermas, they practice much of what he preaches.

The validity of mutual critiques in this debate illustrates how the openness of practical reasoning resists both moral formalism and moral localism. On the one hand, the Frankfurt School theorists and the postmodernists fairly contend that Habermas' model is an abstraction out of a wider context of moral claims, which vitiates the claim of its universality by raising problems of proper application (e.g. to problems of identity). On the other hand, the Frankfurt School theorists and Habermas might agree (1) that collective moral interests are not utterly beyond generalization, however contextualized, (2) that such interests are the ground of a wider freedom, and (3) that with certain qualifications the model of communicative reason is a widely applicable model for emancipatory critique and a strong argument for fundamental elements of collective public interest. Thus universalism is denied an essentially rational practice, while localism is forced to confront argument as a practice with certain formal conditions presupposed by all practitioners of critique.

One finds in this tension between modernism and postmodernism a struggle over the possible closure of critical conditions: on one side, neo-Marxists and Habermasian universalism pull toward stringent and collective standards; on the other, traditionalists and postmoderns resist centrism with localism, difference, and radical contingency. But the structure of the debate is a false dilemma since we cannot choose between collective and individual interests, or between epistemic conditions and the historical openness of an ethics of freedom. By contrast, in those essays which examine the foundations of critical theory, the Frankfurt School theorists manage to avoid these foundational antinomies, and thereby shed some useful light on the heterology of formal, objective, and historical-conventional con-straints on social thought.

Conclusion

> Men seem to be incapable of facing an
> antinomy and not worshipping the terms.　　E. Gilson

A. Philosophy's ambiguous end

Recent discussions of "the end of philosophy" indicate the depth of current interest in the problem of foundations. But our critique of the current debate suggests that this issue can be understood in either a misleading or an illuminating way.

It would be misleading, for instance, to suggest that philosophy is obsolete because its foundationist impulse is necessarily reductive, always oppressive, and ultimately wrong. It is also misleading to conclude that no useful distinctions have been discovered by the search for the most general conditions of knowledge, even if philosophy has discovered no absolute warrant of knowledge or meaning. Likewise it does not follow, as anti-foundationists suggest, that the choice for or against philosophy involves a choice between literary criticism and Plato's philosopher-king, between social nihilism and a universalist prescription for the rational society, or between emancipatory localisms and Skinnerean technocracies.

This all-or-nothing view of the search for critical conditions degenerates into false dilemmas between objectivity and freedom, domination and anarchy. In pragmatic terms the significance of the foundationist debate is not that we must choose between reduction and anarchy, but that we cannot so choose, since neither option works. It is no accident, however, that the terms of the debate seem inevitable, given the genealogy of modern foundationism.

B. Modern epistemological reduction and the genealogy of postmodernism

Arising out of skepticism, modern foundationism sought comfort in the obviousness of intellectual clarity and sensory givenness, aspiring to the critical simplicity and rigor of rationalist (Descartes, Leibniz, Kant) and materialist methods (Hobbes, Bacon, Comte, Marx, radical empiricism). Yet modern philosophy's critical revolution in methodology has met the classic issues (e.g. the status of collectives and individuals, realism and nominalism, objectivity and history, etc.) less with explanatory success than with selective attention in hopes that the scientific method would either decide all points or render the remainder nonsensical. Unhappily, the old positions repeatedly return; and so in the philosophy of science one finds instrumentalist, realist, and hermeneutic interpretations of theory, the lot of which echo the traditional skeptical, realistic, and relativist theories of truth.

Predictably, when we are failed by the obvious, skepticism only returns with greater force. In the wake of modernist deflations, postmodernism *feels* revolutionary, and wants to challenge reason at its roots. Here is where postmodernism overreaches itself with the pretense of global critique. But despite the aura of a postmodern anti-foundationist revolution, the concepts of revolutionary depth and global implication are two notions that postmodernism cannot sustain. This paradox shows that postmodernism has not yet reconciled its critical pretensions with the demands of theory.

The failure of modern epistemological reduction does not validate postmodernism's own sufficiency to the issue of foundations, though it does explain the local and critical character of postmodernism's successes. Incapable of articulating an identity without falling into a covert foundationism, postmodernism settles for a loose collection of reactive stances including such incompatible commitments as Rorty's nominalist pragmatism, Foucault's techno-individualism, Fish's strong conventionism, and Derrida's ultra-late-Hegelian textualism. Because of its vaguely generalized antipathy to centers, systems, reality, and truth, postmodernism can never be very sure what it is, where it goes, or what it can appeal to for its authority.

We do better to note that postmodern anti-foundationism is not *another* revolution in philosophy, but the critique of a failed revolution. When one considers that modernism was a reaction against classical theorizing, postmodernism's genealogical identity comes into focus: i.e. as a skepticism toward an earlier skepticism, a negation of a negation that does not constitute an argument against foundations except in their reductive form. Postmodern localism is a symptom, a cluster of reaction formations against modernism's failure to totalize.

As such, however, the authority of postmodern critique remains in crisis. Ironically, despite its Nietzschean parentage, postmodernism suffers theoretical *ressentiment* while needing more theory. Post-modernism's critical successes finally depend upon something that it cannot recognize, let alone provide: a deep critique of strong foundationism, a critique of foundationist reduction in principle. Postmodern localism is incapable of overcoming its negation of modernism to uncover the impossibility of foundationist reduction.

There is no real progress in the modern/postmodern debate as long as it remains structured by the strong foundationist antinomy, where each side claims to progress merely by changing the type of grounds under consideration in order to command unmastered territories of its opponent's philosophy while ignoring the partiality of its own view. Thus, by abstracting from contexts, modern rationalism excludes the uncertain and the contingent; by reducing knowledge to instrumental efficacy and verification, technology excludes the uncontrollable, though only by begging the question of the value of the ends of action; to deconstruct objectivity by problematizing its language, postmodernism dismisses any but local interests, regardless of technical success, biological needs, and the formal invariance of sign systems. None of these positions gives us a view of foundations we can live with: foundations are neither as univocal as modern philosophy had hoped nor as dispensable as postmodern equivocations often suggest.

As perspectives on tradition, both modernism and postmodernism make limited, though valuable gains. But they leave out too much. Because modernism is too methodologically narrow, and post-modernism is too preponderantly hermeneutic, neither modernism nor postmodernism can explain both what it criticizes and what it requires.

C. The heterology of sciences

The false foundationist dilemma of a privileged method or interpretive freedom obscures the autonomy of the conditions of knowledge and the variety of scientific methods. Oblivious to this misperception, the formal, objective, and human sciences progress according to their own distinct priorities, revealing in practice the inadequacy of the foundationist dilemma to the irreducibility of their grounds.

1. Formal sciences

Since Plato, many philosophers have sought the paradigm of philosophy in mathematics. But other formal sciences have emerged. As Peirce suggested a hundred years ago, semiotics has fulfilled the Kantian revolution in epistemology, completing the rationalist tradition in philosophy by radicalizing it. Semiotics theorizes the openness of thought as a sign process without practical closure, but formalizable in the abstract.

It is no coincidence that literary criticism and psychoanalysis have found the semiotic model useful, insofar as it explodes the Cartesian ideal of reflexive theoretical foundations with its ideal of self-certainty and the absolute subordination of the particular to the general, the contingent to the systemic. Once consciousness is understood as a product of the inferences and interpretations of signs, the Cartesian split between consciousness and its object, and the Cartesian ideal of immediate cognition, are displaced by a process of infinite inference, hypothesis, and interpretation. Finally, it is precisely the semiotic formalization of the thought process which shows the inevitability of this mediacy, and which shows the multiplicity of significations that permeate all real texts, whether intentional or not. Semiotic formalism, that is, not only fails to reduce to a closed system in practice, but opens up thought *in principle* to the universality of hermeneutic question-ability and the process of constituting meaning.

2. Empiricism and objectivity

Where some have turned constitutive models of meaning against knowledge in general, ecological theory has given objectivity and pragmatic invariance new force. Just as post-structuralism fragmented the subject, ecological theory objectified biological contexts as stable systems. In an important contrast between hermeneutic and biological reproduction, while semantic production may be infinitely inde-terminate, biological reproduction is not. Systemic invariance is a concrete, if historical, fact. Members of an ecosystem suffer objective biological conditions which are not infinitely negotiable, but cata-strophically decisive.

Moreover, what is of special interest in ecological theory as an ontology is its success in combining development, complexity, variety, contextual openness, and contextual closure within the same model. This synthesis reveals an invariance of non-essentialist elements in a dynamic system. They are non-essentialistic because the "center" of the system is a dynamic pattern, not an eternal archetype nor the particular members. This gives context a new meaning and status as a scientific factor. In ecological niches patterns of stability have their own systemic-causal force – an objective reality – by way of *positioning* their elements within a process. For this kind of objectivity, being relational rather than atomic, the primary causal force inheres on the level of the systemic pattern rather than by an accumulation of pre-existent lower level forces. Indeed, rather than the rule of context-dissolving-objectivity as is often suggested in hermeneutics, in ecology context *is* objectivity.

Such developments in formal and natural sciences point toward a reconstruction of rationalist and objectivist theorizing in the post-modern scene, though with two important considerations for the new meanings of formal and objective conditions: (a) formal sciences do not define boundaries of empirical sciences (as for Kant), but constitute possible systems whose role in the empirical sciences must be determined empirically (as for Peirce); (b) although formality and objectivity have their place within a world of constituted meanings, their insufficiency to the practical logic of social questions shows the need to distinguish the issues of politics and identity from the issues of formal and natural science. The self-constituted objects of the human sciences imply a fundamental difference: the intervention of practical reason and textuality.

3. Historical and practical sciences

The epistemic claims of objectivity and formality are transformed by the nature of practical, social, or ethical questions where deliberations and interpretations constitute the objects of study. In these contexts, contingency never totally gives way to the necessary.

Here we see the intermediation of the different modes most clearly in the complexity of social constructs. Ecology, for instance, theorizes an objective, biological ground for the common social good insofar as it constitutes the precondition for the survival of the ecosystem. And yet when the ecological issues are translated into political terms, they fragment into other kinds of questions regarding the ideal society.

There are always, of course, those who like the present arrangement. But even among those who do not, there is inevitably further fragmentation along various parameters of interest. As Hugh Stretton notes:

> The Left may want to make wilderness accessible to more and poorer people; environmentalists may want to preserve it from too much use by any people. The Left may want jobs located where environmentalists don't want them. The Left may want high-wage, capital-intensive production of cheap goods; where that squanders energy or pollutes, environmentalists may want lower-paid, labor-intensive production of dearer goods.[1]

Despite their involvement with objective constraints, as soon as ecological issues are conceived in the context of action, they suffer the openness of practical reasoning: i.e. the need to consider numerous possible ends, the heterogeneous parameters and sites of value that constitute the different forms of order, production, and distribution. The environment is not only a technologically pragmatic question, but a moral-political one as well: it remains a choice of freedoms as well as a choice of determinacies. And this is typical of social theory in general: while the global-reach of theory must have its place in critical theory, it can never succeed – the claims of theory can never become total.

Thus it is here, then, in the complexity of the practical sciences that we find the most challenging confluence of the different disciplines with their different standards of knowledge and meaning. When scrutinized carefully, however, it appears that this complexity reduces neither to the facts nor to the arbitrary. There is a confluence of disciplinary practices, an *intermediacy* of epistemic factors that neither displace nor become each other. Insofar as such an object domain is as much historical as natural, critique must be context-specific, though still depending on philosophy to identify the critical conditions of its elements.

D. The other end of philosophy

The current sense that philosophy has returned to fundamental questions of reason's authority and limits – and perhaps without success – has fostered talk of the end of modernism, or even of the end

---

1. *Capitalism, socialism and the environment*, Cambridge University Press, 1976; p. 11.

of philosophy. And indeed, the postmodern situation is a uniquely demanding one, situated as it is between the apparent collapse of strong foundational epistemology and the loose pluralism of the current age. Likewise, the continuing struggle between theoretical reduction and hermeneutic relativism indicates both the force and the frustration of our transitional moment.

Notwithstanding the insights of modern and postmodern perspectives, however, their pretensions to revolutionary significance for foundational thought is exactly what troubles the future of philosophy and critical authority. Likewise, their failures as revolutionary perspectives on philosophy force a reconsideration of the notion of philosophy and foundations, a reconsideration that must avoid the foundationist antinomy of one-or-none. Philosophical progress, in the reconstructed view, is not a matter of greater certainty, or of progress in one direction only, or of finding the right ground; rather, epistemology itself is constituted by a conjunction of grounds that are at once formal, objective, and historically conventional. This is not anti-theory, but a better theory of theory.

In this heterological view, the task of epistemology is to articulate better the epistemic dynamic of the necessary and the contingent. As of old, philosophy must theorize the most general conditions of the various sciences and their relations to each other. But it is saved from reductiveness by its insight into the dialectic of general and particular. Pure sciences, in this case, gain their purity at the expense of their closure over real contexts. Whereas Kant thought Euclidean geometry to be the *a priori* ground of physics, we now think otherwise: Euclidean geometry may work in some areas of physics, and not in others, the truth of which is to be determined empirically. Likewise, semiotics may determine the necessary conditions of meaning in general, but not the meaning of any text in particular, a question which only situated interpretations can decide. Insofar as all existential claims are hypothetical and all *a priori* necessities abstract and formal, knowledge remains a practical compromise between necessary conditions, factual possibilities, and real contexts.

There is no reason why philosophy ought not to seek the most general terms of our understanding with a postmodern understanding of generality. If, as Peirce claimed, logic, phenomenology and epistemology are all empirical sciences, then philosophy can only generalize and specify necessary conditions of the different sciences in dialogue with them. Rather than offering foundational truths as self-evident and fixed, determined abstractly and finally, philosophy determines even its most general truths by theorizing *ex post facto*. Foundational generality is thus inherently ambiguous: it implies both that scientific first principles are *logically* prior to specific scientific practices, and that epistemology's own raw materials are the *conclusions* of those scientific practices. Science is, in other words, a hermeneutic circle.

Moreover, heterology not only suggests that *a priori* certainties stop when we enter the real world, but that mechanistic notions of causation stop when we enter the social realm. Where social questions arise, we must add practical reason to theoretical and technological reason. This means several things. First, as institutions are conventional, whether we know it or not, they are products of history and choice. Second, since institutions are conventional, no rules or utopian blueprints are adequate to say at all times what we must do, whether for the acting individual or the critic of the oppressive society. This is not because there are no facts. Even if objectively oppressive conditions do exist, and even if their causes can be factually determined, their remedies are matters of debate for two reasons: social agendas rest on probable outcomes, and the outcomes are questions of choice as well as fact. Just insofar as practical reason serves a social ideal of freedom, it serves no predetermined end, but reconciles competing visions of the free society according to differing emphases on freedom, equality, security, productivity, and justice. To want something more predetermined is to want a world without freedom.

In light of this reconsideration of foundations, it seems that philosophy need not be local in order to avoid being reductive, nor arbitrary in order to allow freedom. The rejection of self-evidence, certainty, and reduction does not spell the end of general theories or their claims to theorizing the conditions of knowledge. As Peirce aptly put it, philosophy is not like a chain – concerned to make each link indestructible – but like a cord of many threads, increasing its strength by multiplying its threads.[2] The heterological structure of

2. Richard Bernstein pointed to indications of a new consensus in *Beyond objectivism and relativism*, Philadelphia: University of Pennsylvania, 1988; p. 7; and develops this idea more thoroughly in *The new constellation: the ethical-political horizons of modernity/postmodernity*, Chicago, 1992. This latter book has appeared too recently to be fully integrated into this discussion, though a brief comparison is possible.

In line with a heterological foundationism, Bernstein also asks: "Is there a new

that cord is not only the limit of modernism's search for critical conditions, it is also the presupposition of postmodern critiques of modernist reduction. Heterology accounts for both the necessary constraints and the necessary openness of thought. Likewise, in this heterology of constraints lie both the discipline and emancipatory possibilities of the postmodern condition for explanation, theory, and understanding.

way of understanding and practicing critique that escapes this grand Either/Or [of the strong foundational antinomy]?... This is – if not *the* central question – at least *a* central question that is at the very heart of 'modern/postmodern' debates." Likewise, he agrees that "our 'modern/postmodern' situation or predicament is one that defies and resists any and all attempts of reduction to 'a common denominator, essential core, or generative first principle.'" Bernstein's strategy is to turn from Hegel's master metaphor of *Aufhebung* and reconciliation to Adorno's notion of a "constellation," concluding that we cannot "any longer responsibly claim that there is or can be a final reconciliation ... in which all difference, otherness, opposition and contradiction are reconciled. The changing elements of the new constellation resist such reduction. What is 'new' about this constellation is the growing awareness of the depth of radical instabilities" (8–9).

On the other hand, my argument suggests that the depth of the radical foundationist instabilities is not best explained on the basis of the fact that the "elements of the new constellation" are "changing." Rather, I suggest that a heterological foundationism is radical just insofar as it reveals a *permanent*, albeit open, structure within the heterology of foundational elements. Here, I believe, is the origin of emancipatory critique. What is at stake is the matter of a foundational necessity of a non-reductive sort, a necessity that defies reductive reconciliation while avoiding the skeptical implication that all is contingent, all is dispensable. To reduce the issue to change sacrifices the necessity of the underlying structure of foundationist elements to an unaccountable contingency, which too easily succumbs to relativism. By identifying the necessary elements of experience, a heterological foundationism is able to account for both what changes and what stays the same, and thereby account for the failures of both reductive foundationism and relativism.

Bibliography

Adorno, Theodor, *Against epistemology*, Cambridge: MIT Press, 1982.

Apel, Karl-Otto, *Towards a transformation of philosophy*, London: Routledge and Kegan Paul, 1980.

Barthes, Roland, *Mythologies*, New York: Hill and Wang, 1972.

Baynes, Kenneth, James Bohman, and Thomas McCarthy, (eds.), *After philosophy: end or transformation?*, Cambridge: MIT Press, 1987.

Benhabib, Seyla, *Critique, norm and utopia: a study of the foundations of critical theory*, New York: Columbia University Press, 1986.

Berlin, Isaiah, *Karl Marx: his life and environment*, Oxford, 1963.

Bernstein, Richard, *The restructuring of social and political theory*, Philadelphia: University of Pennsylvania Press, 1978.

  "From hermeneutics to praxis," in Wachterhauser, *Hermeneutics and modern philosophy*, 1986.

  Beyond objectivism and relativism: science, hermeneutics, and praxis, Philadelphia: University of Pennsylvania Press, 1988.

  The new constellation: the ethical-political horizons of modernity/postmodernity, Chicago, 1992.

Bernstein, Richard (ed.), *Habermas and modernity*, Cambridge: MIT Press, 1985.

Brooks, Cleanth. "The language of paradox," reprinted in *Critiques and essays in criticism*, ed. Robert Wooster Stallman, New York: Ronald Press, 1949; originally published in *Kenyon Review*, Spring, 1943.

  "Irony as a principle of structure," reprinted in *Contexts for criticism*, (ed.) Donald Keesey, Mountainview, CA: Mayfield, 1987.

Brooks, Cleanth and Robert Penn Warren, *Modern rhetoric*, New York: Harcourt, Brace, Jovanovich, 1979.

Crane, R. S. (ed.), *Critics and criticism*. University of Chicago, 1952, abridged edition.

Dasenbrock, Reed Way (ed.), *Redrawing the lines: analytic philosophy, deconstruction, and literary theory*, Minneapolis: University of Minnesota Press, 1989.

Davies, Paul, *Other worlds*, New York: Simon and Schuster, 1980.

Derrida, Jacques, "Structure, sign, and play," reprinted in *The structuralist controversy: the languages of criticism and the sciences of man*, eds. Eugenio

Donato and Richard Macksey, Baltimore: Johns Hopkins University Press, 1970.

Of grammatology, Baltimore: Johns Hopkins University Press, 1974.

Positions, University of Chicago Press, 1981.

Dreyfus, Hubert, "Holism and hermeneutics," in *Hermeneutics and praxis*, (ed.) Hollinger, 1985.

Dreyfus, Hubert L. and Paul Rabinow, *Michel Foucault: beyond structuralism and hermeneutics*, University of Chicago Press, 1983.

Dummett, Michael, *Truth and other enigmas*, Cambridge: Harvard University Press, 1978.

Durkheim, Emile, *The rules of sociological method*, Glencoe, Illinois: Free Press, 1958.

Eliot, T. S., "Tradition and the individual talent," in *Selected essays*, New York: Harcourt, Brace & World, 1960.

Fetterly, Judith, *The resisting reader: a feminist approach to American fiction*, Bloomington: Indiana University Press, 1978.

Fish, Stanley, *Is there a text in this class?: the authority of interpretive communities*, Cambridge, MA: Harvard University Press, 1980.

"Anti-professionalism," *New Literary History*, Vol. XVII (1985).

"Consequences," in *Against theory: literary studies and the New Pragmatism*, ed. W. J. T. Mitchell, University of Chicago Press, 1985.

"Being interdisciplinary is so very hard to do," *Profession 89*, New York: Modern Language Association, 1989.

Doing what comes naturally: change, rhetoric, and the practice of theory in literary and legal studies, Durham: Duke University Press, 1989.

Foucault, Michel, *The order of things: an archaeology of the human sciences*, New York: Random House, 1970.

The archaeology of knowledge and the discourse on language, New York: Random House, 1972.

Language, counter-memory, practice: selected essays and interviews, Ithaca, New York: Cornell University Press, 1977.

Discipline and punish: the birth of the prison, New York: Random House, 1979.

Power/knowledge: selected interviews and other writings 1972–1977, ed. Colin Gordon, New York: Random House, 1980.

The Foucault reader, (ed.) Paul Rabinow, New York: Random House, 1984.

Politics, philosophy, culture: interviews and other writings: 1977–84, (ed.) Lawrence D. Kritzmann, New York: Routledge, 1988.

Remarks on Marx: conversations with Duccio Trombadori, New York: Semiotext(e), 1991.

Frye, Northrop, "The archetypes of literature," in *Fables of identity*, New York: Harcourt, Brace and World, 1963.

Gadamer, Hans-Georg, "Hermeneutics and social science," *Cultural hermeneutics*, 2 (1975).

Bibliography

Philosophical hermeneutics, ed. David E. Linge, Berkeley: University of California Press, 1976.

Reason in the age of science, Cambridge, MA: Massachusetts Institute of Technology Press, 1981.

Truth and method, New York: Crossroad, 1988.

Gasché, Rodolphe, *The tain of the mirror: Derrida and the philosophy of reflection*, Cambridge: Harvard University Press, 1986.

Habermas, Jurgen, *Knowledge and human interests*, Boston: Beacon, 1968.

Communication and the evolution of society, Boston: Beacon, 1979

The philosophical discourse of modernity, Cambridge: Massachusetts Institute of Technology Press, 1987.

The theory of communicative action, Boston: Beacon, vols. I (1984) and II (1987).

"A review of Gadamer's *Truth and method*," in Wachterhauser, *Hermeneutics and modern philosophy*, 1986.

Harvey, Irene, "The wellsprings of deconstruction" in *Tracing literary theory*, (ed.) Joseph Natoli, Urbana: University of Illinois, 1987.

Hegel, G. W. F., *Phenomenology of Spirit*, trans. A. V. Miller, Oxford: Clarendon Press, 1977.

Heidegger, Martin, *Kant and the problem of metaphysics*, Bloomington: Indiana University Press, 1990.

Held, David, *Introduction to critical theory: Horkheimer to Habermas*, Berkeley: University of California Press, 1980.

Holland, Norman, "Hamlet: my greatest creation," reprinted in Keesey, *Contexts for criticism*, 1987.

Hollinger, Robert (ed.), *Hermeneutics and praxis*, University of Notre Dame Press, 1985.

Hollis, Martin and Steven Lukes (eds.), *Rationality and relativism*, Cambridge: Massachusetts Institute of Technology Press, 1982.

Horkheimer, Max, *Critical theory: selected essays*, New York: Continuum, 1986; including "Notes on science and the crisis" and "Traditional and critical theory."

Hoy, David Couzens (ed.), *Foucault: a critical reader*, Oxford: Basil Blackwell, 1986.

Jameson, Frederic, *The political unconscious: narrative as a politically symbolic act*, Ithaca, New York: Cornell University Press, 1981.

Jay, Martin, *The dialectical imagination: a history of the Frankfurt School and the Institute for Social Research 1923–1950*, Boston: Little, Brown, 1973.

Kant, Immanuel, *Critique of pure reason*, trans. Norman Kemp Smith, New York: St. Martin's, 1965.

Keesey, Donald, *Contexts for criticism*, Mountain View, CA: Mayfield, 1987.

Kellner, Douglas, *Critical theory, Marxism, and modernity*, Baltimore: Johns Hopkins University Press, 1989.

Kuhn, Thomas, *The structure of scientific revolutions*, University of Chicago, 1962.

Leitch, Vincent, *Deconstructive criticism: an advanced introduction*, New York: Columbia University Press, 1983.

Livingston, Paisley, *Literary knowledge: humanistic inquiry and the philosophy of science*, Ithaca: Cornell University Press, 1987.

Lyotard, Jean-François, *The postmodern condition: a report on knowledge*, Minneapolis: University of Minnesota Press, 1984.

MacIntyre, Alasdair, *After virtue: a study in moral theory*, University of Notre Dame Press, 1984.

Marcuse, Herbert, *Negations*, Boston: Beacon, 1968; including "Philosophy and critical theory."

Marx, Karl, *Capital*, Moscow: Progress Publishers, 1971.
  The German ideology, Moscow: Progress Publishers, 1976.

McCarthy, Thomas, *The critical theory of Jurgen Habermas*, Cambridge: Massachusetts Institute of Technology Press, 1978.

Melville, Herman, *The confidence man: his masquerade*, New York: W. W. Norton, 1971.

Mitchell, W. B. T. (ed.), *Against theory: literary studies and the new pragmatism*, University of Chicago Press, 1985.

Ohmann, Richard, *English in America: a radical view of the profession*, New York: Oxford University Press, 1976.

Peirce, Charles Sanders, *Collected Papers*, Cambridge, MA: Harvard University Press, 1932–5.

Popper, Karl, *Conjectures and refutations: the growth of scientific knowledge*, New York: Harper & Row, 1963.

Poster, Mark, *Foucault, Marxism and history: a mode of production versus a mode of information*, Cambridge: Polity Press, 1984.
  Critical theory and post-structuralism: in search of a context, Ithaca: Cornell, 1989.
  The mode of information: post-structuralism and context, University of Chicago Press, 1990.

Putnam, Hilary, "Why reason can't be naturalized," reprinted in *After philosophy: end or transformation?*, eds. Baynes, Bowman, and McCarthy, 1987.

Rabinow, Paul and William M. Sullivan (eds.), *Interpretive social science: a reader*, Berkeley: University of California Press, 1979.

Rawls, John, *A theory of justice*, Cambridge, MA: Harvard University Press, 1970.

Ricoeur, Paul, "Hermeneutics and the critique of ideology" in *Hermeneutics and modern philosophy*, ed. Wachterhauser, 1986.

Rorty, Richard, *Philosophy and the mirror of nature*, Princeton University Press, 1979.
  Consequences of pragmatism, Minneapolis: University of Minnesota, 1982.
  Contingency, irony, and solidarity, New York: Cambridge University Press, 1989.

Saikh, Anwar, *Marxian economics*, New York: Norton, 1987.

Sallis, John (ed.), *Deconstruction and philosophy*, University of Chicago Press, 1987.

Shelley, Percy Bysshe, "A defence of poetry," Boston: Ginn & Co., 1891.

Skinner, B. F., *Beyond freedom and dignity*, New York: Random House, 1971.

Staton, Shirley (ed.), *Literary theories in praxis*, Philadelphia: University of Pennsylvania Press, 1987.

Steiner, Rudolf, *The threefold social order*, New York: Anthroposophic Press, 1966.

Stretton, Hugh, *Capitalism, socialism and the environment*, Cambridge University Press, 1976.

Sullivan, Michael and John T. Lysaker, "Between impotence and illusion: Adorno's art of theory and practice," in *New German Critique*, Fall, 1992.

Taylor, Charles, *Philosophy and the human sciences*, Cambridge University Press, 1985.

Taylor, Charles, *Sources of the self: the making of the modern identity*, Cambridge, MA: Harvard University Press, 1989.

Thompson, John B. and David Held (eds.), *Habermas: critical debates*, Cambridge: Massachusetts Institute of Technology Press, 1982.

Wachterhauser, Brice R. (ed.), *Hermeneutics and modern philosophy*, Albany: State University of New York Press, 1986.

Warren, Robert Penn, "Pure and impure poetry" from *The well wrought urn*, New York: Reynal and Hitchcock, 1947.

White, Hayden, *The tropics of discourse: essays in cultural criticism*, Baltimore: Johns Hopkins University Press, 1978.

White, Stephen K., *The recent work of Jurgen Habermas: reason, justice, and modernity*, Cambridge University Press, 1988.

Wittgenstein, Ludwig, *Philosophical investigations*, New York: Macmillan, 1953.

Index

Index